THE SHADOW PARTY

THE SHADOW PARTY

HOW GEORGE SOROS,

HILLARY CLINTON,

and SIXTIES RADICALS

SEIZED CONTROL OF THE

DEMOCRATIC PARTY

DAVID HOROWITZ
AND
RICHARD POE

THOMAS NELSON
Since 1798

thomasnelson.com

Published in Nashville, Tennessee, by Thomas Nelson, Inc.

Thomas Nelson, Inc. titles may be purchased in bulk for educational, business, fundraising, or sales promotional use. For information, please e-mail SpecialMarkets@ThomasNelson.com.

Library of Congress Cataloging-in-Publication Data

Horowitz, David.
    The shadow party: how George Soros, Hillary Clinton, and sixties radicals siezed control of the Democratic Party / by David Horowitz and Richard Poe.
      p. cm.
    Includes bibliographical references and index.
    ISBN 10: 1-59555-044-5 (hardcover)
    ISBN 13: 978-1-59555-044-6 (hardcover)
    ISBN 10: 1-59555-103-4 (trade paper)
    ISBN 13: 978-1-59555-103-0 (trade paper)
    1. United States—Politics and government. 2. Soros, George—Influence.
I. Poe, Richard. II. Title.
    JK275.H728 2006
    324.2736—dc22

2006021073

Printed in the United States of America
07 08 09 10 11 QW 6 5 4 3 2

To our wives, April Horowitz and Marie Poe,
whose loving support has provided
an isle of peace in the tempest,
and whose counsel has shaped this book
in more ways than anyone will know.

CONTENTS

INTRODUCTION

The war in Iraq marks a new era in America's political life. Never previously has one of America's two major political parties attacked a sitting president and wartime commander-in-chief with the ferocity manifested by leaders of the Democratic Party today. Never before has the country been so divided in the early stages of a war on foreign soil.

Bipartisanship in wartime has been a hallmark of American foreign policy since the Second World War. Republicans displayed it when President Clinton went to war in Bosnia and Kosovo—wars conducted without congressional authorization or UN approval, but which Republican leaders nonetheless supported. Such bipartisanship is strikingly absent in America's war in Iraq. It has been undone by a Democratic leadership committed to more radical goals.

The Democrats' movement to the political left is not new. "Progressive" activists have been carrying out a broad-ranging infiltration of American political and cultural institutions for forty years. Now the effects of that infiltration can be seen in the inability of America's political leaders to form a united front against a clear military threat from abroad.

This book is about the radical forces which are undermining American unity. It identifies the radical leaders and explains their strategy. These activists are organized in two distinct movements, one exerting pressure from below, the other exerting pressure from above. In a 1957 tract, Czech Communist Party theoretician Jan Kozák explained how a small number of communists managed to gain power in Czechoslovakia through parliamentary maneuvers. The trick was to exert pressure for radical change from two directions simultaneously—from the upper levels of government and from provocateurs in the streets. Kozák called this tactic "pressure from above and below."

One way to exert "pressure from below," as Kozák explained, was to fill the streets with rioters, strikers and protesters, thus creating the illusion of a widespread clamor for change from the grassroots. Radicals in the government would then exert "pressure from above," enacting new laws on the pretext of appeasing the protesters in the street—even though the protesters (or at least their leaders) were themselves part of the plot. The majority of the people would have no idea what was going on. Squeezed from "above" and "below," most would sink into apathy and despair, believing they were hopelessly outnumbered by the radicals—even though they were not. Thus could a radical minority impose its will on a moderate majority, even under a democratic, parliamentary system.

In America today, pressure from "below"—the intrusion of street-level radicals into the political process—has already profoundly changed the Democratic Party. This became evident as early as the McGovern campaign of 1972. It has become obvious in recent years that a corresponding pressure "from above" is now closing the pincer from the opposite direction. This movement from "above" is spear-headed by forces, both inside and outside the party, situated at the highest levels of political and financial power. The revolution from above involves key figures from the

Clinton White House, including Hillary Rodham Clinton and her factotum Harold Ickes, along with Bill Clinton's White House chief of staff John Podesta.

The "Lenin" behind this revolution, however, is a man outside the political process altogether. Financial wizard and political manipulator, George Soros is the architect of a "Shadow Party" which operates much like a network of holding companies coordinating the disparate branches of this movement, both inside and outside the Democratic Party, and leading them toward the goal of securing state power. Once attained, that power will be used to effect a global transformation—economic, social and political—a post-Berlin Wall reincarnation of the old radical dream.

In short, this book documents how, through an extraordinary series of political, legal and financial maneuvers, an unlikely network of radical activists and activist billionaires gained *de facto* control over the Democratic Party's campaign apparatus—including both its media "air war" and its get-out-the-vote ground war, and thus over its electoral future. This party within the party (but also outside the party) has no official name, but, without fully comprehending its scope, some journalists and commentators have dubbed it the Shadow Party, a term we have adopted in writing this book.

The Shadow Party is a network of private organizations that exercises a powerful and hidden influence over the Democratic Party, and through it, over American politics in general. It is not a political party per se, and it works outside of the normal electoral system, in pursuance of goals that are not openly disclosed.

The Shadow Party cannot afford to function as an ordinary political party. That would require making an honest, public appeal to voters, and this it cannot do, for its radical vision would offend most Americans. If Americans understood the intentions of the Shadow Party organizers, they would recoil in revulsion and reject its overtures. For these reasons, the Shadow Party network must proceed by stealth. It must (and does) use secretive, deceptive, and extra-constitutional means to achieve its objectives. It must infiltrate government bureaucracies, corrupt public officials and manipulate the press. And it must conceal who and what it is.

The Shadow Party does not confine its activities to the Democratic Party. If it did, it would be less effective. A number of notable Republicans, among them Senator John McCain, have exchanged political favors with the Shadow Party. But the Democratic Party—because it is already a party of the Left—is the focus of the Shadow Party's activities and its chosen instrument. The Shadow Party has not yet achieved its goal of federal power, but since the 2004 election, it has attained a degree of control over the Democratic National Committee and the Democratic Party in general, that is nearly complete.

During the 2004 election cycle, the Shadow Party—headed by a group of leftist billionaires—was able to contribute more than $300 million to the Democrat war chest, and, through its independent media campaigns, to effectively shape the Democrats' message. Despite their defeat at the polls, Shadow Party leaders were intoxicated by their achievement. On December 9, 2004, Eli Pariser, who headed the Shadow Party group MoveOn PAC, boasted to his members, "Now it's our party. We bought it, we own it."[1]

Whom does Pariser mean exactly when he says "we?" What special interests does he represent? Who "bought" the Democratic Party in 2004, and what use do they plan to make of it? The following pages provide answers to these questions. They reveal the radical network that now steers the Democratic Party and shapes its policies. They recount the history of this network and describe its players, tactics and goals. These goals are informed by a fundamental hostility to American institutions—even to the idea of America's sovereignty as a nation.

This is not a book about beating Democrats at the polls. A two-party system is vital to our democracy, and it is because we feel this system is imperiled by the subversion of one of its elements that we have written this book. The issues we seek to raise transcend party identifications and electoral contests. Every American interested in the health of the two-party system has reason to fear the Shadow Party. Ordinary Democrats who have been disenfranchised by the seizure of their party's apparatus have reason to fear it most. Much of the network's power lies in the general ignorance of its existence and purposes, in its ability to conceal its radicalism behind moderate language, and in the kaleidoscopic arsenal of issue-defined front groups, smokescreens of disinformation and public relations spin which the Shadow Party employs.

Radical organizer Saul Alinsky, an early mentor of Senator Hillary Clinton and of many Shadow Party operatives, identified for his disciples the path to power in American politics. Alinsky observed that radicals could achieve revolutionary change without majority support if they understood and exploited the rules of the game. This was the subject of his book, *Rules for Radicals*. The requirements for a radical power grab were a small core of disciplined activists pushing their agendas and a citizenry sufficiently in the dark about its purposes. In these circumstances, a radical minority could impose its will even on a great democracy such as the United States.

Alinsky's theory was tested during the Vietnam War. As he

predicted, a minority of radical activists succeeded in imposing its will on America, without achieving victory at the ballot box. The American people supported the war in Vietnam to its bitter end. Yet, after years of organized chaos on the home front, American leaders grew weary of the internal divisions and yielded to the forces of defeatism. Americans allowed the Left to prevail, not because Americans supported the Left's agenda, but because the Left had a strategy and determination to succeed, while their opponents lacked either the understanding or the will to counter them.

America was not united during the Vietnam era, and our Communist enemies in Hanoi were fully aware of that fact. The harder we fought, the shriller the protest from America's internal opposition became. The radicals' slogan was not "Support a Communist Victory in Vietnam," which would have been rejected by the American people out of hand. The radicals' slogan was "Bring the Troops Home Now." This slogan did not proclaim the radicals' desire that the Communists would win the war—but created the illusion that the anti-war movement cared about America's troops, which it most certainly did not. "Anti-war" activists like the young John Kerry called American soldiers "war criminals," even while minimizing and excusing the genuine war crimes of the enemy.

The radicals' slogan "Bring the Troops Home Now," played on the natural fears and desires of American parents for peace and for a return of their sons. It divided the home front and weakened the national resolve. Eventually it forced an American retreat—and a victory for the Communists in Cambodia and Vietnam. The consequences were brutal—nearly three million Cambodians and Vietnamese were slaughtered by the Communists when they came to power. But they could not have come to power on their own. In every military encounter with American forces, the Communists suffered defeat. Their victory was only possible because the American radicals won.

This book describes forces at work behind the surface of political events, which seek to remake America as a radical utopia. They are driven by the belief that American "hegemony" (as they like to describe it) is harmful and its purposes oppressive. In the name of globalism, they would deny America its nationhood, character and culture. Theirs is a party—a Shadow Party—that is subversive of the American idea itself.

1

THE SHADOW
PARTY'S LENIN

The architect and guiding genius of the Shadow Party, its Lenin—if one is careful with the analogy—is billionaire activist George Soros. Like Lenin, Soros excels at waging revolution from "above"—through manipulation of economic and political forces at the highest levels. However, Soros also resembles Lenin in his diligent cultivation of insurgent forces from "below."

Like the Shadow Party he created, Soros has many layers. On the surface, he is a well-known public figure, a philanthropist and financier who is frequently in the news. Yet another George Soros remains cryptic and elusive, his goals and activities obscured by a smokescreen of denial and calculated misdirection.

Soros denies that he plays any special role in the Shadow Party he has created. He claims that he is just one of its many financial contributors. In fact, as we will show in these pages, Soros founded and organized the Shadow Party personally, and exercises a degree of authority over its operations not unlike that of a corporate president over a company.

Americans need to become better acquainted with Soros and his radical perspective. They also need to familiarize themselves with the sophisticated mechanism he has built for getting his way.

George Soros is one of the most powerful men on earth. A New York hedge fund manager, he has amassed a personal fortune estimated at about $7.2 billion. His management company controls billions more in investor assets. Since 1979, his foundation network has dispensed an estimated $5 billion. Soros claims that his Open Society Institute donates up to $425 million annually to various causes.[1]

For all his wealth, Soros' greatest influence comes not from spending his own money, but from inducing other people to spend theirs. This is most obvious in his approach to the financial markets. Soros' reputation as a financial prognosticator is such that legions of investors hang on his word, and buy or sell at his signal. An op-ed piece by Soros published in the *Wall Street Journal* or an interview broadcast on Bloomberg or CNBC can move vast sums of money in the financial markets, which far exceed Soros' personal spending power. As the *New York Times* once put it, "When Soros speaks, world markets listen."[2]

Through the years, Soros has matched his strength more than once against the economic power of nations, and emerged victorious. He famously shorted the British pound in 1992, wagering $10 billion on a drop in its value. In a desperate bid to keep its currency afloat, the Bank of England tried to buy up pounds as fast as Soros could dump them. However, as more and more investors followed Soros' lead and joined his efforts, the Bank of England eventually gave up. The British pound was devalued, launching a tsunami of financial turmoil from Tokyo to Rome. When it was over, millions of hardworking Britons confronted their diminished savings, while Soros counted his gains. He had personally made nearly $2 billion on the catastrophe, and was henceforth known as "the man who broke the Bank of England."

Breaking the pound sterling was a formidable undertaking. Soros had to risk $10 billion in order to accomplish it. On other occasions, he has wreaked similar havoc by investing nothing more than the time it takes to compose a letter. On 9 June 1993, Soros sent a letter to the *Times* of London suggesting that the German mark was weak. "I expect the mark to fall against all major currencies," he wrote. The statement triggered twenty-four hours of panic selling, which sent the Deutschmark into a tailspin.³ Soros repeated the feat on 14 July 1998, this time with far more destructive consequences, when he suggested in the *Financial Times* of London that the Russian government ought to devalue the ruble by 15 to 25 percent. Panic selling again ensued, plunging Russia into a deep depression.⁴

Few private individuals in the history of finance have possessed the power to break currencies with a single utterance. Soros is one of those few. He likens his influence to the magic of alchemy. In his 1995 book *Soros on Soros*, he wrote, "The alchemists made a big mistake trying to turn base metals into gold by incantation. With chemical elements, alchemy doesn't work. But it does work in the financial markets, because incantations can influence the decisions of the people who shape the course of events."⁵

The possibility that Soros might one day deploy his market alchemy to the disadvantage of the United States has long been a topic of anxious discussion among America's financial watchdogs. Democrat Congressman Henry Gonzalez of Texas—then chairman of the House Banking Committee—expressed this concern in a speech to the Congress on 8 June 1993. "Recent press accounts state that Mr. George Soros, the manager of the Quantum Fund, made over $1 billion betting against the British pound. I am interested in . . . the U.S. bank exposure to Mr. Soros' fund." Gonzalez said.⁶

What Gonzalez feared has come to pass. "I have to disclose that I now have a short position against the dollar." Soros announced on CNN in May 2003. At a time when the US dollar had fallen to a four-year low against the euro, Soros now helped push it lower by informing the world that he had begun cashing in dollars in exchange for euros and other foreign currencies.[7] Soros knows better than most that, when currencies fall, governments often fall with them. His attack on the dollar is an attack on George Bush and on the war Bush is waging in Iraq. Regrettably, it is not the first time Soros has used his financial might to thwart America's War on Terror.

On 26 February 1993, Muslim jihadists struck the World Trade Center the first time, in what was then the most ambitious terror attack ever attempted. Their plan was to knock over the Trade Center's north tower, causing it to fall against the south tower, killing hundreds of thousands of people. To this end, they planted an enormous truck bomb in an underground garage beneath the north tower. The bomb contained more than half a ton of urea nitrate, with a nitroglycerine detonator. It also contained hydrogen cyanide, which the bombers hoped would envelop the blast zone in a cloud of poison gas.

Fortunately, the bomb failed to perform as intended. The cyanide burnt up harmlessly in the blast. The bomb blew a hole six stories deep beneath the Tower, punching through five basement levels, but it failed to undermine the north tower. Thousands were injured and six killed, but the Towers remained.[8]

The Clinton administration handled the first World Trade Center bombing as an ordinary crime. Clinton left the matter to the criminal justice system. Four of the bombers—one Egyptian and three Palestinians—were captured, fingerprinted, mug shot, tried, convicted and sentenced within weeks of the attack. At least three other bombers found refuge in foreign countries, including the team leader, a suspected Iraqi agent named Ramzi Ahmed Yousef.[9] All but one of the seven suspected bombers were eventually caught and convicted. However, US authorities never succeeded in figuring out who ordered the attack in the first place, or in identifying its perpetrators as part of a global terrorist army mobilized against the West.[10]

Much evidence pointed to Saddam Hussein, who had vowed vengeance on America for his defeat in the Gulf War. The terrorist ringleader Yousef had entered the country with an Iraqi passport and was known in New York as "Rashid the Iraqi." Another suspect, Abdul Rahman Yasin, was a US-born Iraqi whose family had taken him back to Iraq to live when he was still a child. After the World Trade Center bombing, Yasin fled to Baghdad, where he was given asylum and, according to one source, a government job. Somehow he eluded US occupation forces when they arrived in Iraq. Yasin remains at large to this day, with a $5 million reward for his capture.

Back in 1993, FBI assistant director James Fox, who then headed the Bureau's New York City office, suspected that the Iraqi intelligence service *Jihaz Al-Mukhabarat Al-A'ma* had orchestrated the bombing, using Islamist volunteers from other countries as cover.[11] However, Fox was not permitted to pursue this line of inquiry. He later confided to terrorism expert Laurie Mylroie that Janet Reno's Justice Department pressured him to ignore any possible involvement by foreign governments. Reno's people "did not want state sponsorship addressed," Fox explained.[12] They simply wanted to arrest and jail the terrorists as common criminals.

President Clinton sought to downplay the attack in every way possible. He pointedly avoided visiting the blast site. In interviews and press conferences, he urged Americans not to "overreact."[13] Following Clinton's lead, New York State governor Mario Cuomo told NBC-TV on 1 March that, "Americans killing one another with guns" posed a bigger threat to public safety than terrorism. Cuomo soliloquized, "We're more threatened by ourselves than we are by foreign terrorists. . . . We're still the most violent place in the world, not because they do it to us but because we do it to ourselves. Terrorism is hardly the problem that the instinct for violence and the refusal to acknowledge it . . . is to us internally."[14]

The passivity and introspection that the bombing evoked from leaders of America's ruling political party—which at the time was the Democrats—served to encourage further attacks. In June 1993, the infamous "blind Sheikh" Omar Abdel Rahman and nine of his followers were arrested for plotting a "Day of Terror" in New York. They planned to bomb UN headquarters, a federal office building, the George Washington Bridge, and the Lincoln and Holland Tunnels, and kill 250,000 people.[15] Investigators soon realized that Rahman was implicated in the earlier World Trade Center attack as well. Several of the bombers involved in the 1993 attack turned out to be followers of Rahman.

Again, Clinton relegated the matter to the criminal justice system. Investigators focused on a small group of low-level perpetrators. Rahman was convicted and jailed, but the global terror network of which his group formed a small but important node went about its business unmolested, enjoying the hospitality and financial support of innumerable friendly regimes in many countries. Had Clinton treated the first World Trade Center attack with the seriousness it deserved, the second attack might not have happened. Tragically, Clinton chose to treat terrorism as an ordinary crime, rather than facing up to what it really was—an act of war against the United States.

We now know that the terrorists who attacked the World Trade Center in 1993 had ties with the al-Qaeda network—the same network that returned on 9/11 to finish the job. George Soros knew this when he wrote his anti-Bush polemic *The Bubble of American Supremacy* in 2002. He knew that eight years of police work had failed to neutralize the terror network and failed to protect the towers. He knew that treating terrorist acts as ordinary crimes does not work. Soros knew all these things, yet he went ahead and wrote, "War is a false and misleading metaphor in the context of combating terrorism. Crimes [like the 9/11 attack] require police work.... In the case of terrorists we *are* dealing with a crime. We need detective work, good intelligence, and cooperation from the public, not military action."[16] Why did Soros write these words, when he surely knew they were not true?

When the second and final attack on the Twin Towers came on 9/11, it brought Wall Street to a standstill. All trading stopped on the New York Stock Exchange until the following Monday, which was 17 September. As the world waited anxiously for Monday's opening bell, the American investment community loyally vowed that it would not let the markets falter. "The patriot in me thinks nothing would be a better slap in the face of some terrible people than a market rally," volunteered money manager Langdon Wheeler in a letter written on Friday, 14 September, urging 100 of his clients to buy stock on Monday. Many shared Wheeler's sentiment. Major companies such as Pfizer, Cisco Systems, FleetBoston Financial and American International Group announced their intention to spend billions of dollars buying back their own stock, in order to help prop up the market. Dozens of giant pension funds with hundreds of billions of dollars under management likewise declared their intention to keep the market afloat through massive buying on Monday. Smaller investors rose up from the grassroots, filling the Internet with chain e-mails calling for an invest-in-America campaign. "Rally the Market on Monday!" one e-mail urged, exhorting patriotic investors to buy 100 shares of their favorite stock before Monday's closing bell.[17]

US officials did what they could to encourage such patriotic investment. The Federal Reserve released a flood of cash into the economy, while regulatory officials pleaded behind the scenes with Wall Street hedge fund managers, asking them to resist the temptation to profit from America's tragedy by short-selling stock in wounded industries. Selling a stock short means betting *against* the stock on the hope that it will *drop* in value—exactly what Soros had done to the British pound. In the stock market, this is accomplished by leasing shares of the targeted stock from a broker, then selling the shares while the price is still high. After the stock crashes, the investor buys back the shares at the new lower price, returns them to the broker, and pockets the profit from the transaction.

The danger of short selling is that it can become a self-fulfilling prophecy, actually helping to depress the market. The shorting investor obviously has a big stake in seeing the stock fall. If it rises, his investment—and then some—is lost. The more shares of the targeted stock short-sellers dump, the lower the price falls. SEC officials feared massive short selling of US securities after 9/11, and tried to discourage it.[18]

Many brokerage houses had lost people in the 9/11 attack. When Monday morning arrived, Wall Street traders observed two minutes of silence to honor the dead, followed by a reaffirming chorus of "God Bless America." Ground Zero rescue workers rang the opening bell at the New York Stock Exchange. Despite these symbolic appeals to national unity, predatory traders drowned out the efforts of America's investor-patriots that day. The Dow Jones Industrial Average plummeted a record 685 points before the closing bell.

Following Monday's market crash, many observers blamed leading hedge funds. Some of these funds made fortunes short-selling the stocks of hard-hit industries such as hotels, auto and other transport-related companies. One financial services insider told NewsMax.com, "We had calls from small people trying to invest $100 to $500. The people were attempting to be patriotic and wanted to invest in America. I find it absolutely sickening and heartbreaking that billionaires investing money for extremely wealthy people are helping to push the markets lower."[19]

One such billionaire was Soros. On Wednesday, 19 September, he was in Hong Kong speaking to a group of business leaders. At a press conference that day, he refused to divulge whether or not his Quantum Fund had been short-selling US assets. Nevertheless, he dropped a useful hint to investors listening. "I don't think you can run markets on patriotic principles," Soros declared.[20] For many Soros followers, that was all they needed to know. It was the signal that he did not support the invest-in-America campaign.

Soros followed this by revealing that he opposed answering the terrorist attacks with a military strike on the Taliban. CNN correspondent Andrew Stevens asked him, "If there is a significant military response by the US on terrorists, what will be the effect on the markets?" Soros replied:

> I think the financial markets are currently afraid of it. I think it's one of the elements of uncertainty that is weighing on financial markets. And I think a lot depends on the response. I think retaliation would definitely have a negative effect, because it would have a negative effect in reality. It would actually be a victory for the terrorists if we now, let's say, inflict—kill innocent civilians. That's the kind of radicalization that they are looking for. But I am confident—and all the signs point to it—that the government is fully aware of this. This is the

advice that they are receiving from Europe and from the Middle East. So actually, I think we are going to be pretty sound in our response.[21]

Soros had just announced to the world, via CNN, that a military retaliation to the most heinous attack in American history would "kill innocent civilians" and hurt global markets. This was also a signal to global markets to respond negatively to such an act of American self-defense.

How then did Soros propose that America should respond? Here Soros grew vague. In his speech that evening at the Asia Society Hong Kong Center, he suggested that America might try to "seal off" Afghanistan, while at the same time taking "constructive steps to improve the world in which we live." But, no invasion:

> We must engage in a concerted effort to eradicate organized terrorism, but we must realize that it is going to be extremely difficult to capture Bin Laden 'dead or alive,' because Afghanistan is very inaccessible.... I think air attacks are largely useless.... [D]uring the Soviet occupation of Afghanistan ... [the mujahideen] were basically living in caves in the mountains, and at night they went down and tilled the soil. They survived the daily bombing raids of the Soviet army pretty well. I think sealing off Afghanistan holds more promise.... I think you could seal off Afghanistan, but that would mean a long siege and we would have to be patient and persistent, and above all, we must avoid creating civilian casualties and demonizing Islam. I am hopeful that this, in fact, will be the policy that the U.S. government follows.... [W]e must match the war on terrorism with constructive steps to improve the world in which we live.[22]

By invoking the experience of the lumbering Soviet invasion and occupation army of 20 years past, Soros misled his audience as to the superior capabilities the US military could bring to bear in the 21st Century. Why he did so is puzzling. Soros is intimately familiar with modern advances in military weaponry, and knew better. He has been a major investor in defense technology since at least 1974, when his Soros Fund began buying up shares of Northrop, Grumman, Lockheed and United Aircraft (subsequently renamed United Technologies). More to the point, Soros was an early pioneer of the "automated battlefield." Beginning in 1975, he invested heavily in such futuristic weapons systems as "smart" bombs, laser-guided artillery, electronic sensors and computerized targeting.[23] In other words, Soros knew how inappropriate it was to compare the weapons and tactics of the Soviet Army circa 1979 with those at the disposal of US forces in 2001.

US and Coalition forces took less than six months to secure Afghanistan, something the Soviets failed to achieve in ten years of fighting. Soros' warning that world markets would respond negatively to US military action proved equally misleading.

On 14 September 2001, economist Brian Wesbury had presented a far more accurate prediction in the *Wall Street Journal*. In an article titled, "The Best Economic Stimulus: Victory" Wesbury wrote, "From an economic perspective, the Bush administration's job in this situation is to reduce risk. And the way to reduce risk is to actively pursue a strategy of eliminating the enemy." Wesbury reminded readers that, "During World War II, the Dow Jones Industrial Average slumped as the Germans marched across Europe. But as U.S. resolve strengthened following Pearl Harbor, the market recovered and the Dow more than doubled between April 1942 and mid-1946. . . . More recently, Saddam Hussein's invasion of Kuwait led to economic turmoil. But the minute bombs started to drop on Baghdad in 1991, stock-market futures soared and never looked back." By contrast, Wesbury

13

noted, America's indecisive conduct of the Vietnam War spooked the markets, as a result of which, from the beginning of the war to its end, the Dow fell 30 percent. "The lesson is clear: A tepid response by the U.S. government toward international terrorism at this juncture will have devastating effects to the long-run health of the U.S. economy. Purposeful military action will reduce the economic risk."[24]

Wesbury was only stating the obvious, and Soros was too smart an investor not to know that he was correct. But Soros was following an agenda that went beyond dollars and cents, beyond fighting terrorism, and beyond any concern for America's best interests. His goal was to end what Henry Luce called "the American Century"—the era of America's dominance in global affairs. In order to meet this objective, Soros would have to stop George Bush from winning the War on Terror.

As the election of 2004 approached—the first since American troops entered Iraq—the public began to learn just what Soros meant when he said in the wake of 9/11 that he intended to "improve the world in which we live." The focal point of this improvement would be removing George Bush as commander-in-chief.

Seven months after American troops entered Iraq and just before the first Democratic primaries, on 29 September 2003, Soros called for "regime change in the United States." He charged that "extremists" had seized the American government and were seeking to dominate the world. He said:

There is a group of—I would call them extremists—who have the following belief: that international relations are relations of power, not of law, that international law will always follow what power has achieved. And therefore the United States

14

being the most powerful nation on earth should impose its power, impose its will and its interests on the world and it should do it looking after itself. I think this is a very dangerous ideology. It is very dangerous because America is in fact very powerful. . . . America being really the dominant power to be in the grips of such an extremist ideology is very dangerous for the world. . . .[25]

A month later, Soros again vowed to drive Bush from office. His language was inflammatory, verging on hysteria. "America under Bush is a danger to the world," Soros told the *Washington Post*. Removing Bush was "the central focus of my life . . . a matter of life and death." Soros then offered: "I'm willing to put my money where my mouth is." How much money, the *Post* asked? Would Soros spend his entire personal fortune to oust Bush? "If someone guaranteed it," he replied. [26]

In the same interview, Soros compared the Bush administration to Nazi Germany. Soros himself had survived both Nazi and Soviet occupation in his native Hungary. He told the *Washington Post*, "When I hear Bush say, 'You're either with us or against us,' it reminds me of the Germans. My experiences under Nazi and Soviet rule have sensitized me."[27] In fact, Bush's statement had been eminently reasonable. For too long, nations pretending to be our friends and allies had been colluding with terrorists on the sly. As long as terrorists found safe harbor anywhere in the world, they would continue to operate. No one could be neutral in such a war. Bush was challenging every nation to stand up and be counted in a struggle against a common foe who threatened every civilized nation alike. Why Soros would object to this policy was unclear, but he objected very strongly.

For the second time in three months, Soros had claimed that

America posed a danger to the world. What exactly did he mean? The following month, December 2003, provided an answer in the form of a new Soros book called *The Bubble of American Supremacy: Correcting the Misuse of American Power.* In it, Soros reiterated his view that the 9/11 attacks did not justify war. "Treating the attacks of September 11 as crimes against humanity would have been more appropriate," he wrote. "Crimes require police work, not military action."[28] It was a line Democratic candidate John Kerry was using in his primary campaign.

More significantly, Soros wrote that America's military response was actually worse, morally, than the original "crime," because, "the war on terrorism has claimed more innocent civilians in Afghanistan and Iraq than have the attacks on the World Trade Center."[29] This was a standard propaganda line of the Left. On such grounds, the allies in World War II would have been judged morally worse than the aggressors who started the war, because the allies won, killing more of the enemy—and inevitably civilians—in the process.

Soros even described the Bush Administration's "pursuit of American supremacy" as more dangerous than Islamist terror,[30] while castigating US leaders for believing that Americans "[had] right on our side."[31] As Soros put it, "Bush equates freedom with American values. He has a simplistic view of what is right and wrong: *We* are right and *they* are wrong. This is in contradiction with the principles of open society, which recognize that *we* may be wrong."[32] Does Soros mean that terrorists may be right?

The bottom line for Soros was that in the middle of the terror war with Islamic radicals, Soros wanted an American president who believed that America may be wrong.

In keeping with this line of reasoning, Soros argued that America's present course would lead to disaster. "I see a certain parallel between the pursuit of American supremacy and the boom-bust pattern that can be observed from time to time in the stock market. The bubble is now bursting."[33] Nations, like stock bubbles, do have a tendency to move from boom to bust, and hopefully back to boom again. However, in regard to America's future, Soros is not content to be a passive investor. He intends to intervene in the process, and not in America's favor. In Soros' vision, America is a threat to world peace and survival. In order to curb the threat, he told an audience at the London School of Economics on 29 January 2004, it is necessary to "puncture the bubble of American supremacy."[34]

The Shadow Party is the institutional manifestation of Soros' anti-American obsession. It is the political spear with which he intends to puncture the bubble of America's influence and success. Coming from anyone else, Soros' threats would sound like idle raving. But Soros is no sidewalk malcontent. He has unprecedented political and financial power for a private citizen and has had real-world experience in putting them to use.

2

HOW SOROS
WORKS

Any journalist who has studied Soros with sufficient attentiveness has learned to greet his public utterances with an ounce of skepticism. At times, Soros evinces what can only be called a professional pride in his skill at deception. His work affords him ample opportunity to hone this talent.

Soros' Open Society foundations have facilitated coups and rebellions in many countries, always ostensibly in the interests of "democratization." In a 1995 *New Yorker* profile Soros told his interlocutor that the "subversive" mission of his Open Society network has required him to wear a variety of masks through the years. In some countries, he would adopt a pro-communist pose while in others he would play the anti-communist. Only Soros himself knew where he really stood—and perhaps not even Soros. "I would say one thing in one country, and another thing in another country," he laughed.[1]

The November 2003 uprising that toppled Georgian President Eduard Shevardnadze is a case in point. While visiting Ukraine, Soros categorically denied press reports linking him to the coup. He told reporters in Kiev on 31 March 2004, "Everything in Georgia was done by its people, not by me. I had nothing to do with it."[2] However, in July, the *Los Angeles Times* quoted Soros thus: "I'm delighted by what happened in Georgia, and I take great pride in having contributed to it."[3] Which version is to be believed? In many ways, the Shadow Party reflects the personality of its creator, an institutional manifestation of its author's fascination with smoke and mirrors. Secrecy, misdirection and

21

disinformation are its stock-in-trade. A fog of deception cloaks its operations at every level.

The financial nerve center of Soros' empire is an investment firm called Soros Fund Management LLC, located at 888 Seventh Avenue in Manhattan. Political operations are facilitated mainly through the Open Society Institute (OSI), whose main office is at 400 West 59th Street. OSI is the flagship of the Soros Foundation Network, whose Open Society Foundations operate in more than 50 countries.

A glance at the top-ranking officers of Soros' Open Society Institute sheds light on the type of expertise Soros values most highly. Its Director of US Advocacy operating from its Washington office is Morton H. Halperin, a former government official with a noteworthy career in left-wing causes. In 1967, the Johnson Defense Department placed Halperin in charge of compiling a secret history of US involvement in Vietnam, based on classified documents. Halperin and his deputy Leslie Gelb assigned much of the writing to left-wing opponents of the war. Not surprisingly, they ended up producing a history that echoed Halperin's long-standing position that the Vietnam War was unwinnable, and ridiculed Presidents Kennedy and Johnson for stubbornly refusing to heed those of their advisors who shared this opinion.

One of Halperin's writers was Daniel Ellsberg. Despite his background as a former Marine and a military analyst for the Rand Corporation, Ellsberg had evolved into a New Left radical. In a personal memoir, *Secrets*, Ellsberg writes that he had already concluded as early as 1967 that, "we were not fighting on the wrong side; we were the wrong side" in the Vietnam War.[4] Evidently Ellsberg had come to view Ho Chi Minh's totalitarian regime as a force for good in the world.

Ellsberg removed the classified documents and released them

to the *New York Times*, which published them as "The Pentagon Papers" in June 1971.[5] This was a clear violation of the Espionage Act of 1918, which forbids the removal of classified documents from government buildings. The government prosecuted Ellsberg, but was forced to drop its case as Nixon's power collapsed during the Watergate intrigues.

Not unlike Ellsberg, Halperin also had a disturbing tendency to abuse his access to top-secret information for the purpose of undermining American policy. At one point, President Nixon and National Security Advisor Henry Kissinger strongly suspected that Halperin was leaking military secrets to the press, in particular, information involving top-secret US military operations in Cambodia. They ordered an FBI tap on his phone. The tap revealed that Halperin stayed in close touch with Daniel Ellsberg long after their professional relationship had ended. On one occasion, FBI agents overheard Halperin, still a consultant to the Nixon White House, discussing political strategies for sabotaging the war effort by cutting off its funding.[6]

Another key Soros appointee is Aryeh Neier, who is president of the Open Society Institute and the Soros Foundation Network. As director of the socialist League for Industrial Democracy, Neier personally created the radical group Students for a Democratic Society, or SDS, in 1959.[7] During the Vietnam War, SDS was the student group most responsible for fanning the flames of unrest on US campuses, and later transformed itself into the terrorist Weather Underground, which declared war on "Amerikkka" and bombed the Pentagon and the Capitol. By that time, however, Neier had moved on to more important projects.

He worked for the American Civil Liberties Union for fifteen years (1963-1978), serving as its director for the last eight of those years (1970-78). Under Neier's leadership, the ACLU helped the

New York Times thwart Nixon's efforts to block publication of the Pentagon Papers through a Supreme Court appeal.[8] Under Neier, the ACLU also issued one of the earliest calls for Nixon's impeachment, in a resolution of 4 October 1973.

Ten days after issuing the resolution, the ACLU launched a nationwide newspaper advertising campaign against Nixon, starting with a full-page statement in the *New York Times* headlined, "Why It Is Necessary To Impeach Richard Nixon. And How It Can Be Done." Putting theory into practice, Neier's ACLU filed suit against Nixon and Kissinger on Morton Halperin's behalf, charging that their FBI wiretap on Halperin's phone had been illegal. In his memoir, Neier writes that testimony from the Halperin lawsuit helped the House Judiciary Committee draw up its articles of impeachment against Nixon.[9]

No doubt impressed by Neier's string of victories against his arch-nemesis Nixon, Halperin himself later joined the ACLU. From 1975 to 1992, he directed an ACLU project called the Center for National Security Studies, which sought to cut US defense spending and hamstring US intelligence capabilities. Halperin also became director of the ACLU Washington office from 1984 to 1992 and head of its "National Security Archives." From this position, Halperin successfully battled to lift a government injunction barring the radical journal the *Progressive* from publishing a recipe for making a hydrogen bomb.[10]

More importantly, Halperin waged open war against US intelligence services, through the courts and the press, seeking to strip the government of virtually any power to investigate, monitor or obstruct subversive elements and their activities.[11] It did not take him long to go the next logical step and argue for abolishing America's intelligence services altogether. "Using secret intelligence agencies to defend a constitutional republic is akin to the ancient medical practice of employing leeches to take blood from feverish patients. The intent is therapeutic, but in the long run the cure is more deadly than the disease," Halperin wrote in his 1976 book, *The Lawless State: The Crimes of the U.S. Intelligence Agencies.*[12]

In a March 1987 article in the *Nation*, Halperin expanded on this theme and, like Ellsberg, took the position that America was the real villain in the Cold War. He wrote, "Secrecy does not serve national security. Covert operations are incompatible with constitutional government and should be abolished."[13] This was a call for unilateral disarming of our intelligence services to match the disarmament of our military, which has long been a staple of the radical agenda.

In hiring Halperin, Soros enabled him to continue his war on America's intelligence services. One of Halperin's principal assignments on the Soros team is to battle "post-September 11 policies that threaten the civil liberties of Americans," which includes blocking the provisions of the Patriot Act that provide new powers to America's intelligence agencies.[14] In this effort, the ACLU, the pro-Castro Center for Constitutional Rights, and other leftist organizations associated with Soros play leading roles.

Soros hired Aryeh Neier in 1993 and Morton Halperin in 2002. In doing so, he put together a team with a common expertise. He has elevated to positions of the highest authority in his Shadow Party two of the men responsible for the political efforts that helped to engineer America's defeat in Vietnam. Today, under Soros' leadership, Neier and Halperin are hard at work on a new project—undermining America's war in Iraq—a task for which their experience uniquely fits them.

As with Vietnam, swaying public opinion against the war in Iraq will not suffice, in and of itself, to bring about US defeat. The

Left knows from experience that US defeat requires a two-phase attack. Phase One is to undermine Americans' will to fight by fostering a spirit of defeatism regarding the war and by casting doubt on its morality. Phase Two is to deprive Americans of their war leader. During the Vietnam War, this was accomplished by forcing President Nixon's resignation.

Both phases were necessary to bring about defeat in Vietnam. In the Iraq War, the Shadow Party is following the same two-step strategy. We might designate the two phases Vietnam II and Watergate II.

Vietnam II encompasses those efforts of the Shadow Party that aim at discrediting, hindering, prolonging and otherwise rendering the war unpalatable to ordinary Americans. Watergate II refers to those efforts designed to inflict upon America a second Watergate crisis, thereby depriving us of America's war leader in a crucial phase of the war. In the early 1970s, it was the resignation of Richard Nixon that encouraged the North Vietnamese to break the Paris Peace Accords by invading and conquering South Vietnam, and the Khmer Rouge to do the same in Cambodia. The impeachment of George Bush would obviously have a similar effect, emboldening our enemies in the Middle East and, indeed, throughout the world.

Open Society Institute funds are heavily involved in operations aimed at implementing Vietnam II and Watergate II. For instance, the Soros-funded Center for Constitutional Rights has already drawn up formal Articles of Impeachment against President Bush, copies of which can be purchased from its website. Another recipient of Soros funding, Amnesty International, has called for the arrest of George Bush, Donald Rumsfeld and other White House officials for alleged mistreatment of Iraqi and other terrorist prisoners. Dr. William F. Schultz, head of Amnesty

International USA issued a statement on 25 May 2005 which said:

> If the U.S. government continues to shirk its responsibility,
> Amnesty International calls on foreign governments to uphold
> their obligations under international law by investigating all
> senior U.S. officials involved in the torture scandal. If those
> investigations support prosecution, the governments should
> arrest any official who enters their territory and begin legal
> proceedings against them. The apparent high-level architects
> of torture should think twice before planning their next vaca-
> tion to places like Acapulco or the French Riviera because they
> may find themselves under arrest as (former Chilean dictator)
> Augusto Pinochet famously did in London in 1998.[15]

In what appears to be a conscious reenactment of its historic
New York Times advertisement of 14 October 1973 calling for the
impeachment of Richard Nixon, the ACLU took out a full-page
advertisement in the *New York Times*, which ran in the 29
December 2005 issue, this time calling for a special counsel to
investigate President Bush's terrorist surveillance program, and
strongly implying that the president should be impeached.
"President Nixon was not above the law and neither is President
Bush," states ACLU Executive Director Anthony D. Romero in
the ad.[16]

Accomplishing such objectives requires an intricate coordination of "inside" activities that fall within the parameters of the
American mainstream (pressures from above) and "outside" activities that draw on the radical grassroots that are openly at war with
the mainstream (pressure from below). Sometimes the need to
work both sides of the fence can result in embarrassing situations,
as, for instance, when *National Review*'s Washington bureau

chief Byron York revealed that Soros' Open Society Institute had contributed to the Lynne Stewart Defense Committee.

Radical attorney Lynne Stewart is a convicted accomplice to terrorism. She was caught on tape helping the imprisoned "blind Sheikh" Omar Abdel Rahman communicate with his terrorist followers. Wrote York, "According to records filed with the Internal Revenue Service, Soros' foundation, the Open Society Institute gave $20,000 in September 2002 to the Lynne Stewart Defense Committee."[17] The reason York was obliged to tease this information from IRS filings, we surmise, is that the data is difficult to find anywhere else.

For instance, it does not appear in any of the Institute's annual reports, nor is it easily retrievable from the Institute's soros.org website. We tried to find it in the most obvious and intuitive way— the way most potential donors, unfamiliar with the website, would have been likely to do it. We typed "Lynne Stewart" and "Lynne Stewart Defense Committee" into the website's general and "advanced" search engines. Our searches produced no links to any Lynne Stewart listing in the Institute's grant database. Only after much rambling around the Internet did we finally locate a page on the FreeRepublic.com message board where an anonymous researcher using the screen name "piasa" just happened to have posted a direct Web address to soros.org's grant listing for the Lynne Stewart Defense Committee. We found the link, but it took luck and persistence. Without "piasa," we might have failed. This experience suggests to us that, prior to Byron York's exposé, potential donors wishing to avoid contributing to charities that fund terrorists might have found it difficult to learn about the Institute's involvement with Lynne Stewart.

The coyness of the Lynne Stewart listing reflects a larger pattern in Soros' Open Socety Institute. This is no accident, as the saying goes. A revealing description of the Institute's record-keeping practices, in fact, comes from its current president, Aryeh Neier. Upon assuming the presidency of the Soros Foundations and the Open Society Institute, Neier found the network's financial records in chaos. "Decisions for the network were generally made by George himself," Neier wrote. "Paper trails either did not exist or were so scant as to be meaningless. George took pride in operating the network in its early years without a budget. . . . The looseness of the finances added to my difficulty in getting a picture of what was being done. . . . [O]nly George himself had an overview of the activities of the whole network."[18]

Neier claims that he "introduced more standard institutional practices" to the operation, but the Lynne Stewart affair suggests that he has a long way to go before attaining anything close to an acceptable degree of financial transparency.

The Institute's purposeful obscurantism is no trivial matter in the philanthropic world, as David Hogberg noted in the *American Spectator* of 5 February 2005. "Both the Ford and Rockefeller Foundations recently instituted policies requiring their grantees to sign a statement saying that its grantees do not support terrorist groups or activities," wrote Hogberg. This was the result of a scandal in which Ford had funded terrorist groups in the Middle East disguised as rights groups and charities. "At the very least, the morally responsible action for OSI grant recipients is to refuse any further OSI money until OSI adopts a similar policy," wrote Hogberg.[19]

Of course, the Institute maintains that it did not view Lynne Stewart as a terrorist when it funded her defense. It viewed her as a "human rights defender." In a 13 October 2004 speech in Oslo, Norway, Institute vice president and director of US programs Gara LaMarche said, "The right to counsel, and its erosion in the

United States since September 11, strikes with particular force at the role of human rights defenders. One troubling trend has been the arrest and prosecution of lawyers and other defenders as 'material witnesses' to terrorism. These include Lynne Stewart, attorney for Sheik Abdul Rahman."[20]

Even at that date, however, Institute officials knew that Lynne Stewart was no defender of "human rights." She is a well-known member of the pro-Communist "legal left" familiar to Aryeh Neier, himself a frequent contributor for the leftist *Nation*. It is no secret in "progressive" circles that Stewart is a self-described revolutionary who advocates the violent overthrow of capitalism followed by the state suppression of people considered "counter-revolutionary" by the new regime. "I don't have any problem with Mao or Stalin or the Vietnamese leaders or certainly Fidel locking up people they see as dangerous," she opined in a November 2002 interview in the Maoist journal *Monthly Review*.[21] In a 1995 interview with the *New York Times*, Stewart said, "I don't believe in anarchistic violence, but in directed violence. That would be violence directed at the institutions which perpetuate capitalism, racism, sexism, and at the people who are the appointed guardians of those institutions."[22]

In keeping with her belief in "directed violence," Stewart has made a vocation of defending violent radicals in court, often as counsel for the radical Center for Constitutional Rights. Her clients have included the Weather Underground terrorist Kathy Boudin, who drove the getaway car during a 1981 Brinks truck robbery in Nyack, New York; David J. Gilbert, who was convicted, along with two comrades, of killing two police officers and a security guard in the same 1981 Brinks truck robbery; Black Panther Willie Holder, who hijacked an airliner to Algiers in 1972 and who allegedly plotted another skyjacking in 1991; and a Palestinian who tried to firebomb a New York synagogue.

It was while defending the "blind Sheikh" Omar Abdel Rahman, however, that Stewart crossed the line and made the transition from terrorist lawyer to terrorist accomplice. Stewart believed passionately in Rahman's cause. Regarding her relationship with the "blind Sheikh," a *New York Times Magazine* article of 22 September 2002 notes, "Stewart was a 'movement' lawyer—she didn't just defend the legal rights of her clients; she also advocated their politics. . . . As Stewart got to know her new client, she came to see him as a fighter for national liberation on behalf of a people oppressed by dictatorship and American imperialism."[23]

Despite Stewart's best efforts, Rahman was sentenced to life in prison on 17 January 1996 for his role in the 1993 World Trade Center bombing and the "Day of Terror" plot. The *Al'Gama'a al-Islamiyya* (Islamic Group) that Rahman heads in Egypt immediately threatened to "hit American interests and personalities" unless US authorities released their leader.[24] Confronted with this threat, Rahman's prosecutor Patrick Fitzgerald imposed "Special Administrative Measures" forbidding the Sheikh to communicate with anyone but his wife and lawyers. All persons allowed access to the Sheikh were forbidden to relay messages back and forth between the cleric and his terrorist followers. The obvious reason for imposing these rules was to prevent Rahman from ordering or encouraging more killings.

Lynne Stewart agreed to these Special Administrative Measures, but then flouted them, helping her client transmit many messages to his flock, including incitements to violence.[25] One technique Stewart employed to smuggle out the Sheikh's communiqués was to distract the prison guard's attention by pretending to make small talk with the Sheikh. While Stewart kept up a stream of blather, much of it quite nonsensical, the Sheikh would speak quietly in Arabic to his interpreter, conveying to him whatever messages he wished to send. Unbeknownst to the conspirators, their intrigues were captured on tape.[26]

The FBI arrested Stewart outside her Brooklyn home on 9 April 2002. She struck a defiant pose at her trial, declaring at one point, "To rid ourselves of the entrenched, voracious type of capitalism that is in this country that perpetuates sexism and racism, I don't think that can come nonviolently. . . . I'm talking about a popular revolution. I'm talking about institutions being changed and that will not be changed without violence."[27] Charged with two counts each of aiding terrorists and lying to federal investigators, Stewart was convicted on 10 February 2005.[28]

Following her arrest, Lynne Stewart's case became a cause célèbre on the left. A "Free Lynne Stewart" movement formed within days. The Center for Constitutional Rights issued a press release characterizing Stewart's indictment as "an attack on attorneys who defend controversial figures and an attempt to deprive these clients of the zealous representation that may be required."[29] Leading the "Free Lynne Stewart" movement was the American Civil Liberties Union (ACLU). Following her conviction, the Massachusetts ACLU issued a statement that read, in part, "[T]he prosecution of Lynne Stewart is a chilling testament to what is being done to individual rights and to the rule of law itself in the name of 'fighting terrorism'. . . . [W]e can only hope that the conviction of Lynne Stewart will be overturned on appeal."[30]

In response to Byron York's exposé, the Open Society Institute tried to distance itself from the Lynne Stewart affair. In an interview with York, Institute spokeswoman Amy Weil volunteered, "More recently, the Institute was asked for additional funding [from the Lynne Stewart Defense Committee] and we turned down that request."³¹ With these words, Weil seemed to imply that Lynne Stewart and her terrorist cause had lost favor with Soros. But had they really? Soros may have stopped giving direct grants to Lynne Stewart, but Weil failed to point out that virtually every other organization taking a prominent role in the "Free Lynne Stewart" movement receives financial support from the Open Society Institute.

No organization has lent more support to Lynne Stewart personally, nor to the legal attack on America's War on Terror, than the American Civil Liberties Union. According to data on file with the Capital Research Center, the Foundation Center, and the Internal Revenue Service, Soros' Institute contributed nearly $19 million to the ACLU during the seven-year period spanning 1998 to 2004—about $2.7 million per year, on average. During this time, the ACLU was busy clogging the courts with lawsuits seeking to stop the use of military commissions to try prisoners of war at Guantanamo Bay, to forbid harsh interrogations of terrorist suspects, to allow Muslims to wear head coverings that obscure their identity in government ID photos, to block the National Security Agency from intercepting telecommunications between terror suspects, and much more.

Perhaps most destructively, the ACLU is spearheading a nationwide effort to induce local governments to declare their jurisdictions "civil liberties safe zones." Cities, towns, counties and states that make such declarations officially repudiate the USA-PATRIOT Act and refuse to cooperate with Homeland Security and the federal counterterror operations authorized by the Act.

As of this writing, eight states and 399 cities, towns and counties have declared themselves "civil liberties safe zones," and another 280 resolutions are reportedly in the works.³² It is perhaps worth noting that Soros' Open Society Institute supports the "civil liberties safe zones" movement not only indirectly through its massive funding of the ACLU, but also directly through financial contributions to the Bill of Rights Defense Committee, which is coordinating the campaign.

3

BORING
FROM WITHIN

As part of their strategy for bringing "pressure from below," George Soros and his Shadow Party pursue alliances with street-level activist groups. Such groups are particularly effective in manipulating local politics. Democratic organizations at the state, county and municipal levels provide easy points of entry for Shadow Party operatives. Once embedded in the party's grassroots infrastructure, they can bore from within.

On 16 August 2005, Soros' Open Society Institute helped launch a new organization called the Progressive Legislative Action Network (PLAN). The Institute's partners in the project include the Soros-funded Center for American Progress run by former Clinton chief of staff John Podesta, the Soros-funded activist group MoveOn, the AFL-CIO, SEIU, AFSCME and the United Steelworkers. Led by Democrat activists David Sirota and Steve Doherty, its purported mission is to seed state legislatures with pre-written, "model" legislation reflecting their leftist goals.[1] However, Soros' involvement with the group makes it highly unlikely that PLAN will restrict its activities to conventional lobbying.

Why the sudden interest in state and local politics on Soros' part? One motivation was noted by the *New York Times*: "The more conservatives succeed in reducing the size and scope of the federal government, the more fiscal freedom the blue states will have to pursue their own idea of a just society."[2] This dovetails neatly with the Left's ongoing campaign to radicalize America from the bottom up, gaining power city by city, county by county, and state by state, in a relentless, political ground war.

Much as Governor George Wallace defied the federal government's orders to desegregate Alabama schools in 1963, the Left now seeks to establish itself in state houses and county seats across the nation, from which it can safely thumb its nose at federal policies it dislikes.

To this end, Soros has transformed his home state of New York into a veritable laboratory for bottom-up revolution. "New York is a state that has more Democrats than Republicans," Soros spokesman Michael Vachon explained. "If we can't gain a foothold here, how can we expect to win on the national level?"[3]

Albany is one of the more heavily Democratic counties in a heavily Democratic state. In the 2004 election, for example, it was generally assumed that the next District Attorney would be a Democrat. The issue for Soros was not how to get a Democrat elected in Albany, but how to get *his* Democrat elected.

Democratic Party stalwart Paul A. Clyne had been Albany DA since 2001, and the Albany County Democrats wanted to keep him there. But Clyne had an Achilles heel. He was tough on drugs, and many voters in his district were not. Clyne favored the 1973 Rockefeller drug laws, the strictest in the nation, many of which were still in force in New York State. Polls showed that a sizeable proportion of New York Democrats wanted the drug laws softened.

Soros saw an opportunity. Working for Clyne was a 34-year-old African American assistant district attorney named P. David Soares. He was ambitious and disgruntled, the perfect profile for a Shadow Party recruit. Soros knew that the Albany County Democrats would put all their money behind Clyne. In order to beat Clyne in the Democrat primary, Soares would need outside help. The full resources of the Shadow Party were brought to bear. An entity calling itself the Working Families Party entered the fray to wage a political "ground war" on David Soares' behalf.

The Working Families Party is a front group for ACORN—the Association of Community Organizations for Reform Now—the largest and most powerful radical activist group in America, about which we will have more to say later. For now, we will simply point out that ACORN is a recipient of Soros' funding, both directly and indirectly, and an integral component of Soros' Shadow Party network.

Steven Kest, ACORN's national executive director, founded the Working Families Party in 1998. The party's website describes the WFP as a coalition formed by ACORN, the Communications Workers of America, and the United Automobile Workers. However, it was Kest who pulled the coalition together, and it is ACORN that clearly dominates the party. To this day, the Working Families Party operates out of ACORN's New York office in Brooklyn. During the 2004 Democratic primary, *New York Sun* reporter William F. Hammond Jr. noted, with some perplexity, that calls to the David Soares campaign in Albany were referred to officials of the Working Families Party in their Brooklyn office, which is, of course, the ACORN office.[4] This provides a glimpse into the Shadow Party's mode of operation, in which lines of authority and accountability are obscured by multi-layered hierarchies of organizations within organizations within organizations.

"The [Working Families Party] was created in 1998 to help push the Democratic Party toward the left," the Associated Press noted on 28 March 2000.[5] In pursuit of this goal, WFP runs radical candidates in state and local elections. Generally, WFP candidates conceal their extremism beneath a veneer of populist rhetoric, promoting bread-and-butter issues designed to appeal

39

to union workers and other blue-collar voters, Republican and Democrat alike.

The Working Families Party benefits from a quirk of New York State election law, which allows parties to "cross-endorse" candidates of other parties. Thus when Hillary Clinton ran for the Senate in 2000, she ran both on the Democratic Party ticket and on the Working Families Party ticket. During the campaign, Hillary spoke at numerous WFP events, most memorably at the party's debut convention, held 26-27 March 2000 at the Desmond Hotel in Albany—an event which the Communist newspaper *People's Weekly World* approvingly called, "a turning point in New York politics."[6]

Before an audience packed with card-carrying members of such union affiliates of the Working Families Party as SEIU, AFSCME, CWA, UAW, and UNITE, left-wing activist Jim Hightower drew applause with such lines as, "They say Wall Street is whizzing. Well, yeah, it's whizzing on you and me. Let's call it exactly what it is—it's class war." After receiving the party's endorsement, Hillary vowed to wage a "people's grassroots campaign," telling a cheering crowd, "I consider this the beginning of a partnership."[7]

Media reports encourage the myth that an ideological rift separates the "centrist" Hillary Clinton from America's radical fringe. However, no sign of this rift can be seen in Hillary's "partnership" with the Working Families Party. "There have been few candidates in history more supportive of our issues than Al Gore and Hillary Clinton," proclaimed WFP campaign literature during the 2000 election.[8] ACORN canvassers fanned out across the state for Hillary, embarking on a massive get-out-the-vote drive.

ACORN's strategy in New York depends heavily on deception, that is, on concealing from the electorate the radical character of the group's ideology. Consider, for example, the bait-and-switch maneuver which ACORN's front group, the Working Families Party, employed in order to gain "permanent" status on the New York State ballot. In order to qualify, Working Families had to win 50,000 votes in at least one election. The fledgling party accomplished this in 1998 by cross-endorsing City Council Speaker Peter F. Vallone, a popular, old-time Queens Democrat who ran for governor in the 3 November 1998 election. Vallone lost the race for governor, but his moderate Democrat politics—utterly incompatible with ACORN's doctrine of militant class struggle—helped lure 51,325 unwitting New Yorkers into voting on the Working Families line, thus qualifying it for ballot status.[9]

Having established itself in this surreptitious manner as a legitimate political party, Working Families went to work throwing its weight around in state politics. It began seeking concessions from major-party candidates, gaining leverage through its power to grant or deny its endorsements. Since the Working Families' endorsement now carries a sizable packet of votes with it, New York politicians, Republican and Democrat alike, go out of their way to court the radical party's favor and to avoid offending its leaders.

Shortly after the party's launch in 1998, co-founder Bob Master—who is also the New York political director of the Communications Workers of America—told the Albany *Times Union*, "We're very clear that we are not abandoning the Democratic Party." Rather, the Working Families Party is attempting to move the Democrats "toward the progressive end of the spectrum," as another party organizer put it.[10]

The movement is spreading. In 2004, the Working Families Party expanded into Connecticut. Its officials promise to set up shop in all ten states where "fusion voting"—that is, cross-endorsement of candidates by multiple parties—is legal. Those states include Arkansas, Connecticut, Delaware, Idaho, Mississippi, New York, South Carolina, South Dakota, Utah and Vermont. What this means for the people of these targeted states can be gleaned, in part, from New York's doleful experience with the Working Families Party.

In the November 2001 city elections, a coalition of far-left politicians led by the Working Families Party won a controlling, veto-proof majority on the New York City Council. The radical activists at ACORN thus gained effective political control over New York City. They accomplished this power grab through careful planning and timing. In 1993, New Yorkers voted in a referendum to restrict local elected officials to two consecutive terms. The new term limits came due in November 2001, at which time a majority of City Council members were forced to step down. This was the moment for which the Working Families Party had been waiting. The City Council was up for grabs.

In the electoral putsch that followed, thirty-eight new members took their seats in the City Council. "Almost a third of the winners ran with endorsements from the extremist Working Families Party . . ." wrote Steven Malanga in the *City Journal*. "More than 60 percent of the new councilmen had backgrounds in government, social services, or community activism."[11]

The newcomers included Hillary's 2000 campaign manager Bill de Blasio and Al Gore's New York campaign manager Eric Gioia. They also included racial arsonists such as Charles Barron, a former Black Panther from Brooklyn, who lost no time arousing controversy. At an 18 August 2002 rally for slave reparations, he declared, "I want to go up to the closest white person and say, 'You can't understand this, it's a black thing,' and then slap him, just for my mental health."[12]

Having achieved its majority, the ACORN-led coalition laid

out a radical agenda. It pressed for laws tightening the Council's grip over city government and stripping the mayor of executive power. Its platform called for a rollback of Giuliani's welfare reforms; a crackdown on New York City police, including a ban on "racial and ethnic profiling;" and the appointment of a politicized Civilian Review Board newly empowered to prosecute police officers. If ACORN and its allies have their way, not only will the City Council raise corporate taxes, increase regulation and empower unions with a battery of new rights, but corporations will be forbidden by law to escape ACORN's persecution through relocation. No corporation will be permitted to leave New York without an "exit visa" issued by the City Council.[13]

While acting locally, Soros' shadow warriors always think globally. On 12 March 2003, the ACORN-dominated New York City Council passed Resolution 549-A, opposing US plans to invade Iraq. "We are sending a message to the president today, at least I am . . . that you can no longer use 9/11 as an excuse for war," declared Charles Barron. Councilwoman Yvette Clark added, "If we're looking for a fight, let's fight poverty, let's fight firehouse foreclosures, let's fight racism and sexism."[14]

Foreign news services had a field day with New York's anti-war resolution. Noted China's *Xinhua News Agency*, "The 31-17 vote in the city hardest hit by the Sept. 11 terrorist attacks came after . . . 100,000 to 350,000 people turned out in the city last month for one of the nation's largest anti-war demonstrations."[15] Germany's *Deutsche Presse-Agentur* added: "Local councils in more than 100 U.S. municipalities large and small have passed similar resolutions."[16] *Channel NewsAsia* reported: "The City Councilors believe that declaring war on another nation was not the way to solve the crisis." "New York says no," proclaimed the *Liverpool Daily Echo* in England.[17]

Of course, many New Yorkers opposed the resolution. Or rather, they would have opposed it had they known about it. To this day, most New Yorkers are unaware that their elected representatives ever issued such an anti-war statement. Local media downplayed the event to the point of invisibility. Almost alone among her journalist colleagues, *New York Post* columnist Andrea Peyser accused the City Council of "disgracing the memory of nearly 3,000 souls who perished in the World Trade Center." Peyser lamented the blow to US troop morale in Iraq, where GIs had named a base in Kuwait City "Camp New York" in honor of the city's sacrifice.[18]

Several council members publicly denounced the resolution, including Democrat Peter Vallone Jr. of Queens, son of the above-mentioned former City Council Speaker Peter F. Vallone. The younger Vallone said, "Just blocks from the Ground Zero, we debate . . . the financial costs of a war. What is the cost of 3,000 lives? In the next attack, when we lose 10,000 people, will that justify the cost? New York City was attacked by terrorists. Saddam Hussein supports terrorists. He is a terrorist." In the same vein, Staten Island Republican Andrew Lanza told his fellow council members, "I suggest that you take a walk down the street and take a long, hard look at that gaping hole in the ground, at that gaping hole in our lives."[19]

Clearly the City Council no longer spoke for ordinary New Yorkers. An alien force had taken the city government by stealth. That force was the Shadow Party, acting through the radical activist network ACORN, which in turn operated under cover of one of its many front groups, The Working Families Party.

On 4 February 2004, New York City's ACORN-dominated City Council went a step beyond the resolution, approving an ordinance that declared the Big Apple a "civil liberties safe zone," meaning that the city officially renounces the USA-PATRIOT Act and refuses to cooperate with federal counterterror operations authorized under that act. This was part of the national movement described in Chapter 2, organized by the American Civil Liberties Union and other left-wing groups. Once again, local media failed to draw attention to the legislation, and most New Yorkers, to this day, have no idea it was ever passed.[20]

The City Council takeover and the refusal to cooperate with Homeland Security in fighting the terrorist threat was the work of the same Working Families Party that later came to the assistance of Soros candidate David Soares in 2004. Like Hillary Clinton before him, Soares ran on the Democrat and Working Families Party tickets simultaneously. The *Daily News* later concluded, "The key to Soares' success was the WFP, which launched a low-profile door-to-door campaign for Soares months ago and ran phone banks from its city offices. The Albany machine was caught napping."[21] Hailing Soares as "The People's Prosecutor," the radical *Village Voice* identified the source of the campaign's success:

> In this primary contest, both the Soares and Clyne campaigns spent more than $100,000, but Soares had the more aggressive field operation. About 500 volunteers worked on his behalf, making calls or knocking on doors. In the weeks leading up to the primary, volunteers spoke with more than 20,000 voters. On election day, a 10-car caravan snaked through the county, blaring messages of support from local politicians. Soares visited Albany's housing projects, starting on the 12th floor of each building and working his way down, urging people on every floor to get out and vote.[22]

Clyne attempted to counter the Shadow Party forces by exposing his opponent as a stalking horse for Soros. One of his campaign flyers bore the headline, "DON'T BE FOOLED." It warned, "A New York City drug legalization group is trying to buy the Albany County District Attorney's Office." Clyne was referring to the Drug Policy Alliance, headed by former Princeton University professor Ethan Nadelmann. Soros hired Nadelmann away from Princeton in 1994 to run his nationwide drug legalization campaign, which today functions mainly through The Drug Policy Alliance. Founded by Soros, the group receives about one-third of its financial support from Soros' OSI, and Soros himself sits on its board. Of the $121,776 that the Working Families Party siphoned into David Soares' campaign, $81,500 came from the Drug Policy Alliance Network, which is the political arm of the Drug Policy Alliance.

In other words, Nadelmann's Soros-controlled group donated *indirectly* to the David Soares primary campaign, by giving money to the Working Families Party, which then passed the money on to the Soares campaign. This arrangement was clearly illegal. Among its many irregularities, the most obvious is that it violates a New York State law forbidding political parties from meddling in the primaries of other parties. For example, Republicans cannot try to influence the outcome of a Democratic primary by helping one Democrat candidate over another. Likewise, the Working Families Party may not support one candidate over another in a Democratic primary. Yet that is exactly what the Working Families Party did in the case of David Soares, when they supported him over his Democrat rival Clyne. Despite its illegality, the strategy worked. Soares won both the primary and the general election. Today he is district attorney of Albany County.

Efforts to hold the Shadow Party accountable for its misdeeds were feeble, half-hearted and ineffective. On 14 October 2004, New York State Supreme Court Justice Bernard J. Malone Jr. ruled that the Working Families Party had indeed violated state Election Law 2-126 by contributing to Soares' primary campaign. However, the judge seemed at a loss as to how to enforce the law he had just cited. He indicated that a criminal investigation might be in order, but seemed unsure who should conduct it.

To this end, the judge sent copies of his 15-page decision to the New York State Board of Elections, to state Attorney General Eliot Spitzer, and to Albany County district attorney Paul Clyne. The judge noted, however, that, if Clyne's office undertook an investigation, Clyne himself could not conduct it, since he was an interested party. Clyne, for his part, sensibly stated that he wanted nothing to do with the case. His conflict of interest was too glaring. He asked Judge Malone to appoint a special prosecutor instead, but the judge declined.

That left state Attorney General Eliot Spitzer holding the ball. Would Spitzer enforce the law? Evidently not. His spokesman Darren Dopp dashed any such hopes when he announced that Spitzer's office was willing to review the judge's decision, but that such an investigation really ought to be handled by the state Board of Elections or some local prosecutor.[23]

With that announcement, all hope of enforcing New York State's election law came to an end. The district attorney's office of Albany County passed quietly from Democrat control into the control of George Soros' Shadow Party. "Never before, at least in my experience in New York State, has such a conscious, orchestrated, two-tiered scheme to evade the contribution limits of the election law ever been devised, let alone successfully executed," marveled James Featherstonhaugh, an attorney for the Clyne campaign.[24] The *New York Post* editorialized, "So it seems that

Soros . . . has successfully gamed the system, using his wealth to unseat a DA who wouldn't toe his line."[25]

As for the chief beneficiary of all this fuss, the man whom the *New York Sun* dubbed the new "Sheriff of Albany," Soares wasted no time putting New York State politicians on notice that they had plenty to fear from him. The new District Attorney announced that he would not shrink from pressing criminal charges against the political Brahmins of the state capital. "We can't expect an 18-year-old on the street corner to respect the law if the people who make the laws and enforce the laws aren't held accountable," he told the *New York Sun*. "We're going to prosecute all offenses occurring in Albany County."[26]

Left-wing state senator Eric Schneiderman, whose district covers Manhattan and the Bronx, praised Soares: "He's an absolute straight arrow. Think about what an independent district attorney could do about cleaning up the swamp in Albany. This is 'Mr. Smith Goes to Washington'—with subpoena power. It's someone, finally, who isn't in on the deal."[27] This was nonsense, of course. David Soares is very much in on the deal. It just happens to be a different deal: Soros' deal.

Attorney General Eliot Spitzer's refusal to investigate the Soares scandal points to a deeper dysfunction in the heart of New York State's law enforcement hierarchy. Spitzer, a Democrat, has long used his office for frankly political ends—most notably to further the career of Hillary Clinton. During the 2000 Senate campaign when Hillary won her seat, Spitzer's bullying of Hillary's critics won him the nickname of Hillary's "pit bull." In 2000, Hillary built her campaign largely around a report that Spitzer issued, in a most timely fashion—December 1999—just as election season got underway. The report charged New York City police with racial profiling. Hillary used Spitzer's report to accuse

Mayor Giuliani of running a brutal police state, targeting innocent blacks. Police-bashing became the dominant refrain of her
campaign.

In the middle of the campaign, Spitzer helped Hillary's cause
by intimidating conservative radio talk host Sean Hannity of
WABC-NY. On 8 July 2000, Hannity had invited author Laura
Ingraham onto his show to talk about her new book, *The Hillary
Trap*. Hannity originally scheduled Washington DC defense
attorney Keith Waters, former president of the National Bar
Association, to defend Hillary on his show. However, spin doctors
for the Democratic National Committee pressured Hannity at
the last minute to replace Waters with Spitzer. Calling into the
show by phone, Attorney General Spitzer took a drubbing from
Hannity and hung up during a commercial, in a huff. He did not
let the matter rest there, however. Hannity's producer Eric
Stanger alleges that, moments after Spitzer hung up on Hannity,
Stanger received a call from Spitzer. The state Attorney General
complained angrily that he had been rudely treated on the show
and threatened retribution against Hannity. Stanger recounts this
exchange:

> SPITZER: I fully intend to use the capacity of the Office of
> Attorney General to act on this.
> STANGER: Sir, is that a threat?
> SPITZER: You can take that however you want. Well, no, what
> I meant was that I'm going to call my friends in
> local government and tell them to boycott your
> show. [28]

Even radical civil rights attorney Ron Kuby had to admit that
Spitzer had crossed the line. Kuby—who also happens to be a

WABC-NY radio talk show host—accused Spitzer of "an outrageous abuse of power," suggesting that Spitzer's alleged threat "is arguably a criminal offense, it is arguably an impeachable offense."[29]

Spitzer played the partisan pit bull at the 2004 Democratic National Convention in Boston. Noting that the upcoming Republican convention in New York would coincide with the third anniversary of the 9/11 attacks, Spitzer warned Republicans, before a crowd of cheering delegates, "We're going to hear a lot about September 11. I say this to the Republican Party: With all respect and deference, do not dare use 9/11 for political purposes .... [I] say to the Republicans, do not go there. It would not be fair and right and we will not let you do it."[30]

The people of New York did not elect Eliot Spitzer Attorney General so that he could run political interference for Hillary Clinton, threaten conservative talk show hosts and lecture Republican leaders on what they should or should not say at their own convention. They elected him to enforce the law. The allegations of fraud, money laundering and other illegalities surrounding George Soros' manipulation of the election of David Soares provided Spitzer with a perfect opportunity to perform the duties he was actually elected to perform. Yet he showed no interest in taking action.

When it comes to cleaning up Shadow Party corruption, Hillary's pit bull has no teeth. Perhaps that is because the political fortunes of Hillary and Soros are integrally linked.

4

SOROS AND
HILLARY

The 2004 Take Back America Conference held in Washington marked a watershed of sorts. It was the first time that Hillary and Soros had appeared together on the same stage at any public, mass-media event on US soil. Until 3 June 2004, Soros and Hillary had gone to great lengths to conceal their collaboration from the public eye. At the Take Back America conference, they let the cat out of the bag. The respect and affection they plainly feel for each other was fully on display.

Hillary introduced Soros to the audience with these words: "Now, among the many people who have stood up and said, 'I cannot sit idly by and watch this happen to the country I love,' is George Soros, and I have known George Soros—(applause)—for a long time now, and I first came across his work in the former Soviet Union, in Eastern Europe, when I was privileged to travel there, both on my own and with my husband on behalf of our country. . . . [W]e need people like George Soros, who is fearless, and willing to step up when it counts. So, please join me in welcoming George Soros."[1]

Soros' speech touched on many issues, but the most instructive were the comments he made on the abuses at the Abu Ghraib prison in Iraq. Soros said, "I think that the picture of torture in Abu Ghraib, in Saddam's prison, was the moment of truth for us, . . . I think that those pictures hit us the same way as the terrorist attack itself, not quite with the same force because in the terrorist attack we were the victims. In the pictures we were the perpetrators, others were the victims. But, there is, I'm afraid, a direct connection between those two events, because the way President Bush conducted the war on terror converted us from victims into perpetrators."[2] The audience of Democrats burst into applause at these words.[3]

In the beginning of his speech, Soros had praised Hillary with a warmth and admiration that seemed every bit as sincere as hers: "I'm very, very proud to be introduced by Hillary. I've seen her in operation. I have great, great admiration for her. I've seen her deliver a speech in Davos about open society that explained the ideas better than anybody else that I've heard. I've seen her visit Central Asia, where I have foundations, and she was very effective, more effective than most of our statesmen in propagating democracy, freedom, and open society."[4]

The speech in Davos to which Soros referred had been delivered by Hillary at the 1998 meeting of the World Economic Forum in Switzerland. Soros and Hillary attended together. For Hillary, the Davos junket came as a welcome break, a chance to escape the mounting impeachment crisis then consuming the Clinton White House. Hillary's friendship with Soros deepened during that stressful period of her life. One source close to Hillary's inner circle states that Soros came to visit Hillary at the White House during the impeachment proceedings, during a tense period when she was receiving only her most intimate and trusted friends.[5] Evidently, Hillary counted Soros among her confidants at that point.

No details of their early friendship are publicly available, yet it is clear that Hillary has known Soros "for a long time," as she put it. Hillary states that she first became aware of Soros through his work in the former Soviet Union. On 22 November 1994, the Clintons feted the new Ukrainian president Leonid Kuchma at the White House. Press reports indicate that Soros attended the dinner party. Hillary traveled to Central Asia in November 1997, visiting several of the former Soviet republics. Among the cities she visited was Bishkek, the capital of Kyrgyzstan, where she cut the ribbon for the opening of the American University of Kyrgyzstan, and received its first honorary degree. In her acceptance speech, Hillary praised the work of Soros' Open Society Institute, which had funded the university.

In November 1998, Hillary also made a two-day trip to Haiti, during which she toured US-funded healthcare facilities, in the company of two of the facilities' financial backers, George Soros and William H. Gates Sr., the father of Microsoft founder Bill Gates. Beyond these slender facts, we know little about the early years of their relationship. Neither Hillary nor Soros has seen fit to write about each other in their books, and the Washington press corps, for the most part, has avoided any mention of their long and ever-deepening friendship.

One exception to this rule was a *Newsweek* report of 11 May 1998, which hinted that Soros may have offered Hillary a job with his foundation network. "Friends daydream about her [Hillary] becoming head of UNICEF, or even UN secretary-general. More likely: some sort of global foundation, aided by friends such as financier George Soros or World Bank president James Wolfensohn," wrote Howard Fineman.⁶ Why did Fineman consider it "more likely" that Hillary might take a job with Soros than with the United Nations? Perhaps he was just guessing. Then again, Fineman appears to have had access to unusually good sources for his story. He shared a byline on the article with reporter Matthew Cooper, who is married to Mandy Grunwald, a close Hillary advisor and personal friend.

Hillary may or may not have considered working for Soros, but, if she had, she would have found the ideological climate of his

Open Society Institute familiar and gratifying. With few exceptions, the causes Soros champions are precisely those dearest to Hillary's heart, such as rationing health care, rolling back gun rights and extending the voting franchise to convicted felons.

Hillary's radicalism is deep-rooted and fundamental, bearing the clear imprint of her early mentor Saul Alinsky. Hillary met the Chicago radical through a leftwing church group to which she belonged in high school.⁷ They stayed in close touch until Alinsky's death. Hillary's 1969 senior thesis at Wellesley College was a 75-page salute to Alinsky.⁸ It contained excerpts of his forthcoming book, *Rules for Radicals*, which he had allowed Hillary to read before the book's publication in 1971. Upon her graduation, Alinsky offered Hillary a full-time organizer job with his Industrial Areas Foundation. She declined only because Yale Law School seemed to offer a superior path for infiltrating the Establishment.⁹

Hillary's efforts to cultivate a "moderate" or "centrist" public image faithfully reflect Alinsky's teachings. In *Rules for Radicals*, Alinsky pronounces a harsh judgment on the Sixties New Left. Rather than winning over the masses, the New Left went out of its way to shock, horrify and alienate the masses, he charged. He condemned flag-burning, Maoist slogans and the disheveled hippie style. "If the real radical finds that having long hair sets up psychological barriers to communication and organization, he cuts his hair. . . . As an organizer, I start from where the world is, as it is, not as I would like it to be. . . . That means working in the system," Alinsky scolded.¹⁰

Alinsky envisioned a special role for white, middle-class activists such as Hillary, whom he saw as potential emissaries to the American heartland. "[E]ven if all the low-income parts of our population were organized—all the blacks, Mexican-Americans, Puerto Ricans, Appalachian poor whites—if through some genius of organization they were all united in a coalition, it would not be powerful enough to get significant, basic, needed changes," Alinsky warned. Only by winning support among the white majority could activists hope to achieve "basic" change in America. Alinsky called for a proliferation of "middle-class organizations" and "middle-class guerrillas."[11] He wrote: .

> Organization for action will now and in the decade ahead center upon America's white middle class. That is where the power is. . . . Our rebels have contemptuously rejected the values and way of life of the middle class. . . . [I]t is useless self-indulgence for an activist to put his past behind him. Instead, he should realize the priceless value of his middle-class experience. His middle-class identity, his familiarity with the values and problems, are invaluable for organization of his "own people."[12]

Alinsky was a master of infiltration. He viewed revolution as a gradual—even orderly—process, best accomplished by infiltrating and manipulating institutions with deep roots in the community, such as churches, unions, ethnic organizations and local political machines. In Alinsky's native Chicago, few institutions had deeper roots or wider influence than organized crime. The pragmatic Alinsky wooed gangsters as lovingly as he courted ward bosses, bishops and school superintendents.

Ironically, the city of Al Capone also happens to have given birth to modern, "liberal" criminology. Alinsky had a foot in both worlds. He pursued a master's degree in criminology at the University of Chicago from 1930 to 1932.[13] UC's radical sociologists defended and romanticized gangsters as victims of social injustice. Alinsky went further, pursuing actual alliances with mobsters. He personally befriended Frank Nitti, Capone's lieutenant.

Nitti had taken charge of Capone's empire after the mobster's imprisonment on tax charges in 1931. Alinsky later boasted that Nitti, "took me under his wing. I called him the Professor and I became his student."[14] In 1932, Alinsky married the daughter of a prominent Chicago bootlegger.[15] He remained on friendly terms with gangsters all his life.[16]

Alinsky's real power came not from the criminal underworld, however, but from Wall Street—specifically, from the wealthy, "socially-conscious" patricians who funded his activism. A skilled fundraiser, Alinsky managed to smooth-talk some of America's wealthiest philanthropists into underwriting his Industrial Areas Foundation—an organization dedicated to waging class warfare in America. He prided himself on his ability to "use the strength of the enemy against itself"—a strategy he called "mass jujitsu."[17] "I feel confident that I could persuade a millionaire on a Friday to subsidize a revolution for Saturday out of which he would make a huge profit on Sunday even though he was certain to be executed on Monday," Alinsky once quipped.[18]

His early benefactors included department-store mogul Marshall Field III; Sears Roebuck heiress Adele Rosenwald Levy; and Gardiner Howland Shaw, an assistant secretary of state in the Roosevelt administration.[19] Alinsky's skill at seducing the rich ultimately brought him into the inner sanctum of American power, among the tight circle of Wall Street families whose influence can make or break presidents. One such kingmaker was Katharine Graham, an early friend of Alinsky whose family newspaper, the *Washington Post*, would one day topple Richard Nixon.[20] Graham inherited the *Post* from her parents, Agnes and Eugene Meyer. It was the Meyers who provided Alinsky with the cash and publicity that catapulted him to national prominence in 1945.[21]

In 1944, the University of Chicago Press signed Alinsky to

write a book promoting his vision of a new American radicalism. Six months before its publication, Agnes Meyer, who co-owned the *Washington Post* with her husband Eugene, lionized Alinsky and his movement in a six-part series titled "The Orderly Revolution." President Truman ordered 100 reprints of Meyer's series.[22] By the time Alinsky's manifesto, *Reveille for Radicals*, hit the bookstores in January 1946, he was already famous. *Reveille* became a national bestseller, and Mrs. Meyer began funding Alinsky's Industrial Areas Foundation.

He learned to wield power quietly, below the radar. During the Sixties, major media ignored him, yet Alinsky's hidden hand directed some of the decade's most potent insurgencies. The War on Poverty bureaucracy was filled with Alinsky's acolytes. The infiltration began in 1961, when Robert Kennedy appointed Columbia University sociologist Lloyd Ohlin to direct the newly-formed Office of Juvenile Delinquency. Ohlin had learned the Alinsky model of orderly revolution at its source, the University of Chicago sociology department, where Ohlin earned his Ph.D. He co-wrote an influential book called *Delinquency and Opportunity* with Richard Cloward, a colleague at Columbia University. Published in 1960, it argued that juvenile delinquency resulted from a dearth of economic opportunity, which could be cured, they implied, only through radical social change.

In 1964, President Johnson declared war on poverty and appointed Sargent Shriver to the post of "poverty czar." Ohlin and his radical colleagues slipped comfortably into Shriver's new Office of Economic Opportunity, which funded such programs as VISTA, Head Start, Job Corps and the Community Action Program (CAP). Now the Alinskyites had their hands on the federal money spigot. Ohlin and his colleagues directed the very first CAP grant into a program at Syracuse University through which

Alinsky personally trained community activists.[23] The federal government spent more than $300 billion on War on Poverty programs in the first five years. Much of this money went to street radicals such as Alinsky.

During the Sixties, Alinsky's under-the-radar influence was such that even Bobby Kennedy fell under his spell. Following his brother's assassination, RFK began drifting leftward, in search of a base for his presidential ambitions. He met Cesar Chavez in 1966, forging an alliance with the popular union leader in order to gain political capital.[24] It happens that Chavez was an Alinsky protegé. Alinsky's foundation had recruited him in 1952, and provided much of his early funding and training.[25] RFK's friendship with Chavez brought him directly into Alinsky's inner circle. In 1967, Alinsky launched a civil rights shakedown of the Eastman Kodak Company in Rochester, New York, accusing the company of failing to hire enough black workers. Kennedy pulled strings behind the scenes on Alinsky's behalf. Alinsky later wrote, "I had an understanding with the late Senator Robert Kennedy to advise him when we were ready to move [against Eastman Kodak]. In my discussions with Kennedy, I found that his commitment was not political but human. He was outraged by the conditions in the Rochester ghetto."[26]

It is pointless to speculate what might have developed from Alinsky's growing friendship with Kennedy, had an assassin's bullet not cut short the alliance on 5 June 1968. But Alinsky was fated to form one last, significant alliance before he died—in hindsight, perhaps the most influential of his career. This was his alliance with young Hillary Rodham. It was she who would carry the torch of Alinsky's "orderly revolution" into the 21st century.

She has already carried that torch into the US Senate. The rate of Hillary's ascent through the Democratic hierarchy suggests that she will carry it much farther. As a newcomer who had never before held elective office, Hillary's nomination for a Senate seat from New York was unusual. Political parties ordinarily award such positions to veteran campaigners with long track records of success. Even more unusual was the speed with which Hillary rose to party leadership, winning plumb committee assignments, which normally should have gone to more senior colleagues.

In January 2003, for instance, Hillary was appointed chairwoman of the powerful Senate Democratic Steering and Coordination Committee. This job gave her authority to make or break Senate Democrats by blocking or approving their committee assignments. One Senate aide confided, "The other Democrats resent her. But they're so weak, their weakness permits her to grow."[27]

Hillary also secured control of the Democrat money machine. When Clinton loyalist Terry McAuliffe ran for chairman of the Democratic National Committee in February 2001, rivals backed off and ceded the job to McAuliffe, under pressure from the Clintons.[28] This left McAuliffe—and thus Hillary—in charge of official fundraising for the Democratic Party. By the time McAuliffe stepped down in favor of Howard Dean in February 2005, neither Dean nor any other Democrat was in a position to challenge Hillary's hegemony.

Hillary further consolidated her hold on Democrat fundraising by launching HillPAC in January 2001. This monstrously well-funded political action committee enabled Hillary to provide campaign funds to political allies. When the McCain-Feingold Act of 2002 barred political parties from collecting "soft-money" donations—that is, unlimited contributions that are not reported to the Federal Election Commission—Hillary helped set up a network of independent fundraising groups—what we now call the

Shadow Party—which could continue collecting unlimited donations outside official party channels. These groups were only nominally independent, however, since George Soros and Harold Ickes—both Hillary allies—coordinated their activities.

Thus did the junior senator from New York succeed in getting a tight grip on the Democratic Party's "levers of control," as Emmett Tyrrell Jr. noted in his book, *Madame Hillary*.[29] The speed with which she accomplished it was breathtaking. "Hillary Rodham Clinton has . . . utterly [taken] over the Senate Democrats and the party itself—inside and out—and she has done it in a mere two years," Tyrrell marveled.[30]

Hillary and her partner George Soros remain secretive about many details of their collaboration, and with good reason. A political partnership between them would be illegal—expressly forbidden by the campaign finance laws incorporated into the McCain-Feingold Act.

Hillary shares with Soros a fascination with deception and subterfuge. Her penchant for Byzantine intrigue is reflected throughout her organization. This point came through in a *New Republic* cover story titled, "Welcome to Hillaryland." Its author Ryan Lizza informs us that the term "Hillaryland" is an affection-ate nickname that Hillary's operatives have bestowed upon what Lizza calls "the vast political empire . . . unrivaled in Democratic politics" which is Hillary Clinton's political machine. Lizza plainly sympathizes with Hillary politically, and, in his article, strove mightily to present her and her team in the most positive light. Even so, the Machiavellian character of Hillaryland reveals itself repeatedly in Lizza's article.

"The person who actually manages this expansive operation is almost unknown in political circles," writes Lizza. "She rarely talks to the press . . . never appears on television. She declined to cooperate with this article. Her name is Patricia Solis Doyle . . ."[31] Declined to cooperate? Here is an eyebrow-raiser. Ryan Lizza is a left-leaning writer for a magazine whose pro-Democrat sympathies are well-known. Doyle's refusal to cooperate with this friendliest of all possible interviewers suggests a level of paranoia beyond the usual. Even more striking is an anecdote Lizza recounted in his piece:

> One day I was walking down the street and bumped into a tier-one Hillary adviser. We gossiped about Hillaryland, and he cryptically suggested that Harold Ickes, one of the architects of Hillary's 2000 Senate campaign, and a devoted Hillary man, was no longer a key player. This seemed like big news. When Hillary first decided to run for Senate, it was Ickes who sat with her in the White House residence with a giant map of New York, explaining the challenges she faced. Hillaryland without Ickes is inconceivable. It turned out that the word on the street (literally) was wrong. It was some kind of complicated misdirection, something one often encounters in Hillaryland.[32]

The nature of this "complicated misdirection" is revealing. Lizza was told that Harold Ickes had fallen from favor, that he was no longer a player in Hillaryland. Evidently, his source hoped that Lizza would parrot this disinformation in his article, passing along the deception to his readers. But why? Lizza writes:

> Hillaryland experts offered me two contradictory explanations: Either my source was trying to *sideline* Ickes, an old White House rival, or *protect* Ickes, whose work with 527s requires him to maintain some distance from Hillaryland. But, for the record, Ickes is still an influential adviser. As the case of the Ickes

riddle shows, getting answers to simple questions is always a little harder in Hillaryland."

For all the obstruction Lizza encountered in Hillaryland, he emerged from his trials with an important piece of information. Some "Hillaryland experts" suggest that his source was trying to *protect* Ickes by spreading a false rumor that Ickes had fallen out of favor with Hillary. It would protect Ickes because his "work with 527s requires him to maintain some distance from Hillaryland." In short, the complex crossings between the Democratic Party and Shadow Party need to remain hidden from unwanted scrutiny.

Just as George Soros functions as the unofficial chairman of the Shadow Party, Harold Ickes functions as its unofficial CEO. Ickes runs the network of 527 committees, 501(c)3s, 501(c)4s and other private, non-profit groups that Soros wove together to form the Shadow Party. Federal law expressly bars private fundraising groups of this sort from coordinating their activities with national political parties or with national political candidates such as Hillary Clinton. To whatever extent Ickes is facilitating such coordination, he is violating federal election law. What Ryan Lizza may be telling us in his article is that some of Hillary's people are sufficiently concerned about Ickes' role that they are going out of their way to mislead reporters into thinking that Ickes has been expelled from Hillary's inner circle, even though he has *not* been expelled. Welcome to Hillaryland—and Sorosville.

5

INSIDE SOROS

George Soros was not speaking idly when he told an audience at the London School of Economics that he meant to "puncture the bubble of American supremacy." His Shadow Party is funding and facilitating a national movement that could very well achieve that result. By following the same game plan that toppled Nixon and undermined US military efforts in Vietnam three decades ago, Soros and his dream team may well succeed in their goal of causing history to repeat itself. It may be appropriate, at this point, to ask the question: What's in it for Soros himself?

According to Soros, all of his political and philanthropic activities are directed towards one goal—fostering what he calls the "open society." The term was coined in 1932 by the French philosopher Henri Louis Bergson. Bergson defined as "closed" those societies whose moral code is tribal and chiefly concerns the good of the tribe itself. Those societies which base their morality upon "universal" principles, which seek the good of all mankind, Bergson defined as "open." Bergson himself converted from Judaism to Catholicism on the grounds that Christianity is "open" whereas Judaism is "closed." Subsequently, the Viennese-born philosopher Karl Popper took Bergson's concept a step further. Popper argued that even Christianity is insufficiently "open" because it excludes people who do not embrace its beliefs. To be truly "open," a society must accord equal respect to all beliefs, showing no favoritism toward any particular one. A truly open person never assumes that his beliefs are superior to someone else's and never forgets his own fallibility. One who claims possession of "ultimate truth" is an "enemy" of the open society, wrote Popper.

As a Jew who fled his native Austria to escape the Nazis, Popper brooded over the clash between democratic and totalitarian societies which so tragically divided his generation. He came to see totalitarianism, in all its forms, as the final and inevitable result of "closed" thinking, that is, the failure to respect other people's beliefs. Popper laid out his views in an influential book *The Open Society and Its Enemies*, published in 1945. It was in the form Popper had given it that George Soros first encountered the notion of "open" and "closed" societies. Soros studied under Popper at the London School of Economics, and later referred to him as "my spiritual mentor."[1] Soros would later mold his foundation network around Popper's vision. The Open Society Institute and its global network of Open Society foundations draw their names from Popper's concept.

Soros' attempts to apply Popper's ideas to the real world demonstrate the impracticality of those ideas. In the real world, societies that are unwilling to defend their values are overrun by enemies who lack such inhibitions. There are no open societies in Soros' globalist sense. Every civilization holds certain assumptions about what sort of behavior is acceptable and unacceptable, and no civilization can stand that is unwilling to enforce its beliefs.

Even a system as tolerant, open and "universal" as American democracy cannot live up to Popper's ideal. The American founders believed in self-evident truths. Popper did not. The founders regarded liberty as an absolute right, derived not from government but from "Nature's God." The rights enshrined in the Declaration are called "inalienable" precisely because they are seen as God-given. To deny individuals liberty was to violate the "Laws of Nature," as Jefferson famously wrote in the Declaration of Independence. Popper held no such beliefs. In his view, men were doomed to grope blindly for truth, by trial and error. No matter how hard they searched, they would never find it.

Soros' anti-American agenda begins with his critique of America's birth certificate. In *The Bubble of American Supremacy*, Soros argues that "the Declaration of Independence is also open to different interpretations." According to Soros, the principles of the Declaration "are not self-evident truths but arrangements necessitated by our inherently imperfect understanding."[2] Because these founding principles have no special sanctity and represent no timeless truths, Soros views them as disposable. They can be changed at will, to fit the radical fashion of the day. And, indeed, rewriting the US Constitution happens to be one of Soros' pet projects.

On 8-10 April 2005, Yale Law School hosted a conference called, "The Constitution in 2020," promoted as an effort to produce "a progressive vision of what the Constitution ought to be." Its website listed Soros' Open Society Institute as a sponsor.[3] In fact, of the five organizations hosting the event, three were recipients of Soros funding.

The five sponsors were the American Constitution Society, the Yale Law School, the Arthur Liman Public Interest Program at Yale, the Open Society Institute, and the Center for American Progress. The American Constitution Society and the Center for American Progress are both Shadow Party fronts—the latter headed by former Clinton chief of staff John Podesta. One of its founders was Morton Halperin, director of US advocacy for Soros' Open Society Institute and executive director of the Open Society Policy Center. Halperin's official biography at the Center now lists him as a senior fellow there. Soros helped launch both groups, and both have received major funding from the Open Society Institute.[4]

Where Soros goes, Hillary Clinton cannot be far behind. The junior senator from New York played a quiet but significant role in founding the American Constitution Society.[5] While the Society's website does not acknowledge any formal affiliation with Hillary, the *National Law Journal* reports that she serves on its Board of Advisors.[6] Hillary is also reported to be a power behind the scenes at the Center for American Progress, which one insider characterized as "the official Hillary Clinton think tank."[7]

Leaving nothing to chance, Soros made sure that his progressive Constitutional Convention would be widely promoted on college campuses. For this purpose, he deployed yet another subdivision of his Shadow Party, a group called Campus Progress, whose website touted the event with the headline, "An Invitation to Help Design the Constitution in 2020." Founded in January 2005, Campus Progress is the student outreach arm of the Soros-funded Center for American Progress. Its director is David Halperin, a former speechwriter for the Clinton White House and—not incidentally—the son of Morton Halperin, who, as noted above, serves as director of US advocacy for Soros' Open Society Institute and executive director of the Open Society Policy Center. As noted above, the senior Halperin was also a co-founder of Soros' Center for American Progress.[8]

The Halperin family has deep roots in Soros' Shadow Party. Many readers will recall that Mark Halperin, who is political director of ABC News, issued a memo to his reporters during the final weeks of the 2004 campaign, instructing them to slant the news in favor of Democrat candidate John Kerry. Mark Halperin is another son of Morton Halperin. Mark and David Halperin are brothers.[9] In addition to directing Campus Progress, David

Halperin served as founding executive director of the Soros-funded American Constitution Society. He also co-founded the Internet company Real Networks with left-wing billionaire and Shadow Party funder Rob Glaser.

It should be clear, at this point, that Soros was not just one among several sponsors of "The Constitution in 2020." Shadow Party operatives and front groups ran the whole show. We might think of it as a Shadow Constitutional Convention.

Attendees report that conference leaders pushed for a "Second Bill of Rights" based upon Franklin D. Roosevelt's "Four Freedoms" (freedom of speech, freedom of worship, freedom from want and freedom from fear). How any government would go about banishing "want" and "fear" from human life is not exactly clear, but the sheer magnitude of the project ensures that any government attempting it would require authoritarian powers beyond those available in a representative republic such as ours. We should hardly be surprised that Soros wishes to rewrite the Constitution, given the scope of his ambitions. Nor should we be surprised that the speakers at the Shadow Constitutional Convention harped so incessantly on the "evolutionary character of constitutional law."[10] Before Soros can transform US society into a socialist utopia, our Constitution will need to undergo a great many "evolutionary" changes. Commenting on the Yale event, John Hinderaker wrote in the *Weekly Standard*:

> The left makes no secret of its intentions where the Constitution is concerned. It wants to change it, in ways that have nothing to do with what the document actually says. It wants the Constitution to enshrine its own policy preferences—thus freeing it from the tiresome necessity of winning elections. And how will the Constitution be changed? Through

a constitutional convention, or a vote of two-thirds of the state legislatures? Of course not. The whole problem, from the liberal perspective, is that they can't get democratically elected bodies to enact their agenda. As one of the Yale conference participants said: "We don't have much choice other than to believe deeply in the courts—where else do we turn?" The new, improved Constitution will come about through judicial re-interpretation.[11]

In his effort to dismantle the American founding and remake the society it shaped, Soros goes beyond his teacher. Popper was, in fact, a great admirer of America. Three years before his death in 1991 Popper wrote: "It was my first trip to the United States in 1950 that made an optimist of me again. That first trip tore me forever out of a depression caused by the overwhelming influence of Marxism in postwar Europe. Since then I have been to America twenty or maybe twenty-five times, and each time I have been more deeply impressed."[12]

Soros arrived in America with a very different attitude. Having lived in England for nine years, Soros traveled to New York in 1956 for one reason only—to make money on Wall Street. He had no interest in planting roots in America. In fact, he set himself a deadline of five years, during which he hoped to save $500,000, and after which he meant to return to Europe. "It was my five-year plan," Soros told his biographer Michael T. Kaufman. "At the time, I did not particularly care for the United States. I had acquired some British prejudices; you know, the States were, well, commercial, crass, and so on."[13]

Soros ended up staying in America, even becoming a citizen in 1961. Yet his later writings suggest that he never shed his initial disdain. On the contrary, he seemed to invent new and ever more imaginative reasons for despising his adopted country as the years passed. "Who would have thought sixty years ago, when Karl Popper wrote *Open Society and Its Enemies*, that the United States itself could pose a threat to open society? Yet that is what is happening, both internally and externally," Soros concluded in *The Bubble of American Supremacy*.[14]

In seeking to prove that George Bush's America poses a "threat to open society," Soros has to stretch Popper's ideas beyond recognition. When Popper made his first visit to the United States in 1950, America was engaged in a Cold War with Communist totalitarianism. President Truman was, at that very moment, aggressively purging Communist sympathizers from government positions. In accordance with Truman's Executive Order of 22 March 1947—the so-called "Loyalty Order"—more than six million individuals were investigated and about 500 lost their government jobs over a five-year period. "All of this was conducted with secret evidence, secret and often paid informers, and neither judge nor jury," wrote Douglas T. Miller and Marion Nowak in their book *The Fifties: The Way We Really Were*.[15]

It is difficult to see how the America that so excited Popper in 1950—the America of the Truman Doctrine, the Loyalty Order and Joe McCarthy—could be seen as more "open" in the Popperian sense, than the America of George Bush, against which Soros has declared all-out war. Yet that is precisely what Soros asks us to believe—that America was more "open" in the 1950s than it is today. "This is not the America I chose as my home," he complained in 2004.[16]

"Open society stands for freedom, democracy, rule of law, human rights, social justice, and social responsibility as a universal idea," Soros declares in *Open Society: Reforming Global Capitalism*.[17] This is as close as he gets to defining what he means

73

by "open society." Like Karl Marx and generations of socialists, Soros prefers not to offer a blueprint of the promised future, even as he works to dismantle the present. "In my foundation network, we have never defined open society. Had we done so, the organization would have become more rigid; as it is, flexibility has been our hallmark."[18]

Flexibility indeed. As America confronts hostile cultures that seek its destruction, Soros argues that it must defer to cultural tastes:

> Pure reason and a moral code based on the value of the individual are inventions of Western culture; they have little resonance in other cultures. . . . The Western intellectual tradition ought not to be imposed indiscriminately on the rest of the world in the name of universal values.[19]

Here Soros reveals a contradiction in his vision of the "Open Society." His proscription against imposing "open society" on others, coupled with his refusal to describe the future he seeks, suggests that the "critical" aspect—the destructive aspect—of his mission is what motivates and defines it, and the positive, idealistic aspect is a blank slate for his progressive vanguard to one day define. In other words, it is merely a smokescreen for whatever agendas the revolutionaries may wish to pursue. With unexpected candor, Soros admits that he finds destruction easier than creation. Regarding his "democratization" efforts in the former Soviet bloc, he told the *New York Times* in 1990, "[W]hen our aim was to break open a closed system, we supported the iconoclasts. Now the task is to build an open system. It is much harder to do this. . . . In a way it is much more boring. Building is always more effort than destroying."[20]

The focus of Soros' complaint against President Bush is the belief Bush shares with most Americans that the "Western form of representative democracy" is the best form of government yet devised, and that other nations would benefit from adopting it. Soros does not share this belief. He condemns the Bush Administration for seeking to impose "representative democracy" on Afghanistan, Iraq and other Islamic countries. After all, who are we to say that our ideas are superior to theirs? "When President Bush says, as he does frequently, that 'freedom' will prevail, in fact he means that America will prevail. . . . In a free and open society, however, people are supposed to decide for themselves what they mean by freedom and democracy and not simply follow America's lead."[21]

While Soros condemns George Bush for his evangelical fervor in spreading democracy, Soros himself is engaged in a similar missionary enterprise. By his own estimate, Soros has spent more than $5 billion over the last 25 years to spread his doctrine of the "open society," and institute it in existing societies. Yet, if the Open Society has no clear definition, and no one has any right to impose his version of it on anyone else, then what exactly is Soros and his Open Society network doing?

British journalist Neil Clark offers a cynical answer to this question. In Clark's view, the "open society" is little more than a fig leaf for Soros to hide his greed:

> [S]oros deems a society "open" not if it respects human rights
> and basic freedoms, but if it is "open" for him and his associates
> to make money. And, indeed, Soros has made money in every
> country he has helped to prise "open." In Kosovo, for example,
> he has invested $50m in an attempt to gain control of the Trepca
> mine complex, where there are vast reserves of gold, silver, lead

and other minerals estimated to be worth in the region of $5bn.
He thus copied a pattern he has deployed to great effect over the
whole of eastern Europe: of advocating "shock therapy" and
"economic reform," then swooping in with his associates to buy
valuable state assets at knockdown prices.[22]

Clark has a point in that Soros' tendency to mix business
with his political missionary operations often makes it difficult
to see where one activity ends and the other begins. But while it
is evident that Soros is all but incapable of letting a good business opportunity pass him by, on another level, he appears to
believe his own press. He genuinely sees himself as a missionary—a reformer, a liberator, an apostle for a vaguely imagined
society that will replace the one we have.

"My goal is to become the conscience of the world," Soros
immodestly confessed to his biographer Michael Kaufman, in a
moment of candor that could give megalomania a bad name.[23] The
enigmatic billionaire has many times described himself as a "failed
philosopher." In *Open Society: Reforming Global Capitalism*, Soros
writes ruefully, "Every philosophical argument is liable to raise
endless new questions. . . . Once I spent three years of my life trying to work out my philosophy, and I ended up where I began."[24]

Soros is referring to a period from 1963 to 1966 when he
worked for a staid, slow-moving Wall Street brokerage house
which left him plenty of spare time to indulge his private passion
for philosophy. He devoted three years to writing a philosophical
treatise called *The Burden of Consciousness*, in which he expounded
on the nature of "open" and "closed" societies, but never finished
the book. This failure marked the end of his dream to return to
England and devote himself full-time to studying philosophy. In
his 1995 book, *Soros on Soros*, he recalls:

There came a day when I was rereading what I had written the day before, and I couldn't make sense of it. I realized that I was spinning my wheels. That was when I decided to get back into business. I thought that I had some major new philosophical ideas, which I wanted to express. I now realize that I was mainly regurgitating Karl Popper's ideas. But I haven't given up the illusion that I have something important and original to say.[25]

If Soros' philosophizing tends to take him around in circles, it is probably not so much because he is a poor philosopher, but because he has undertaken an impossible task: to rationalize a life—his own—which defies rationalization.

On 5 November 2003, Soros created a stir by showing up for a meeting of the Jewish Funders Network, a New York society dedicated to encouraging Jewish philanthropy. Soros' disdain for Jewish charities is well known, so his sudden appearance at the event struck many as puzzling. Uriel Heilman of the Jewish Telegraphic Agency wrote:

> Associates said Soros' appearance . . . was the first they could ever recall in which the billionaire . . . had spoken in front of a Jewish group or attended a Jewish function. Soros' first known funding of a Jewish group came in 1997, when his Open Society Institute's Emma Lazarus Fund gave $1.3 million to the Council of Jewish Federations, and when Soros gave another $1.3 million to the Jewish Fund for Justice, an anti-poverty group.[26]

In fact, Soros had come to the Jewish Funders meeting in order to drum up support for his anti-Bush campaign. He approached the topic in what some observers thought a peculiar way. From the podium, Soros called on fellow Jews to acknowledge what he called their own role in provoking anti-Semitism around the world. "There is a resurgence of anti-Semitism in Europe," he said. "The policies of the Bush administration and the Sharon administration contribute to that. . . . If we change that direction, then anti-Semitism also will diminish."[27]

To illustrate his point, Soros cited a 16 October 2003 speech by Malaysian Prime Minister Mahathir Mohamad, in which the Prime Minister (since retired) had charged that, "Jews rule this world by proxy."[28] Soros mused, "I'm also very concerned about my own role because the new anti-Semitism holds that the Jews rule the world." In calling attention to his "own role" in fostering anti-Semitism, Soros seemed to imply that some of his financial maneuvers might have helped fuel anti-Jewish feeling, particularly in Malaysia, where he was widely accused of causing a collapse of the national currency, in 1998.[29]

Soros' remarks at the meeting scandalized many Jews. "Let's understand things clearly: Anti-Semitism is not caused by Jews; it's caused by anti-Semites," said Elan Steinberg, senior adviser at the World Jewish Congress. Abraham Foxman, national director of the Anti-Defamation League, commented: "If [Soros] sees that his position of being who he is may contribute to the perception of anti-Semitism, what's his solution to himself—that he give up his money? That he close his mouth?"[30]

Soros' uneasy relationship with the Jewish community and his rejected faith (a reflection also of his uneasy relation with the country he adopted) goes back many years. Born in Budapest on 12 August 1930, Soros originally bore the name György Schwartz. His parents were non-practicing Jews. Soros' father, Tivadar, was a lawyer. However, his marriage into a prosperous merchant family gave him leisure to indulge his true passion: the promotion of

Esperanto, an artificial language created during the 1880s. Esperantists hoped to wipe out nationalism by persuading everyone in the world to drop their native tongues and speak Esperanto instead. Swept up in this globalist fantasy, Tivadar mastered Esperanto and in 1936 changed his family name to Soros—an Esperanto verb, in the future tense, meaning "will soar."

When the Nazis occupied Hungary in 1944, Tivadar and his family went into hiding. Taking on false identities as Christians, they survived the Holocaust. Soros writes that life under Nazi and Communist rule shaped his character in unexpected ways. One effect was to darken his attitude toward fellow Jews. He never forgot how Hungary's *Judenrat*, a Jewish Council set up by the Nazis, betrayed Jews in exchange for special privileges.[31] At one point, the *Judenrat* recruited him and other Jewish youngsters to hand out leaflets deceptively persuading unwitting Jews to turn themselves in for deportation to the death camps. Soros showed one of the leaflets to his father. It ordered the recipient to report to a certain synagogue with a blanket and two days' worth of food. Tivadar asked his son if he understood the significance of the order.

"I can guess. They'll be interned," replied the thirteen-year-old boy.

Tivadar told his son to go ahead and deliver the messages, but to warn each recipient that it was a deportation summons. Afterwards, his father told young Soros to stop running errands for the *Judenrat*. "George had liked the excitement of being a courier but he obeyed his father without complaint," observes Soros' biographer Michael Kaufman.[32] Inasmuch as young Soros understood so clearly the significance of his work for the *Judenrat*, it is revealing that he derived such enjoyment from it. More revealing still is the fact that Soros would cite this incident, so many years later, as a reason for disliking fellow Jews. On what basis can he condemn the collaborators of the *Judenrat* for their betrayals while exempting himself from moral judgment? Granted, Soros was only a teenager when he faced these trials, yet boys his age were fighting and dying all over Europe.

Tivadar saved his family by splitting them up, providing them with forged papers and false identities as Christians, and bribing Gentile families to take them in. George Soros took the name Sandor Kiss, and posed as the godson of a man named Baumbach, an official of Hungary's fascist regime. Baumbach was assigned to deliver deportation notices to Jews and confiscate Jewish property. He would bring young Soros with him on his rounds.[33] Appearing on the PBS television show, *Adam Smith's Money World* on 15 April 1993, Soros said of his wartime activities, "I was adopted by an official of the ministry of agriculture, whose job was to take over Jewish properties, so I actually went with him and we took possession of these large estates. That was my identity. So it's a strange, very strange life. I was 14 years old at the time."[34] Later, on 20 December 1998, Soros faced tougher questioning from Steve Kroft of *60 Minutes*:

KROFT: You're a Hungarian Jew . . .

Mr. SOROS: Mm-hmm.

KROFT: . . . who escaped the Holocaust . . .

Mr. SOROS: Mm-hmm.

KROFT: . . . by posing as a Christian.

Mr. SOROS: Right.

KROFT: And you watched lots of people get shipped off to the death camps.

Mr. SOROS: Right. I was 14 years old. And I would say that that's when my character was made.

KROFT:	In what way?
Mr. SOROS:	That one should think ahead. One should understand and anticipate events and when one is threatened. It was a tremendous threat of evil. I mean, it was a very personal experience of evil.
KROFT:	My understanding is that you went out with this protector of yours who swore that you were his adopted godson.
Mr. SOROS:	Yes. Yes.
KROFT:	Went out, in fact, and helped in the confiscation of property from the Jews.
Mr. SOROS:	Yes. That's right. Yes.
KROFT:	I mean, that sounds like an experience that would send lots of people to the psychiatric couch for many, many years. Was it difficult?
Mr. SOROS:	Not at all. Not at all. Maybe as a child you don't see the connection. But it was—it created no problem at all.
KROFT:	No feeling of guilt?
Mr. SOROS:	No.[35]

This from the man who aspires to be "the conscience of the world."

When the Communists occupied Hungary, they presented young Soros with a new set of moral challenges. He insists to this day that Communism repelled him, yet admits that he told his father in 1946, "I'd like to go to Moscow to find out about Communism. I mean that's where the power is. I'd like to know more about it."[36] Better than any of his moral ideals or pronouncements, the statement "that's where the power is" sums up the compass by which Soros has guided his life.

Tivadar persuaded his son to go to England instead. His advice came none too soon. In January 1947, Stalin installed the Communist dictator Matyas Rákosi in Hungary. Born Matthias Rosenberg, he was a Hungarian Jew who had lived many years in the USSR. Returning with the Red Army, Rákosi plunged his native Hungary into a bloodbath of purges, show trials, mass deportations and executions. Soros has never revealed what effect the Jewish dictator Rákosi might have had on his already tenuous sense of "tribal loyalty," to use Soros' phrase. Nor has he offered any opinion as to whether Rákosi's embrace of Communist "universalism" was in any way preferable to the Zionists' embrace of "tribalism." Whatever his thoughts may have been, Soros, then 17, left his homeland for England in August 1947, after seven months of Rákosi's terror.

Around 1980, when working as a successful New York hedge fund manager, Soros found himself yearning to make a difference in the world. But his estrangement from Judaism left him groping for a purpose. In his 1991 book, *Underwriting Democracy*, he confessed: "As I looked around me for a worthy cause, I ran into difficulties. I did not belong to any special community. . . . I never quite became an American. I had left Hungary behind and my Jewishness did not express itself in a sense of tribal loyalty that would have led me to support Israel."[37]

In 1995, Soros told the *New Yorker*, "I don't think that you can ever overcome anti-Semitism if you behave as a tribe. . . . The only way you can overcome it is if you give up the tribalness." This is exactly the rule by which the young Soros lived—and survived— as a collaborator in fascist Hungary. The *New Yorker* suggested to Soros that his opposition to "tribalness" implied an opposition to the very concept of a Jewish state. Soros replied "testily." He said: "I don't deny the Jews their right to a national existence—but I don't want to be part of it."[38] As usual, however, this is only a half-truth, since Soros never hesitates to advocate policies whose execution would surely result in Israel's destruction. "I suspect that Hamas will have to be brought into the peace process before it can be fully successful," he wrote in *Soros on Soros*.[39] How bringing in a terrorist organization openly committed to the destruction of Israel—and to the killing of Jews as Jews—could make the Arab-Israeli peace process successful Soros failed to explain.

At times, Soros has characterized the founding of Israel as a pathological reaction by certain Jews obsessed with emulating their Nazi oppressors—"a process of victims turning persecutors," as he describes it in *The Bubble of American Supremacy*, in a phrase chillingly applicable to himself. Citing criminological data from US prisons, Soros pointed out that "some of the most violent criminals in U.S. jails" were abused when young. "An abused youth chooses a perpetrator as his role model and starts imitating him," Soros explained. Thus did Jewish victims of the Nazis emulate their oppressors and become persecutors of Palestinians.[40]

"When you look at the way Jews react to persecution," Soros wrote in another book, "you'll find that they tend to follow one of two main escape routes. Either they transcend their problem by turning to something universal or they identify with their oppressors and try to become like them. I came from an assimilationist family and I have chosen the first route. The other alternative is Zionism, the founding of a nation where the Jews are in the majority."[41] Soros thus implies that he escaped the cycle of "victims turning persecutors" only because his parents rejected their Jewish heritage. "I grew up in a Jewish anti-Semitic home," he once quipped.[42] What Soros misses in these reflections is the fact that he survived by assimilating to Nazism, an option unacceptable to most and, in practice, open to only a few.

In 1947 Soros made his way to England, where he gained admission to the London School of Economics and studied with Popper. Philosophy entranced him, but the world of finance offered him a future and he took it. After graduating in 1952, he joined the London brokerage firm Singer & Friedlander, where he mastered the obscure art of international arbitrage. In 1956, he moved to New York and began work as a stock trader. Eventually he landed a job as a portfolio manager at Arnhold and S. Bleichroeder Inc., an investment bank catering to old money, with roots going back to 1803 Berlin. The firm's blue-chip clientele had once included Germany's "Iron Chancellor," Otto von Bismarck. Soros' career blossomed in New York, due partly to his drive and intellect and partly to the help and guidance of top-level global investors whose favor he courted.

While he moved among these worldly powers he did not give up his philosophical longings. It was during his stint with Arnhold and S. Bleichroeder that he wrote the bulk of his treatise *The Burden of Consciousness*. Soros chose an apt environment for this work. In 1959, he moved to Greenwich Village, on Christopher Street, an unusual destination for a financier in those days. The neighborhood became famous during the Fifties for its poetry readings, jazz clubs and "beatnik" intelligentsia. When Soros arrived, the beatniks were giving way to the emerging Sixties counterculture, of which Greenwich Village was an early epicenter. Soros had married and moved with his wife to a new location in the Village on Sheridan Square in 1961. A son joined the family in 1963.[43] Soros has written and spoken little about this period of his life, but he lived half a decade in the Village, and the experience surely influenced him in countless ways.

We do not know to what extent Soros mingled with the Village intelligentsia when he lived there, but certain notable habitués of the neighborhood's salons and coffeehouses were destined to have an impact on Soros in later years. The influential socialist Michael Harrington, for example, held court almost nightly at the White Horse Tavern, barely half a block from Soros' Sheridan Square apartment. In the early Sixties, Harrington served on the board of the League for Industrial Democracy, along with Aryeh Neier, whom Soros would later hire to lead his foundation network.

While Soros labored over his manuscript of *The Burden of Consciousness*, Harrington too was writing a book. Published in 1962 under the title *The Other America*, it argued that post-war prosperity had failed to eliminate poverty in America, that an "invisible" underclass of about 50 million people suffered desperate want, and that something must be done.[44] Harrington called for a "war on poverty," though he was vague on particulars. "There is no point in attempting to blueprint or detail the mechanisms and institutions of a war on poverty in the United States," he wrote. "There is information enough for action. All that is lacking is political will."[45] President Johnson read and admired Harrington's book. *The Other America* is widely credited with inspiring Johnson's War on Poverty—a well-intended but ultimately disastrous program whose perverse effects helped give birth to Soros' own Shadow Party.

Another Village personality of the era ended up playing a more personal role in Soros' life. The poet Allen Ginsberg frequented Village hangouts during the period Soros lived there. A red-diaper baby who spent summers as a boy at the Communist Party's Camp Nicht-Gedeiget in the Catskills, Ginsberg grew up to be a New Left radical, whose activities earned him a place on the FBI's "Dangerous Subversive" list in 1965.[46] While there is no evidence that Soros met Ginsberg during his Village years, they certainly did meet, possibly around 1980. Ginsberg became Soros' "life-long friend," according to Kaufman.[47] By the mid-1980s, the poet was a frequent guest at Soros' plush Fifth Avenue apartment and his El Mirador estate on Long Island.[48] When dissident Hungarian playwright and director István Eörsi visited New York in 1981, Soros and Ginsberg reportedly showed him a "wild time" on the town.[49]

Soros has few real friends, but the late Allen Ginsberg was apparently one of them. This raises questions. Another life-long friend of Soros, Wall Street financier Byron Wien, has commented, "He [Soros] wants to achieve certain objectives—he gets his satisfaction from that, not from human relationships. George has transactional relationships. People get something from him, he from them."[50]

What did Soros and Ginsberg get from each other? At the very least, they reinforced one anothers' radical inclinations. Ginsberg was one of America's foremost promoters of marijuana, LSD and other sources of chemical "enlightenment." Soros claims that it was Ginsberg who persuaded him to champion drug legalization.[51] Ginsberg was also a fierce advocate of the Palestinian cause. He traveled to Israel in 1988 and compiled a dossier on Israeli censorship of Palestinian media. Working with a committee of pro-Palestinian Jews in New York, which included Arthur Miller, Norman Mailer, Erica Jong, Susan Sontag and others, Ginsberg organized the signing and dispatch of a formal protest letter to the Israeli government, demanding press freedom for Palestinian journalists in the occupied West Bank and Gaza Strip. The letter made headlines in the *New York Times*.[52] With regard to the selective application of the rules of "open society," Soros had plainly found a kindred spirit.

Soros' Village interlude ended when he moved his growing

family—his daughter was born in 1965—into more spacious and conventional quarters on Central Park West. He applied himself to trading with renewed enthusiasm and, in 1969, he and an associate, Jim Rogers, struck out on their own, starting what would later become known as the Quantum Fund, the cash cow of Soros' global empire.

In business, his eerily prescient investments marked him as the man to watch on Wall Street. When he bought up oil drilling and equipment stocks in 1972, everyone thought he was mad. But one year later the Arab states imposed an oil embargo that forced oil prices through the roof. No one had ever heard of an "automated battlefield" back in 1975. But Soros invested heavily in "smart" bombs, laser-directed artillery shells and computerized missiles, the same weapons that destroyed Saddam Hussein's army in the Gulf War 16 years later.[53]

Between 1979 and 1981, the Quantum Fund quadrupled in value, from $100 million to $400 million. At this juncture, *Institutional Investor* magazine named Soros "the world's greatest money manager." He was just getting warmed up. In September 1992, he shorted the British pound, as noted in Chapter 1. Wagering $10 billion that it would sink in value against the German mark, Soros bought deutschmarks and dumped pounds, while the Bank of England tried to counter him by doing the reverse. After weeks of maneuvering, the counter effort failed, and the British were forced to devalue the pound by 20 percent. 16 September became forever known as "Black Wednesday" among London traders.[54] Soros' profit from the crash was nearly $2 billion. In June 1994, *Financial World* magazine hailed Soros as the top earner on Wall Street, noting that his 1993 profits "exceeded the gross domestic product of at least 42 member nations of the UN."[55] New vistas unfolded. "The man who broke the Bank of

England" had become a player, not only in financial markets, but in the struggle for power and dominance among nations and empires.

From a moral standpoint, Soros defined himself when he set up shop in the dying Soviet Union. As a self-styled crusader for Open Society, he found himself in a unique position to foster a new democracy in the ruins of Soviet Communism, if that had been his priority or design. But instead, Soros approached this opportunity as he had other crossroads in his life—specifically his confrontations as a Jew with the Nazi regime and then with the Communists in Hungary. He assimilated to the corrupt system already emerging and milked profits from a vulnerable people. This proved more seductive than attempting to create a better future in post-communist Russia. The choice eerily recalled Soros' self-revealing comment to his father as a 17-year-old contemplating a move to Stalin's Russia: "That's where the power is."

Soros' road to power, in this instance, as in others, was through his philanthropic enterprises. His motives in pursuing philanthropy have been often questioned. In 1995, the London *Sunday Times* noted: "[Soros'] investment fund did not pay taxes in the United States between 1969 and 1986, enjoying a 'free ride' that netted him and his investors billions of dollars. Until the American Tax Reform Act [of] 1986 was passed, [Soros'] Quantum Fund legally avoided paying a cent." The *Times* went on to observe that, "all [Soros'] philanthropy began in 1987, the first year he and his fund had to pay taxes. Charitable matters are tax deductible and Soros says his aim is to give away half his yearly income, the maximum he can deduct."[56]

In fairness to Soros, he actually began dabbling in philanthropy as early as 1979. In 1984, he launched his first Open

Society Foundation in Hungary. But it is also true that his giving remained modest until 1987. That year, he opened his Moscow office, and his philanthropy quickly swelled to its now-legendary proportions. "My spending rose from $3 million in 1987 to more than $300 million a year by 1992," he wrote.[57]

There is no question but that Soros spreads a lot of money around. On the other hand, his critics have long argued that his philanthropic spending is "merely a smoke screen for empire building," in the words of the *New Yorker*'s Connie Bruck. Soros admitted to Bruck that his philanthropy opened doors to political influence—influence (as Soros failed to add) that could be translated into profits. When he first began doling out money in Central Europe, "People like the dictator in Romania, Iliescu, suddenly became very interested in seeing me.... [M]y influence increased."[58]

The entanglement of his goals as philanthropist, politician and profiteer became particularly acute in the chaos of post-Communist Russia, where the temptations were more abundant than usual. In 1992, when the Clintons took office, they inherited the historic task of redefining America's relationship with the collapsed Soviet empire and helping to rebuild a society in its ruins. The Clintons' Russia policy proved a spectacular failure, in large part because they delegated so much of its execution to George Soros and others like him.

From the beginning, President Clinton chose to deal with Russia and the former Soviet states through private back channels, circumventing normal State Department procedures. He appointed what became known as a "troika," three officials endowed with extraordinary authority over US-Russian relations. This troika included Strobe Talbott at the State Department, Lawrence Summers at Treasury and Vice President Al Gore.[59]

Talbott had been Bill Clinton's roommate and fellow Rhodes Scholar at Oxford University. He was the first of the troika to be appointed, and was the leader of the group. On 19 January 1993, Clinton invented a new title for Talbott, naming him Ambassador-at-Large to Russia and the New Independent States. Ten weeks later, Clinton further solidified Talbott's power by appointing him chairman of a "Supercommittee" or Steering Committee on the former Soviet Union. *Business Week* accordingly dubbed Talbott the Clinton administration's "Russian policy czar."[60]

To guide him through the mysterious by-ways of the former Soviet states, Clinton's new "Russian policy czar" turned to a businessman with experience in the region: George Soros. Regarding Soros' freelance statesmanship during this era, Talbott told the *New Yorker* in 1995: "I would say that [Soros' policy] is not identical to the foreign policy of the U.S. government—but it's compatible with it. It's like working with a friendly, allied, independent entity, if not a government. We try to synchronize our approach to the former Communist countries with Germany, France, Great Britain—*and* with George Soros." Talbott added that he considered Soros "a national resource—indeed, a national treasure."[61]

Anne Williamson, a journalist who specializes in Russian affairs, remarked in an interview, "The Clintons welcomed Soros with open arms. Soros performed services for the Clintons, and in return received wide latitude for his business ventures in the former Soviet bloc. Soros not only expanded his fortune under Bill and Hillary, but he also fit in with their countercultural zeitgeist. Through them, Soros found a public platform to espouse his wacky politics. With Bush in power, Soros no longer has that kind of influence. That's a big part of what's driving him crazy."[62]

Soros clearly relished the high-level access he enjoyed during the Clinton years. In 1995, he told PBS talk show host Charlie Rose, "I like to influence policy. I was not able to get to George Bush [Senior]. But now I think I have succeeded with my influence. . . . I do now have great access in [the Clinton] administration. There is no question about this. We actually work together as a team."[63]

The period of Soros' financial and political suzerainty coincided with Russia's wholesale collapse into corruption and anarchy. David Ignatius of the *Washington Post* held the Clinton administration largely to blame. "Let's call it Russiagate," he wrote in an article of 25 August 1999, in which he decried, "the lawlessness of modern Russia and the acquiescence of the Clinton administration in the process of decline and decay there." Ignatius concluded, "What makes the Russian case so sad is that the Clinton administration may have squandered one of the most precious assets imaginable—which is the idealism and goodwill of the Russian people as they emerged from 70 years of Communist rule. The Russia debacle may haunt us for generations."[64]

Soros was deeply immersed in the quicksand of corruption which engulfed Russia during the '90s. After years of preparation, he began his big power play in May 1989, when he began funding a young Harvard economist named Jeffrey Sachs to develop an economic reform plan for Poland. Soros paid Sachs and his team through his newly-founded Stefan Batory Foundation in Warsaw. The young economist favored "shock therapy"—a sudden lifting of price controls, currency controls, trade restrictions and investment barriers which would plunge the country instantly into the icy waters of free-market competition. The idea was to get the pain of the transition over with as quickly as possible. Poland implemented Sachs' plan on 1 January 1990. Hyperinflation immediately soared out of control.[65] "It was very tough on the population, but people were willing to take a lot of pain in order to see real change," Soros wrote later.[66] Ultimately, Poland's "big bang" was deemed a success.

Soros and Sachs went to Moscow next, seeking to persuade Mikhail Gorbachev to try shock therapy in the Soviet Union. Gorbachev rejected their plan, which angered Soros. Later, when Gorbachev tried to secure loans from Western lenders, Soros undermined him, denouncing the Soviet leader in the press and predicting that his reforms would fail.[67] Soros' attack damaged Gorbachev's reputation in the West, impeding his access to foreign aid.[68] As the Soviet economy faltered, Gorbachev's hold on power weakened. Kremlin hardliners attempted a coup in August 1991, setting off a chain reaction of events that ended in Gorbachev's ouster. The coup itself failed, but the Soviet Union split up, and Gorbachev was obliged to resign. Boris Yeltsin emerged as Russia's new leader.

Yeltsin proved more cooperative than his predecessor. Now Soros and Sachs could finally get down to the serious business of implementing their shock therapy plan. Russia lifted its price controls on 2 January 1992. The life savings of ordinary Russians went up in smoke as inflation hit 2,500 percent. This was only the beginning. What followed was one of the greatest economic catastrophes in history.

Over the next four years, a cabal of corrupt officials and businessmen, both Russian and American, used their government connections to hijack Russia's privatization process for personal gain. They bought up the crown jewels of Russia's economy for a fraction of their worth in rigged auctions and stole billions of dollars from foreign aid loans earmarked for economic development projects. Russia scholar Peter Reddaway estimates that between 1992 and 1996, "Although 57 percent of Russia's firms were privatized, the state budget received only $3-5 billion for them, because they were sold at nominal prices to corrupt cliques."[69] By 1996, a group of seven Russian businessmen had managed to gain control of 60 percent of Russia's natural resources, including its precious oil and gas reserves. Through their manipulations behind the scenes, this group exercised *de facto* control over the country, for which reason the Russians called them "oligarchs."[70] It is largely due to widespread disgust with the corrupt reign of the oligarchs that so many Russians look with favor today upon Vladimir Putin's iron-fisted but orderly rule.

Throughout the '90s, Sachs and Soros wielded enormous influence in Russia. From 1995 to 1999, Sachs headed the Harvard Institute for International Development, through which Harvard University provided economic development assistance to needy countries. Much as Strobe Talbott delegated important aspects of US-Russian diplomacy to George Soros during the '90s, the United States Agency for International Development likewise delegated to the Harvard Institute the job of overseeing Russia's transformation to a market economy. This put Sachs and his team in the position of official economic advisors to Boris Yeltsin, representing the US government. Russians called them the *Garvardniki*—the Harvard boys.[71]

The *Garvardniki* could make or break Russian officials by deciding who would get foreign aid grants and who would not. Their influence over Yeltsin was such that he frequently bypassed the Russian Parliament, issuing presidential decrees to enact the Harvard team's reforms. At times, the men from Harvard would even draft Yeltsin's decrees with their own hands.[72] All of this meddling in Russia's internal affairs might have been excusable and even commendable, had the *Garvardniki* proved wise and trustworthy counselors. All too often, however, they used their influence to push bad policy for selfish reasons. The Harvard Institute's Russian operations quickly became a hotbed of corruption, as its envoys exploited their access to Yeltsin and the Russian oligarchs for personal gain.

Jeffrey Sachs has not been accused of profiting personally from these activities. Nevertheless, the cloud of scandal which consumed the Institute on his watch reflects poorly on his leadership, to say the least. Sachs resigned as director of the Institute on 25 May 1999, even as US Justice Department investigators were probing its Russian operations.[73] Harvard shut down the scandal-ridden Institute in January 2000, but not soon enough to avoid a Justice Department lawsuit charging Institute personnel with fraudulent misuse of USAID funds. Harvard settled the case out of court for $26 million—a mere wrist slap considering the damage the Institute had done to the Russian economy and to US-Russian relations.[74] Oddly, the Russia scandal left no perceptible marks on Professor Sachs' reputation. As we shall see in Chapter 11, his career is flourishing today as never before.

Throughout the '90s, George Soros navigated the breakers of Russia's economic turmoil like a champion surfer, finding the experience energizing, exhilarating and highly profitable. A reporter for the New Republic asked Soros in 1994 how he should describe to his readers the immense power and status the mighty philanthropist enjoyed in the former Soviet states. Soros replied, "Just write that the former Soviet Empire is now called the Soros Empire."[75]

The Soros Empire was short-lived. By 1998 federal investigators in the United States were scrutinizing billions of dollars in illegal transfers flowing out of Russia through the Bank of New York and other US financial institutions. As the magnitude of the pilferage began leaking into Western media, foreign aid and foreign investment slowed to a trickle. Everything finally came to a screeching halt on "Black Monday," 17 August 1998, when Russia was forced to devalue the ruble and default on its debt. Rep. Jim Leach, head of the House Banking Committee, announced on 1 September 1999 that the Russia scandal could prove to be "one of the greatest social robberies in human history." Based on preliminary inquiries, Leach declared that he was "very confident" that at least $100 billion had been laundered out of Russia, an unknown portion of which may have been diverted from the International Monetary Fund and other foreign aid loans.[76]

Journalist Anne Williamson, appearing before Leach's House Banking Committee on 22 September 1999, explained to a panel of stunned congressmen how so many US taxpayer dollars had managed to go missing in Russia. She told the committee that the Clintons had set up an "international patronage machine." Clintonites in the guise of "consultants" to the Russian government requested and received loans, virtually at will, through such international lending agencies as the IMF, the World Bank, the US Agency for International Development, the Overseas Private Investment Corporation and the Export-Import Bank. Few questioned the loans, said Williamson, because the Clinton administration had designated Russian "privatization" a "national security" priority. Much of the money simply vanished into offshore accounts and the New York Stock Exchange. Other monies were invested in Russian junk bonds, privatization auctions and other lucrative schemes. A handful of inside players, Russian and American alike, got rich, while the average Russian—not to mention the US taxpayer—got fleeced.[77]

Soros insists that his own investments in Russia were squeaky clean. This is debatable. His privileged access to Kremlin officials and friendly oligarchs helped lubricate many deals. Anne

Williamson notes that Soros invested in Russia's second-largest steel mill, Novolipetsk Kombinat, and in the Russian oil firm Sidanko.[78] Joining Soros in these purchases was the Harvard Management Company, which invests Harvard University's multibillion-dollar endowment fund. Soros and Harvard Management purchased shares in Novolipetsk and Sidanko in 1995, through rigged auctions. Technically speaking, the bidding was closed to foreigners. Soros and Harvard Management evaded the no-foreigners rule by making their purchases through the Sputnik Fund—an investment group tied to the powerful Russian oligarch Vladimir Potanin.[79]

To Soros' evident discomfort, the topic of Sidanko and Novolipetsk came up during his testimony in a Congressional hearing. On 15 September 1998, a full year before the Russian scandal exploded in the press, Soros appeared before Leach's House Banking Committee as a friendly witness. Most of the queries put to him were deferential to the point of fawning. But at one point Representative Spencer Bacchus asked a searching question. "Mr. Soros, you have agreed with Chairman Leach's statement that crony capitalism was one of the main problems in Russia. . . . But could not someone consider you as maybe one of the insiders in Russia, as maybe one of the cronies . . . ?"

Soros denied it. He said he avoided any deals in Russia that smacked of cronyism or special favors. But Rep. Bacchus reminded Soros that he had acquired shares in "a large oil company which . . . has more reserves than Mobil Oil." The congressman was referring to the privatization of Sidanko Oil. "I would say that that was part of the crony stuff that was going on," Soros finally conceded.[80] The Leach Committee never got to the bottom of the Russian imbroglio, which was hushed up more quickly and forcefully than any other Clinton scandal.

Russia is not the only country where Soros' business ethics have come into question. A French court convicted him of insider trading in connection with a takeover attempt on the Société Générale bank. The charges against Soros carried a possible two-year prison sentence, though the Paris Court of Appeals graciously let him off with a $2.9-million fine on 24 March 2005. Soros lost a second appeal on 14 June 2006. [81]

Even his admirers struggle to reconcile Soros' predatory financial maneuvers with his carefully cultivated image as a philanthropist and humanitarian. Soros claims that he can compartmentalize the two functions. Conscience clouds an investor's judgment, he says. Therefore, he sets aside conscience when playing the markets. "When I sold sterling short in 1992 . . . I was in effect taking money out of the pockets of British taxpayers," he admits in *The Crisis of Global Capitalism: Open Society Endangered.* "But if I had tried to take social consequences into account, it would have thrown off my risk-reward calculation, and my profits would have been reduced."[82]

It all comes out in the karmic wash, argues Soros, because once he has executed a deal and made money, he can then use his profits for the betterment of humanity—as he conceives it. Soros once told the British paper the *Observer*: "I realized [as a young man] that it's money that makes the world go round, so I might as well make money. . . . But having made it, I could then indulge my social concerns."[83] These social concerns, of course, are indistinguishable from the betterment of Soros, the self-appointed "conscience of the world."

6

STRATEGY FOR
REGIME CHANGE

"THIS IS STOLEN LAND!"

"CHICANO POWER!"

"IF YOU THINK I'M ILLEGAL BECAUSE I'M
MEXICAN, LEARN THE TRUE HISTORY
BECAUSE I'M IN MY HOMELAND."

"WE DIDN'T CROSS THE BORDER,
THE BORDER CROSSED US."

These were just some of the slogans waved aloft—along with red-white-and-green Mexican flags—by hundreds of thousands of demonstrators who took to the streets across America on the weekend of 25-26 March 2006. In Los Angeles alone, as many as half a million protesters jammed the thoroughfares and brought the city's traffic to a halt. Some protesters burned American flags and a few fought with police.

The immediate pretext was a proposed crackdown on illegal immigration then under debate in Congress. However, the larger issue was a blunt demand for open borders, for the unconditional right of foreigners to cross US borders at will, and to work or settle in the USA without restriction. It was a vision of an Open Society without end.

Joshua Hoyt, the executive director of the Illinois Coalition for Immigrant and Refugee Rights, told the *Los Angeles Times*, "There has never been this kind of mobilization in the immigrant community ever. They have kicked the sleeping giant. It's the beginning of a massive immigrant civil rights struggle."[1]

More accurately, it was the beginning of a massive new Shadow Party operation. Soros allies and front groups played a central role in orchestrating the rallies. Activists for the public-sector union SEIU reportedly "took care of security" in Los Angeles and provided bus transportation for protesters.[2] Teacher unions encouraged high school students to demonstrate and turned a benevolent eye on tens of thousands of truancies. The following groups—all funded by George Soros' Open Society Institute—helped to organize them:

Association of Community Organizations for Reform Now (ACORN)

American Friends Service Committee (AFSC)

Center for Community Change (CCC)

League of United Latin American Citizens (LULAC)

Massachusetts Immigrant and Refugee Advocacy Coalition (MIRA Coalition)

Mexican-American Legal Defense and Educational Fund (MALDEF)

National Council of La Raza

The Gamaliel Foundation[3]

The Open Society Institute has given $648,200 to MALDEF. La Raza has received over $1.7 million. By far, the most generous grants have gone to the Center for Community Change, which has received more than $5.2 million from Soros' Institute in recent years. Better known by its acronym CCC, the Center engages in "community organizing" in low-income neighborhoods, using techniques pioneered by Saul Alinsky.

On the Monday following the pro-immigration marches, the Center held a prayer service near the Capitol, attended by about 300 radical clergy, including Roman Catholic nuns, priests and monks.[4] The use of clergy in a high-profile media event was a quintessentially Alinsky touch.

The executive director of the Center for Community Change is Deepak Bhargava, a former ACORN organizer who later worked with Arianna Huffington to stage the Soros-funded Shadow Conventions in 2000. Bhargava is a major player in the Soros network.

Prominent among the left-wing luminaries on Bhargava's board of directors is Peter Edelman, the husband of radical civil rights lawyer Marian Wright Edelman. Both are Clinton loyalists and have played a special role in the political life of Hillary Clinton for nearly 40 years. A former aide to Robert F. Kennedy, Peter Edelman contacted young Hillary in 1969 after *Life* magazine featured her Wellesley College commencement speech in a cover story glorifying student activists.[5] From that point, the Edelmans took a proprietary interest in Hillary's career. It was they who recommended Hillary for an appointment to the House Judiciary Committee's Watergate investigative team in 1974, when she was fresh out of Yale Law School, at age twenty-six.[6] Later, Hillary did legal work for the Children's Defense Fund, which Marian Wright Edelman founded. Peter Edelman served the Clinton White House.

What interest does Soros' Shadow Party have in encouraging mass immigration? One answer lies in voter demographics. The more immigrants enter the country, and the more quickly their citizenship is processed, the more voters the Left is likely to gain. Republicans have made impressive inroads into the Hispanic vote under George W. Bush's leadership, but first-generation immigrants still vote Democrat in overwhelming numbers. For most, it is not an ideological choice. Even those immigrants whose sympathies lie with the Republican Party often vote Democrat for practical reasons. Most have relatives eager to join them in America, and they know that immigration policies will always be looser under a Democrat regime.

In his book *The Truth About Hillary*, former *New York Times Magazine* editor Edward Klein warns that Hillary's advisors have already crunched the numbers for a presidential victory in 2008 and that racial demographics are the key. Due to immigration and high minority birth rates, several red states will turn blue by 2008, they claim. Democrats need only retain their present share of black and Hispanic voters for Hillary to win by a healthy margin. According to Klein, four red states now turning blue are Texas, Ohio, Iowa and Missouri. Between now and 2008, blacks, Hispanics and other minorities in Texas will grow from 49.5 to as much as 54 percent of the population. Hillary expects to add these states to presumed victories in New York, California, Florida, New Jersey and Massachusetts, giving her 212 electoral votes—only 58 votes short of victory. Winning Michigan, Illinois, and Pennsylvania would put Hillary "over the top."[7]

On a deeper level, Shadow Party support for the March 2006 pro-immigration rallies probably reflects the usefulness of such spectacles in manipulating mass psychology. Epic grievances and high-profile street actions provide the energy and fuel of progressive movements. They unsettle ordinary citizens, conjuring up images of revolutionary ruptures and civil unrest. Anxiety is the soil in which radical change takes root. Generating such anxiety is essential to the Shadow Party's strategy for regime change.

Soros and his Shadow Party comrades did not invent the politics of demagoguery and racial division. They are merely practicing—and expanding—politics familiar on the Democratic Left. Consider Democrats' reaction to Reagan's victory in 1981 and his call for reducing the size of the federal government. They attacked Reagan's budget as an assault on black people. By 1982, Democrats were openly predicting violence in the streets. There was only one problem. The demagogues making these threats did not want to do the rioting themselves. They wanted black people to do it for them.

"Large scale protest in the United States now seems certain," wrote social scientists and progressive activists Richard A. Cloward and Frances Fox Piven in the *Nation* at the time. "Riots or Marauding Gangs—Will They Strike Our Cities?" asked the headline of a Neal Pierce column in the *Washington Post*. New York City Municipal Assistance Corporation chairman Felix Rohatyn predicted "a very hot summer ahead," noting that "violence is the handmaiden of despair."

Juan Williams, then a young, African American columnist for the *Washington Post*, noted these alarums and responded: "If Liberals Need Riots, Let Whites Do It:" "The tom-toms of progressive thinking are beating out the message that this summer blacks should riot. . . . Well, as a young black, I'd personally prefer the beach. . . . [R]iots would mean living through days and nights of fear and watching neighborhoods just now on the mend from the '60s devastated again. . . . [A]sking black people to riot again is asking too much."[8]

Noting that "this country has not seen a good white riot in years," Williams continued, "What the liberals need is not to have blacks out on 14th Street again. No, what they need is to have blacks, like me, with reporters' notebook in hand, covering it in a white neighborhood."

Williams spoke for many black Americans who had decided they no longer wanted to provide the fodder for the Left's racial arson. This was a blow to Democrat planners.

Beating the tom-toms no longer brought out the warriors. Williams' rebuff must have come as a particularly cruel disappointment to the two aforementioned social scientists whom Williams cited by name in his article, Richard A. Cloward and Frances Fox Piven, both key operatives of the Shadow Party network.

In the Sixties, Cloward and Piven had practically invented the strategy of exploiting black rage to advance the cause of "social justice." Their formula even bore their names: the Cloward-Piven strategy.

On 11 August 1965, the black district of Watts in Los Angeles erupted in violence after police used batons to subdue a man suspected of drunk driving. Riots raged for six days, spilling over into other parts of the city, leaving 34 dead. Democrats used the tragedy to promote an expansion of the welfare state, sponsoring new government programs to address the problem of the inner city poor. On the radical end of the spectrum, Cloward and Piven viewed the spreading violence as an opportunity for revolution.

Barely three months after the fires of Watts had subsided, they began privately circulating mimeographed copies of an article they had written called "Mobilizing the Poor: How it Could Be Done." In their view, destruction could be a creative force. While liberals funded welfare programs, Cloward and Piven proposed to overload the welfare system and destroy it.

When the Cloward-Piven strategy paper was published six months later as an article in the *Nation*,[9] it electrified the Left. Activists were abuzz over the plan, which was variously dubbed the "crisis strategy," the "flood-the-rolls, bankrupt-the-cities strategy" or just simply the "Cloward-Piven strategy." It would become the play book for Shadow Party radicals working for "regime change."

Cloward was then a professor of social work at Columbia University. His co-author Piven was a research associate at Columbia's School of Social Work. (She now holds a Distinguished Professorship of Political Science and Sociology at the City University of New York.) In their article, the authors charged that the ruling classes used welfare to weaken the poor and preserve the "system." By providing a social safety net, the rich doused the fires of potential rebellion. As radicals, Cloward and Piven wanted to fan those flames.

Poor people can advance, Cloward later explained to the *New York Times*, only when "the rest of society is afraid of them."[10] Rather than placating the poor with government hand-outs, activists should work to sabotage and destroy the welfare system. The collapse of the welfare state would ignite a political and financial crisis that would shake the foundations of society. Poor people would rise in revolt. Only then would "the rest of society" accept their demands.

The rebellion could be ignited by exposing the inability of the welfare state to meet the "real needs" of the poor. The strategy would be to overload the welfare system with a flood of new applicants and cause it to go bankrupt. The number of Americans subsisting on welfare—about 8 million at the time—probably represented less than half those technically eligible for full benefits, the authors noted. They proposed a "massive drive to recruit the poor *onto* the welfare rolls." Cloward and Piven calculated that persuading even a fraction of the potential welfare recipients to demand their entitlements would bankrupt the entire system. The demands would break the budget and jam the bureaucratic gears into gridlock. The result would be "a profound financial and political crisis" that would unleash "powerful forces . . . for major economic reform at the national level."

Their article called for "cadres of aggressive organizers" to use "demonstrations to create a climate of militancy." Intimidated by black violence, politicians would appeal to the federal government for help. Carefully orchestrated media campaigns carried out by friendly journalists would promote the idea of "a federal program of income redistribution" in the form of a guaranteed living income for all, working and non-working people alike. Local officials would grab hold of this idea like drowning men reaching for a lifeline. They would apply pressure on Washington to implement the idea. With major cities erupting in chaos like Watts, Washington would have to act.

This was the plan detailed in the *Nation* on 2 May 1966. While the Cloward-Piven strategy never achieved its goal of ushering in a Marxist utopia, it provided a blueprint for many parallel campaigns. The Shadow Party has adopted the Cloward-Piven formula, applying it to many sectors of public life, with a devastating efficiency its creators never envisioned.

Cloward and Piven launched a "Welfare Rights Movement" based on their original plan. They recruited a radical black organizer named George Wiley to lead it. Wiley never captured the media spotlight as did other black militants of his era, such as Huey Newton and Angela Davis. But he was able to inflict more damage on America's body politic than any of the better-known icons of radical politics. The secret to Wiley's effectiveness was the strategy that Cloward and Piven had devised.

Born in New Jersey and raised in Rhode Island, Wiley joined the Syracuse University faculty in 1960 as a professor of chemistry. There he founded the Syracuse chapter of the Congress for Racial Equality (CORE) and became its first chairman. Wiley's radicalism was fueled, in part, by his wife, a white graduate student, née Wretha Frances Whittle, whom he married in June 1961. Wretha

Wiley was an early member of Students for a Democratic Society. SDS leader Tom Hayden stayed with the Wileys' when he visited Syracuse in 1962.[11]

George Wiley rose quickly in the civil rights movement, resigning his post at Syracuse University in November 1964 to become associate national director of CORE, second-in-command to national director James Farmer. Farmer was a giant in the civil rights movement, having organized the Freedom Rides in 1961. His commitment to non-violent action was no longer fashionable, however. By 1965, CORE's ranks were filling with black nationalists, and Farmer announced his retirement. Wiley tried to succeed him, but the nationalists blocked his way, ridiculing Wiley for his buttoned-down style and integrationist views.

Seeing that he had no future at CORE, Wiley looked for other options. He met with Cloward and Piven in January 1966, at a radical organizers' meeting in Syracuse called the "Poor People's War Council on Poverty." Wiley listened to their plan with interest.[12] He left CORE the same month, launching his own activist group, the Poverty Rights Action Center, with headquarters in Washington DC.[13] In a calculated show of militancy, Wiley now exchanged his business suits for dashikis, jeans, battered shoes and a newly-grown Afro.[14]

Cloward and Piven courted Wiley aggressively. They knew that their plan could spark a nationwide movement, but it lacked a proper leader. They needed an experienced organizer with vision, charisma and—most important of all—street credibility. Wiley could be that organizer, they thought. Ironically, Wiley was not from the inner city, but from the black middle class. Like the late Stokeley Carmichael and other middle-class leaders of Sixties black power movements, however, Wiley could speak the language of the streets when necessary.

Regarding the Cloward-Piven strategy, Wiley told one audience: "[A] lot of us have been hampered in our thinking about the potential here by our own middle-class backgrounds—and I think most activists basically come out of middle-class backgrounds—and were oriented toward people having to work, and that we have to get as many people as possible off the welfare rolls." However, Wiley went on, "I think that this [Cloward-Piven] strategy is going to catch on and be very important in the time ahead."[15]

After a series of mass marches and rallies by welfare recipients in June 1966, Wiley declared "the birth of a movement"—the Welfare Rights Movement.[16] In the summer of 1967, Wiley founded the National Welfare Rights Organization (NWRO), moving it into his office in Washington DC. Wiley then set to work putting the "crisis strategy" into effect. His tactics closely followed the recommendations laid down in the *Nation* article. Wiley's followers invaded welfare offices—often violently—bullying social workers and loudly demanding every penny to which the law "entitled" them. By 1969, NWRO claimed a dues-paying membership of 22,500 families, with 523 chapters across the nation.[17]

In a summary account of Wiley's tactics, the *New York Times* reported in 1970, "There have been sit-ins in legislative chambers, including a United States Senate committee hearing, mass demonstrations of several thousand welfare recipients, school boycotts, picket lines, mounted police, tear gas, arrests—and, on occasion, rock-throwing, smashed glass doors, overturned desks, scattered papers and ripped-out phones."[18] These methods proved effective. "The flooding succeeded beyond Wiley's wildest dreams," wrote Sol Stern in the *City Journal*. "From 1965 to 1974, the number of single-parent households on welfare soared from 4.3 million to 10.8 million, despite mostly flush economic times."[19]

The National Welfare Rights Organization pushed for a "guaranteed living income," as prescribed by Cloward and Piven, which it defined, in 1968, as $5,500 per year for every American family with four children. Wiley employed the battle cry, "Fifty-five hundred or fight!" raising it the following year to, "Sixty-five hundred or fight!" Wiley never made headway with his demand for a living income. Nevertheless, the tens of billions of dollars in welfare entitlements that Wiley and his followers managed to squeeze from state and local governments came very close to sinking the economy, just as Cloward and Piven had predicted.

In their 1966 article, Cloward and Piven had given special attention to New York City, whose masses of urban poor, leftist intelligentsia and free-spending politicians rendered it uniquely vulnerable to the strategy they proposed. Noting that New York City was already expected to shell out $500 million in annual benefits to the 500,000 people on its welfare rolls in 1966, Cloward and Piven calculated that, "An increase in the rolls of a mere twenty percent would cost an already overburdened municipality some $100 million" per year. A twenty percent increase was well within reach. It could be accomplished not only by adding new people to the rolls, but also by prodding current welfare recipients to register for additional benefits, such as "special grants" for clothing, household equipment and furniture. At the time, city welfare agencies were paying about $20 million per year in "special grants." Cloward and Piven estimated that they could "multiply these expenditures tenfold or more," draining an additional $180 million annually from the city coffers.[20]

Cloward and Piven had chosen their target shrewdly. George Wiley and his welfare radicals terrorized social workers in cities across the country, but their greatest success came in New York. New York City's arch-liberal mayor John Lindsay, newly elected in November 1966, capitulated to Wiley's every demand. An appeaser by nature, Lindsay's preferred strategy was to calm racial tensions by taking "walking tours" through Harlem, Bedford-Stuyvesant and other troubled areas of the city. This made for good photo-ops, but failed to mollify Wiley's cadres and the masses they mobilized, who wanted cash. "The violence of the [welfare rights] movement was frightening," recalls Lindsay budget aide Charles Morris.[21] Black militants laid seige to City Hall, bearing signs saying, "No Money, No Peace." One welfare mother famously screamed at Mayor Lindsay, "It's my job to have kids, Mr. Mayor, and your job to take care of them."[22]

Lindsay answered these provocations with ever-more-generous programs of appeasement in the form of welfare dollars. Soon after taking office in 1966, he appointed Mitchell Ginsberg to the post of welfare commissioner. An associate dean at the Columbia University School of Social Work, Ginsberg was a colleague of Cloward and Piven, who shared their radical views. He surrounded himself with welfare-rights activists and set to work dismantling every procedure for screening (and potentially disqualifying) welfare applicants. By 1968 the rejection rate for applicants had fallen from 40 percent in 1965 to 23 percent. The *Daily News* nicknamed the new welfare commissioner "Come-and-Get-It" Ginsberg.[23]

New York's welfare rolls had been growing by twelve percent per year already before Lindsay took office. The rate jumped to 50 percent annually in 1966.[24] During Lindsay's first term of office, welfare spending in New York City more than doubled, from $400 million to $1 billion annually.[25] Outlays for the poor consumed 28 percent of the city's budget by 1970. "By the early 1970s, one person was on the welfare rolls in New York City for every two working in the city's private economy," Sol Stern wrote in the *City Journal*.[26]

Crucial to Wiley's success was the cooperation of radical sympathizers inside the federal government, who supplied Wiley's movement with grants, training, and logistical assistance, channeled through federal War-on-Poverty programs such as VISTA, as Wiley organizer Hulbert James acknowledged. "Welfare rights organizations in this country were developed primarily by VISTA," James conceded in 1969.[27] Among other perks, Wiley's NWRO received free legal aid and free office space from the notoriously left-wing Legal Services division of the Office of Economic Opportunity. Johnson administration officials awarded NWRO a $435,000 contract in 1968.[28]

With Richard Nixon's election later that year, however, the tide began to turn and Wiley's federal subsidies began drying up. So did the public's patience for the sort of violent tactics Wiley promoted. As money tightened, NWRO's leaders began turning on each other. White activists were driven from leadership positions by militant black nationalists. In a repeat of his experience at CORE, Wiley himself came under attack for his middle-class background. A poor people's organization should be run by poor people, the insurgents declared. Pressure grew to fill every leadership slot with welfare recipients, rather than with the professional activists who had previously led NWRO.

In December 1971, Wiley threw in the towel, announcing his resignation in a *New York Times* interview. He said that he would start a new group called The Movement for Economic Justice. But the new organization never got off the ground. Wiley died in a boating accident on 8 August 1973, and the welfare rights movement died with him.

The National Welfare Rights Organization limped along without Wiley, finally closing its doors in 1972. Its stormy and influential history had lasted only six years. Wiley's movement had been an economic disaster for American taxpayers and a social catastrophe for millions of poverty-stricken Americans who, thanks to Wiley's efforts, became locked in the cycle of welfare dependency. For its radical masterminds, however, the disaster could be (and was) looked on as a triumph. As a direct result of the overloading of its welfare rolls, New York City—the financial capital of the world—effectively went bankrupt in 1975. The entire state of New York was nearly taken down with it. Radicals reveled in their victory. The Cloward-Piven strategy had proved its effectiveness.

To this day, most Americans have never heard of Richard Cloward or Frances Fox Piven. New York City has not forgotten their achievement, however. In 1998, Mayor Rudolph Giuliani reviewed the effects of their strategy, without naming its authors. Noting that the number of people on welfare in the Big Apple had skyrocketed from 200,000 to nearly 1.1 million between 1960 and 1970, Giuliani said: "This wasn't an accident, it wasn't an atmospheric thing, it wasn't supernatural. It was the result of policies, choices, and a philosophy that was embraced in the 1960s and then enthusiastically endorsed in the City of New York. . . . This is the result of policies and programs designed to have the maximum number of people get on welfare."[29]

The *New York Times* learned that an earlier draft of Giuliani's speech had identified Cloward and Piven by name, but their names had been edited out of his final speech. The *Times* rushed to the defense of the two radicals with a 9,800-word sympathetic retelling of their story in its Sunday magazine, and a savage attack on Giuliani's welfare reforms. The article stated:

> In an early draft of his presentation, Giuliani even rounded out
> his history by citing two Columbia University professors

whose audacious role in the welfare explosion is now all but forgotten. In plotting what they called the "flood-the-rolls, bankrupt-the-cities strategy," Richard A. Cloward and Frances Fox Piven literally set out to destroy local welfare programs. By drowning the cities in caseloads and costs, they hoped to build support for a more generous Federal solution, preferably a guaranteed national income. What's also all but forgotten now is that the strategy almost worked.[30]

Neither leftist nor mainstream media ever again mentioned the Cloward-Piven strategy. Nor did Cloward and Piven ever again reveal their intentions quite as candidly or publicly as they had in their 1966 article in the *Nation*. They learned to tailor their message to a more conservative era. Meanwhile, their activism continued, and with it their strategy of overloading the "system" in the hope of causing a breakdown. Cloward and Piven wasted no tears over the end of welfare. With professional aplomb, they simply broke camp and moved on to the next battlefield, seeking fresh applications for their crisis strategy. Their persistence paid off. George Soros and his Shadow Party were waiting in the wings for their distinctive expertise.

7

MARCHING
ORDERS

The next project Richard Cloward and Frances Fox Piven undertook was to launch what would become known as the Voting Rights Movement. This was ironic, for Cloward and Piven did not believe in voting. They despised America's electoral system every bit as much as they despised its welfare system, and for much the same reason. They believed that welfare checks and voting rights were mere bones tossed to the poor to keep them docile. The poor did not need welfare checks and ballots, they argued. The poor needed revolution.

In their 1977 book, *Poor People's Movements: Why They Succeed, How They Fail,* Cloward and Piven took stock of the radical movement as a whole, analyzing what they regarded as notable but temporary successes, such as the movements for industrial workers' rights, unemployed workers' rights, civil rights and welfare rights, and trying to determine which tactic worked and which failed. Their conclusion, as a reviewer in the *Nation* summarized it, was that "the poor cannot rely either on organization or the ballot to advance their interests; the only means they have of securing justice is disruptive protest.... Rent strikes, crime, civic disruptions are the politics of the poor."[1]

Not only was voting ineffective in fostering radical change, but the charade of the "electoral process" actually served the interests of the ruling classes, the authors averred. Voting provided a safety valve to drain away the anger of the poor. It distracted the poor from more fruitful methods of political action. "[E]lectoral political institutions channel protest into voter activity in the United States, and may even confine it within these

119

spheres if . . . the electoral system appears responsive . . ." argued Cloward and Piven.[2] This was unfortunate, they wrote, because, "as long as lower-class groups abided by the norms governing the electoral-representative system, they would have little influence. . . . [I]t is usually when unrest among the lower classes breaks out of the confines of electoral procedures that the poor may have some influence," as, for example, when poor people engage in "strikes," "riots," "crime," "incendiarism," "massive school truancy," "worker absenteeism," "rent defaults," and other forms of "mass defiance" and "institutional disruption."[3]

Poor people lose power "when leaders try to turn movements into electoral organizations," Cloward and Piven wrote in 1981. That is because the "capability of the poor" to effect change lies "in the vulnerability of societal institutions to disruption, and not in the susceptibility of these institutions to transformation through the votes of the poor." Channeling mass protest movements into voting movements is a form of ruling-class cooptation, the authors charged. It "leads to muting and, in the end, to the dissipation of the political power of the poor."[4]

Of the two major parties, the Democrats posed a greater threat of cooptation, the authors implied, since Democrats pretended to represent the lower classes. As long as the poor believed they could get what they wanted by voting Democrat, their energies would be channeled into useless "voter activity," rather than strikes, riots, "incendiarism" and the like. By holding out the false hope of change through the system, Democrat politicians lulled the poor into complacency.

What should radicals do?

Cloward and Piven drew on their past experience for an answer. Ten years earlier, when they determined that the welfare state was acting as a safety valve for the establishment, they resolved to destroy the welfare state. The method of destruction they chose was drawn from the teachings of Saul Alinsky.[5] "Make the enemy live up to their own book of rules," Alinsky wrote.[6] And so they did, challenging the welfare state to pay out every penny to every person theoretically entitled to it. Alinsky called this sort of tactic "mass jujitsu"—using "the strength of the enemy against itself."[7]

Now Cloward and Piven had concluded that the Democratic Party also acted as a safety valve for the establishment. How would one go about applying "mass jujitsu" to the Democratic Party? Simple. You would force the Democrats to live up to their own book of rules. If the Democrats say they represent the poor, let them prove it. Cloward and Piven did not think they could. Fear of disruptive, McGovern-style insurgencies had left Democrat "oligarchs" wary of mobilizing new constituencies whose loyalties might prove fickle. If confronted with a militant new voting bloc of the poor, Democrats would resist it, Cloward and Piven predicted. They would be exposed as hypocritical shills for the rich.

Cloward and Piven presented their plan in a December 1982 article titled, "A Movement Strategy to Transform the Democratic Party," published first in the radical bulletin *Ideas for Action* and subsequently in the left-wing journal *Social Policy*. Once again, the Left was buzzing over Cloward and Piven. The *Nation* mischievously noted, "Cloward and Piven propose a progressive version of a voter registration drive—a strategy which has the appeal of appearing (and being) as patriotic as the League of Women Voters and the Boy Scouts."[8] Its wholesome appearance would be deceptive, however. Cloward and Piven would do to the voting system what they had previously done to the welfare system. They would flood the polls with millions of new voters, drawn from the angry ranks of the underclass, all belligerently demanding their voting rights. The result would be a catastrophic disruption of America's electoral system, the authors predicted.

The authors hoped that the flood of new voters would provoke a backlash from Democrats and Republicans alike, who would join forces to disenfranchise the unruly hordes, using such time-honored expedients as purging valid voters from the rolls, imposing cumbersome registration procedures, stiffening residency requirements, and so forth. This voter suppression campaign would spark "a political firestorm over democratic rights," they wrote. Voting rights activists would descend on America's election boards and polling stations much as George Wiley's welfare warriors had flooded social services offices. "By staging rallies, demonstrations, and sit-ins . . . over every new restriction on registration procedures, a protest movement can dramatize the conflict . . . ," wrote Cloward and Piven. "Through conflict, the registration movement will convert registering and voting into meaningful acts of collective protest."[9]

The expected conflict would also expose the hypocrisy of the Democratic Party, which would be "disrupted and transformed," the authors predicted.[10] A new party would rise from the ashes of the old. Outwardly, it would preserve the forms and symbols of the old Democratic Party, but the new Democrats would be genuine partisans of the poor, dedicated to class struggle. This was the radical vision driving the Voting Rights Movement.

Cloward and Piven called on many of their old comrades from the Welfare Rights Movement to assist them in the new project. Large numbers of George Wiley's former activists now worked for a group called ACORN, which was itself an offshoot of Wiley's National Welfare Rights Organization. ACORN founder Wade Rathke, a white man, had been a Wiley protegé.

Born and raised in New Orleans, Rathke attended Williams College in Massachusetts for two years, where he joined Students for a Democratic Society, dropping out of school to become a full-time activist. In June 1969, an Alinsky-trained organizer named Bill Pastreich hired Rathke to help start a chapter of the National Welfare Rights Organization in Springfield, Massachusetts.[11] Rathke and Pastreich were soon arrested for incitement to riot after leading a demonstration of welfare mothers in Springfield that erupted into a rock-and-bottle-throwing melée.[12]

George Wiley took note of Rathke's special talents and soon found a use for them. In June 1970, Wiley sent him to organize Little Rock, Arkansas, working on the NWRO payroll.[13] Black nationalists in Wiley's organization were already harassing and pushing out whites like Rathke, and Wiley sensed that his own days with the group might be numbered. The "Arkansas experiment" was an attempt by Wiley to start fresh, with a new type of community organizing network that would reach out to whites, blacks, poor people and blue-collar workers alike. Arkansas was chosen because it was poor, 35 percent black, and because its liberal governor Winthrop Rockefeller had brought a generous helping of War-on-Poverty money into the state, via the Office of Economic Opportunity.[14]

Rathke called his new group the Arkansas Community Organizations for Reform Now or ACORN. Later, as he opened chapters in other states, he changed the name to Association of Community Organizations for Reform Now. Powered by massive funding from VISTA and other federal programs, ACORN grew quickly, expanding from one state to twenty in six years.[15]

From the beginning, ACORN downplayed welfare rights and focused on issues with a wider appeal, such as fighting for a "living wage." It lobbied state and local governments to adopt a minimum wage considerably higher than that mandated by the federal government.

Virtually all of ACORN's founders and top organizers had come out of the National Welfare Rights Organization. They were disciples of George Wiley and Saul Alinsky, thoroughly schooled in the Cloward-Piven strategy, which they called "breaking the bank." The Cloward-Piven strategy formed the basis of many ACORN programs. In future years, the organization would involve itself in activities as diverse as seizing and renovating abandoned buildings, union organizing, forming and running political parties, advising banks on how to comply with federal guidelines mandating investment in low-income neighborhoods, and much more. The common threads running through every ACORN program are money and power. The programs are designed to make money and to enhance ACORN's power.

Today ACORN claims some 175,000 dues-paying member families, and more than 850 chapters in 75 US cities.[16] "Walk through just about any of the nation's inner cities," wrote *City Journal*'s Sol Stern in 2003, "and you're likely to find an office of ACORN, bustling with young people working 12-hour days to 'organize the poor' and bring about 'social change.' The largest radical group in the country, ACORN . . . boasts two radio stations, a housing corporation, a law office, and affiliate relationships with a host of trade-union locals. Not only big, it is effective, with some remarkable successes in getting municipalities and state legislatures to enact its radical policy goals into law."[17]

Following a meeting with high-level Citigroup executives in New York, at which he hammered out details of a long-term consulting contract whereby ACORN would advise Citibank on housing loans, Wade Rathke remarked on his blog, "It was hard not to think about the fact that I had last been in the building a dozen years ago with 1,200 ACORN members when we marched . . . to the building on Park Avenue to protest our inability to get Citibank to do right in any way. . . . Somehow in one of those exquisite tactical miracles of planning, execution, and a hundred tales of discipline and courage everything came together and we managed to break through security and police and get everyone into the downstairs of the building as well as a fair contingent upstairs to negotiate for a much denied meeting with Citibank officials."[18]

Rathke has come far since then. He no longer has to break into buildings to win audiences with Fortune 100 executives. Now he walks through the front door. In another sign of ACORN's rising status, the very first grant awarded by the Bill Clinton Foundation, on 3 February 2006, went to Rathke's group. Clinton gave ACORN $250,000 to help Hurricane Katrina evacuees collect government benefits such as Earned Income Tax Credits.[19]

ACORN founder Wade Rathke plays a special role in the Shadow Party, providing a liaison between many of its most critical operations. He is a union leader, political powerbroker, street-level community organizer and foundation executive, all in one. In addition to serving as Chief Organizer of ACORN, Rathke is also deeply involved with Andrew Stern's radical, public-sector union SEIU, one of the Shadow Party's most important cash cows. He is president and co-founder of SEIU's southern conference, a member of SEIU's executive board, and founder of its Local 100 in New Orleans.

Rathke also co-founded the Tides Foundation with Drummond Pike. Today he is Board Chairman of its sister group, the Tides Center, and sits on the Board of Directors of the Tides Foundation. The Tides "family" of organizations is a nerve center of radical Shadow Party activity. George Soros has given more than $17 million to the Tides Center since 1999.

One of Rathke's fellow Board members at Tides is civil rights attorney Maya Wiley, the daughter of George Wiley. She formerly served as an advisor to the Director of US Programs for George Soros' Open Society Institute and as a consultant to the Open Society Foundation—South Africa. She co-founded and runs the Center for Social Inclusion, a Soros-funded organization dedicated to fighting "structural racism." The Center for Social Inclusion bills itself as "A Project of the Tides Center."

Given Rathke's exceptionally powerful network and his deep roots in the welfare rights movement, it was only natural that Cloward and Piven would turn to Rathke for help when they set out to launch their "voting rights" movement in 1982. That year, two new organizations came into being. One of them, Project Vote, was an ACORN front, launched by former NWRO organizer and ACORN leader Zach Polett. The other, Human SERVE, was founded by Cloward and Piven themselves, along with a former NWRO organizer named Hulbert James. Together with ACORN, these groups would form the vanguard of the Voting Rights Movement.

All three of these organizations set to work lobbying energetically for the so-called Motor-Voter law, which Bill Clinton ultimately signed in 1993. When President Clinton signed the National Voter Registration Act on 20 May 1993, Cloward and Piven stood behind him, in places of honor, at the ceremony.

Having achieved their goal, Cloward and Piven dissolved Human SERVE. Today, the National Voting Rights Institute, founded by John Boniaz in 1994, carries the torch of the "voting rights" movement, with support from George Soros.

The Motor-Voter bill eliminated many controls on voter

fraud, making it easy to register but difficult to determine the validity of new registrations. Under the new law, states were required to provide opportunities for voter registration to any person who showed up at a government office to renew a driver's license or apply for welfare or unemployment benefits. "Examiners were under orders not to ask anyone for identification or proof of citizenship," notes *Wall Street Journal* columnist John Fund in his book, *Stealing Elections*. "States also had to permit mail-in voter registrations, which allowed anyone to register without any personal contact with a registrar or election official. Finally, states were limited in pruning 'deadwood'—people who had died, moved or been convicted of crimes—from their rolls."[20]

Just as they swamped America's welfare offices in the 1960s, the Cloward-Piven team now sought to overwhelm the nation's understaffed and poorly policed electoral system. The law quickly led to what John Fund called, "an explosion of phantom voters."[21]

Leftist activists flooded the polls with bogus registrations. Election officials who dared to complain were intimidated with lawsuits and cries of "racism."[22] Richard Cloward defended the mess he had created by telling CBS News in 1996, "It's better to have a little bit of fraud than to leave people off the rolls who belong there."[23]

Throughout the 1990s, US elections descended ever deeper into a maelstrom of confusion and chaos, culminating in the Florida recount crisis of 2000. On the eve of the 2000 election, in Indiana alone, state officials discovered that one in five registered voters were duplicates, deceased, or otherwise invalid.[24] How this slipshod paperwork affected the final vote count from state to state has never been tallied, but the cloud of confusion hanging over the election served leftist agitators well. "President Bush came to office without a clear mandate," George Soros declared. "He was elected president by a single vote on the Supreme Court."[25] Once again the "flood-the-rolls" strategy had done its work. Cloward, Piven and their disciples have introduced a level of fear, tension and foreboding to US elections heretofore encountered mainly in Third World countries.

8

OPENING
THE DOOR

No one knows when George Soros first conceived the idea of creating the Shadow Party. However, we do know that important elements of the plan appear to have solidified as early as 1994. It was a bad year for Democrats—the year of the Gingrich Revolution. Midterm elections that year shifted power to Republicans on a massive scale. For the first time since 1946, Republicans won a majority in the House (230-204) and in the Senate (52-48), both at the same time. Newt Gingrich became Speaker of the House, with a ten-point "Contract with America," which called for strengthening national defense, slashing government waste, cutting taxes and balancing the budget. The Republican Revolution had begun.

Many Democrat strategists at the time blamed their defeat on television advertising. They accused Republicans of flooding the networks with "attack" ads, and running the "nastiest" campaign in recent memory. "[W]e all need a shower after this election," wrote *Boston Globe* columnist Ellen Goodman. She accused Republicans of running a "$350 million sales pitch" based on "nastiness," "negativism," "hostility" and "attack ads."[1] The most effective "attack ads" employed by Republicans in 1994 were aimed not so much at particular Democratic candidates as at their leaders, Bill and Hillary Clinton. Neither Bill nor Hillary was running for any office that year, but the Clinton legacy—particularly Hillary's quasi-socialist plan for a national health system—haunted every Democrat contestant. The mid-term elections became a referendum on the Clinton

Administration's tack to the left, and the couple who were responsible for it.

In local races across the country, Republicans ran TV ads using newly available "morphing" technology. A local Democrat candidate would appear on the screen, then slowly his face would morph into that of Bill Clinton. This simple device did nothing more than remind voters that their local Democratic candidates belonged to the same party as President Clinton. This was one of the "nasty" messages that proved devastating for Democrat candidates across the nation. Even more effective was the barrage of television advertisements targeting Hillary and her healthcare plan. Clinton advisor Sidney Blumenthal attributes the Republican victory of 1994 almost entirely to the power of these anti-Hillary messages. In his memoir, *The Clinton Wars*, he writes:

> [Hillary's Health Security Act] reached the floor of the Congress at a treacherously dangerous stage of his term . . . very close to the Congressional elections. . . . And when health care failed, the blame fell directly on both Clintons. . . . In the face of extravagantly funded enemies who were dominating the airwaves with their advertising, Clinton's political response was sputtering and feeble. . . . [T]he collapse of health care reform overshadowed Clinton's presidency.[1]

As the media battle over Hillarycare grew more intense during the summer of 1994, the Shadow Party—or at least certain alignments of activists who would later become prominent in the Shadow Party—made their first, coordinated effort to sway public opinion through the use of front groups posing as "non-partisan" academic or public service organizations.

In July 1994, three such front groups released studies within days of each other, all purporting to represent a "non-partisan" position, yet all defending Hillarycare and darkly insinuating that political advertising had become a threat to democracy.[3] The first of these studies came from Ralph Nader's consumer group Citizen Action, whose 18 July report claimed that medical and insurance interests had spent $26 million between January 1993 and May 1994 in an effort to kill Hillarycare. "Health-care special interests have focused their campaign contributions to subvert, delay, weaken and otherwise undermine comprehensive reform," complained Citizen Action director Michael Podhorzer.[4]

One week later, on 23 July, the Center for Public Integrity released a study charging that special interests had spent $100 million in an 18-month period trying to influence the Hillarycare debate one way or the other. Funds for the CPI study came from the public-sector union AFSCME—the American Federation of State, County, and Municipal Employees—led by radical Gerald McEntee.[5] Two days later, the Annenberg Public Policy Center at the University of Pennsylvania—a brand new institution founded that year—released a third study, which found that more than $50 million had been spent on advertising either for or against Hillarycare. "We are witnessing the largest, most sustained advertising campaign to shape a public policy decision in the history of the republic," said the Annenberg Center's Kathleen Hall Jamieson.[6] The Annenberg study was funded by the Robert Wood Johnson Foundation, about which we will have more to say presently.[7]

Anger and frustration crackled through the prose of these "non-partisan" studies. For months, anchors on the major television networks had featured Hillary's health plan in their newscasts, talk shows and public interest programs, giving the plan free promotion on a scale no money could buy. Democrats relied heavily on this type of voluntary support from ideological sympathizers in the network media. They were furious to discover that a private group of healthcare insurers could undo all their work with a single, $14-million ad campaign, such as the "Harry and Louise" series, that informed American voters through simple skits that the government plan would take away many cherished freedoms, such as their right to choose their own doctor.

By purchasing their own air time, Hillary's opponents had demonstrated that they could counter the effects of the network producers by putting their message directly to the people. This threatened the Democrats' then still intact media monopoly. Something had to be done.

Enter George Soros. Only three weeks after the congressional election, Soros spoke before a small group of two hundred people, mostly physicians, at Columbia University's school of medicine.[8] On the surface, his speech seemed apolitical. He spoke mainly about a new initiative he was launching called the Project on Death in America. In typical Soros fashion, this project had two purposes, one overt, the other covert.

Its overt purpose was to help the elderly and the terminally ill go to their deaths more comfortably, by providing hospices, pain reduction and other sorts of "palliative" care, designed not to cure them but simply to help them relax, feel better and accept the inevitable. But the Project on Death also had a covert purpose, which was almost certainly its real purpose. That purpose was to save money by rationing healthcare—specifically by denying expensive care to people who were deemed hopeless or whose lives were not considered worth saving for one reason or another. Under Soros' proposal, many gravely ill people would be given "palliative" care instead of real care, which was much less expensive. Soros explained:

Can we afford to care for the dying properly? The number of people dying in the United States currently stands at 2.2 million annually. Increases in cancer and AIDS deaths and the aging of the baby boomers will cause this figure to climb faster than the population.... The fear is that the dying of the elderly will drain the national treasury.... [B]ut [a]gressive, life-prolonging interventions, which may at times go against the patient's wishes, are much more expensive than proper care for the dying.[9]

Hillary's healthcare proposal featured a similar plan to ration care for the elderly.[10] Indeed, the widespread—and quite accurate—perception that Hillarycare would *decrease* rather than increase the amount of healthcare available to Americans contributed greatly to its overwhelming rejection by the public. Viewed in this light, Soros' Project on Death in America can be seen as a back-door effort to salvage a key feature of Hillarycare. Over the next ten years Soros' OSI and the Robert Wood Johnson Foundation—which had funded the Annenberg Center's study decrying the role of political advertising in defeating Hillarycare—together poured $200 million into the Project on Death in America.

Soros' speech at Columbia's medical school made it clear that he shared Hillary's views on rationing healthcare. No doubt he also shared Sidney Blumenthal's concern about how easily Hillary's opponents had managed to kill her plan through TV advertising. Perhaps that is why Soros chose to end his speech with what appeared on the surface an odd change of subject. He announced to his audience that he intended to "do something" about "the distortion of our electoral process by the excessive use of TV advertising."[11]

It is usually a good idea to take Soros seriously when he

announces a new initiative. He has the money, the will and the resources to put his plans into effect. In his Columbia medical school speech, Soros meant what he said. It was not long before his promise to curb the "use of TV advertising" in American elections came to pass. And it was through this effort that the Shadow Party, as we know it today, emerged full-blown into public life.

Only eight months after Soros' speech at Columbia, Republican Senator John McCain and Democrat Senator Russ Feingold joined forces to propose a "sense of the Senate" resolution calling for "comprehensive campaign finance reform legislation."[12] They thus set into motion the juggernaut that would ultimately give us the McCain-Feingold Act of 27 March 2002.

From the beginning, McCain-Feingold was a political Trojan Horse. Its stated purpose did not reflect its actual purpose. Its stated purpose was to clean up politics by tightly regulating the amount of money political parties and candidates could accept from donors. Its actual purpose, to use Soros' words, was to curb the "use of TV advertising" in American politics. "Television ads are doubly corrupting: They substitute misleading, negative sound bites for honest statements, and they are paid for by donor (read: special-interest) money," wrote Soros in his 2000 book *Open Society: Reforming Global Capitalism.*[13]

Any doubts about the intentions of the McCain-Feingold legislation were dispelled by its actual results. As we shall see, the spending caps imposed by McCain-Feingold were widely ignored, in many cases by the very politicians who had pushed for them most strongly. Rather than limiting the amount of money in politics, the passage of McCain-Feingold ushered in a record increase in political contributions. This development seemed to provoke mostly shrugs from the chief proponents of "campaign finance reform" who populated Soros' many and increasingly effective front groups.

The real impact of McCain-Feingold has been to regulate political *speech* rather than finances, and it accomplished this with a vengeance. The legislation bars private organizations, including unions, corporations and citizen activist groups, from advertising for or against any candidate for federal office on TV or radio 60 days before a general election, and 30 days before a primary. Only official political parties may engage in "express advocacy" for or against a candidate during that black-out period. The law does grant an exemption, however, to major (Democrat-leaning) media networks. Unlike ordinary citizens, major media networks may use the airwaves and cable networks to say whatever they like about any candidate on their news reports and talk shows during the 60- or 30-day black-out period. Thus the law grants to a handful of media organizations what amounts to a government-enforced monopoly on political speech during election season.

Many people assumed the Supreme Court would strike down McCain-Feingold. But they were proved wrong. In a move that stunned civil libertarians, the Supreme Court approved McCain-Feingold on 10 December 2003 by a one-vote margin.[14] In a dissenting opinion, Judge Antonin Scalia wrote:

> Who could have imagined that the same Court which, within the past four years, has sternly disapproved of restrictions upon such inconsequential forms of expression as virtual child pornography, tobacco advertising, dissemination of illegally intercepted communications and sexually explicit cable programming would smile with favor upon a law that cuts to the heart of what the First Amendment is meant to protect: the right to criticize government?[15]

In its original form, McCain-Feingold regulated political speech only on television and radio. The Internet remained free, at least for the moment. US District Judge Colleen Kollar-Kotelly closed that loophole on 18 September 2004, when she ordered the Federal Election Commission to extend McCain-Feingold's censorship power over the World Wide Web. The FEC commissioners dutifully went to work devising rules and regulations to control political speech on the Internet, including the speech of individual bloggers. Commissioner Bradley Smith dissented, warning that "grassroots Internet activity is in danger."

The six FEC commissioners were evenly divided between three Democrats and three Republicans. All three Republicans, including Smith, wanted to appeal Judge Kollar-Kotelly's ruling on censoring the Internet, which the FEC had the right to do. However, all three Democrats on the Commission refused to appeal the ruling. Consequently, the FEC moved forward with its plans for Internet regulation. In an interview with CNET.com, Smith warned that the FEC might regulate virtually "any decision by an individual to put a link on their home page, set up a blog, send out mass e-mails, any kind of activity that can be done on the Internet." What Smith's fellow commissioners were proposing, in effect, was to calculate what they thought would be the cash value of any activity by politically-inclined bloggers on behalf of a party or candidate and regulate that activity as they would any other sort of "in-kind" political contribution. Failure on the part of bloggers to report their political writings would be a federal offense. Smith asked:

> Would a link to a candidate's page be a problem? If someone sets up a home page and links to their favorite politician, is that a contribution? ... How do we measure that? Design fees, that

sort of thing? The FEC did an advisory opinion in the late
1990s . . . saying that if you owned a computer, you'd have to
calculate what percentage of the computer cost and electricity
went to political advocacy. It seems absurd, but that's . . . the
direction Judge Kollar-Kotelly would have us move in.[16]

An explosion of blogger outrage ensued. "I will continue to
link to campaign websites whenever I want. . . . If they put me
into jail for it, so be it," stated blogger Roger L. Simon. Blogger
Tom Smith at Right Coast declared, "[T]hey can stop us from
blogging . . . when they pry our keyboards from our cold, dead
fingers." Bowing to public pressure, the FEC backed down from
its decision and released guidelines that appear to exempt most
bloggers from regulation.[17] However, UCLA law professor Eugene
Volokh warns that the guidelines are complex and ambiguous.
Moreover, future court decisions may overturn them.[18]

Such are the ominous implications of the McCain-Feingold
legislation. The real question is, how did such an anti-demo-
cratic law get formulated and passed by the US Congress in the
first place? That is where George Soros and his Shadow Party
come in.

The Shadow Party emerged from the cauldron of corruption
known as the Pewgate scandal. Most Americans have never heard
of Pewgate, yet all are affected by its results.

Ryan Sager of the *New York Post* broke the Pewgate story on 17
March 2005. He charged that the McCain-Feingold Act—officially known as the Bi-Partisan Campaign Reform Act of 2002
(BCRA)—was pushed through Congress by fraud. Beginning at
least as early as 1994, and perhaps earlier, Sager reported a group
of non-profit foundations began bankrolling "experts" and front
groups whose purpose was to bamboozle Congress into thinking

that millions of Americans were clamoring for "campaign finance reform"—even though they were not.[19]

As Sager reported, a former program officer of the Pew Charitable Trusts named Sean P. Treglia, claimed to have masterminded the scheme. Treglia boasted of his achievement during a taped conference in March 2004 at USC's Annenberg School for Communication (an institution run by a former Clinton official, which receives funding from Soros' OSI). Treglia has worked at Annenberg since September 2003 as "senior advisor for democracy initiatives," in which capacity he is tasked with training journalists to cover campaign finance issues. On 12 March 2004, Treglia delivered a speech to a sympathetic audience of journalists, academics and other experts, on the topic of "Covering Philanthropy and Nonprofits Beyond 9/11." *New York Post* reporter Ryan Sager obtained a videotape of that talk.

"I'm going to tell you a story that I've never told any reporter," Treglia said on the tape. "Now that I'm several months away from Pew and we have campaign-finance reform, I can tell this story." According to Treglia, proponents of "campaign finance reform" faced a problem—Americans did not want the kind of "reform" they were proposing. The movement "had lost legitimacy inside Washington because they didn't have a constituency that would punish Congress if they didn't vote for reform," Treglia explained. And so he devised a plan.

Since the "reformers" had no constituency, they would simply create one—or rather, the illusion of one. They would use foundation money to buy "experts" and front groups across the nation, to generate outcries for "campaign finance reform." Some front groups were created from scratch. In other cases, existing nonprofit groups were paid handsomely to climb on the "campaign finance reform" bandwagon. Flush with foundation money, these front groups would beat their breasts unceasingly for "campaign finance reform," putting on an energetic show for a tiny audience of 100 Senators and 435 members of Congress. Says Treglia, "The target audience for all this activity was 535 people in Washington. The idea was to create an impression that a mass movement was afoot—that everywhere they looked, in academic institutions, in the business community, in religious groups, in ethnic groups, everywhere, people were talking about reform."[20]

The *New York Post* reports that, from 1994 to 2004, Pew and its allies dispensed $140 million to promote campaign finance "reform," of which 88 percent—$123 million—came from just eight foundations, as follows:

Pew Charitable Trusts	$40.1 million
Bill Moyers' Schumann Center for Media and Democracy	$17.6 million
Carnegie Corporation of New York	$14.1 million
Joyce Foundation	$13.5 million
George Soros' Open Society Institute	$12.6 million
Jerome Kohlberg Trust	$11.3 million
Ford Foundation	$8.8 million
John D. and Catherine T. MacArthur Foundation	$5.2 million
Total	$123.2 million

Source: The New York Post[21]

Some of the more notable recipients of Pewgate money included groups posing as government ethics "watchdogs." Soros' OSI alone gave $1.7 million to the Center for Public Integrity, $1.3 million to Public Campaign, $650,000 to the Alliance for Better Campaigns, $625,000 to Common Cause, $300,000 to Democracy 21, $275,000 to Public Citizen and $75,000 to the Center for Responsive Politics.[22] Other Pewgate foundations contributed to these "watchdog" groups as well. In addition, a significant portion of Pewgate funds went into academic institutions such as the Annenberg Centers at the University of Pennsylvania and the University of California, and the William J. Brennan Center for Justice at New York University. Soros' OSI alone gave more than $3.3 million to the Brennan Center between 1999 and 2003.

Some Pewgate funds were used to buy favorable media coverage. Sager reports that the Carnegie Corporation paid the *American Prospect* magazine $132,000 to publish a special issue pushing campaign finance reform. National Public Radio has spent at least $860,000 of Pewgate funds on programs spotlighting the role of money in politics.[23] In his efforts on behalf of Pewgate, PBS icon Bill Moyers raised media manipulation to the status of an art form. As president of the Schumann Center for Media and Democracy since 1990, Moyers himself was the number-two Pewgate donor. However, as a journalist, Moyers also *received* Pewgate money and also promoted front groups funded by Pewgate foundations.

Through his Public Affairs Television company, Moyers produces documentaries for PBS newsmagazines such as *Frontline*. As a Pewgate operative, Moyers' special relationship with PBS provided him with a bully pulpit for getting the message out about campaign finance reform. Journalistic ethics took a back seat to the political cause. In a June 1999 PBS special "Free Speech for Sale," Moyers interviewed three campaign finance reformers— Bert Neuborne of the Brennan Center, Charles Lewis of the Center for Public Integrity, and Bob Hall of Democracy South— without disclosing that all three represented organizations funded by Moyers' own Schumann Center.[24] By that time, Moyers had personally produced eight hours of programming promoting campaign finance reform.

Some Pewgate money found its way into the hands of politicians, notably Senator McCain of Arizona, the Republican cosponsor of the McCain-Feingold Act. McCain's Reform Institute for Campaign and Election Issues received generous funding from several Pewgate foundations, including the Carnegie Corporation of New York, the Jerome Kohlberg, Jr. Revocable Trust, and George Soros' OSI. McCain's Institute also received funding from such ultra-leftist sources as the Tides Foundation, the Proteus Fund, Echosphere and the Educational Foundation of America. Indeed, the Reform Institute's website reveals that almost all of McCain's funders who have contributed more than $50,000 are left-wing foundations.[25]

Pewgate's tentacles reach even to the US Supreme Court. Many of the legal arguments upon which the court based its 10 December 2003 decision to uphold McCain-Feingold derived from data cooked up by the Soros-funded Brennan Center at New York University. "[A]lmost half the footnotes relied on by the Supreme Court in upholding [McCain-Feingold] are research funded by the Pew Charitable Trusts," Treglia boasted in his videotaped speech.[26]

As noted above, the Brennan Center received more than $3.3 million from Soros' Open Society Institute. It also received $1.4 million from the Carnegie Corporation, $1 million from the Ford Foundation and $600,000 from the Pew Charitable Trusts. During the three-year legal battle over McCain-Feingold in the US Supreme Court, McCain-Feingold's defenders based key portions of their case on research provided by the Brennan Center—research that turned out to have been "deliberately faked," in the words of Weekly Standard editor David Tell.[27]

The bogus research sought to defend McCain-Feingold's regulation of political advertising—an aspect of the bill which four out of five Supreme Court justices later condemned as an infringement of free speech. The portion of the bill in question was the so-called Snowe-Jeffords Amendment—now in force—which prohibits corporations, unions and most non-profits from using unregulated political contributions to buy political ads on radio or TV 30 days before a primary and 60 days before a general election.

During the court challenges, Brennan Center analysts argued that the Snowe-Jeffords Amendment would place no undue restrictions on legitimate political speech, but would affect mainly "sham-issue ads." A "sham-issue ad" is one that attempts to persuade viewers to vote for a particular candidate without overtly pronouncing any of the prohibited "magic words," such as "Vote for Joe Schmoe" or "Vote against Joe Schmoe." An ad that uses the magic words is guilty of "express advocacy." By law, "express advocacy" ads can be purchased only with "hard money"—that is, political contributions that are reported to the FEC and subject to FEC limits and regulation.

Political operatives who have raised large quantities of unregulated money—that is, political contributions that are not reported to the FEC and are not subject to FEC limits—therefore find themselves in a quandary. They cannot use their unregulated money to buy "express advocacy" ads. So they do the next best thing. They buy TV ads that avoid the "magic words" but nevertheless hold forth on political issues in such a way as to encourage people to vote one way or the other in a particular race.

Critics call these "sham-issue ads." Common sense seems to dictate that "sham-issue ads" are just as legitimate as any other sort of political ad, and entitled to the same First Amendment protection. However, ceaseless lobbying by Pewgate-funded "public interest" advocates has succeeded in convincing many jurists and journalists that "sham-issue ads" are inherently odious. Operating on the assumption that "sham-issue ads" are evil and therefore unworthy of First Amendment protection, the Brennan Center embarked on an effort to prove, through "scientific" research, that the Snowe-Jeffords Amendment would suppress only small numbers of "true" or "legitimate" issue ads, while greatly impeding the dissemination of evil "sham-issue" ads.

David Tell dissected the Brennan Center's research in a 26 May 2003 article in the *Weekly Standard*. Among other outrages, Tell revealed that Brennan Center political scientist Jonathan Krasno had clearly admitted in his funding proposal to the Pew Charitable Trusts that the purpose of the proposed study was political, not scholarly, and that the project would be axed if it failed to yield the desired results. Tell wrote that Krasno's paper, "'Issue Advocacy: Amassing the Case for Reform,' dated February 19, 1999, explained that '[t]he purpose of our acquiring the data set is not simply to advance knowledge for its own sake, but to fuel a continuous multi-faceted campaign to propel campaign reform forward.' Dispassionate academic inquiry was so alien to the spirit of the thing that Brennan promised to suspend its work midstream, pre-publication, if the numbers turned out wrong. 'Whether we proceed to phase two will depend on the judgment of whether the data provide a sufficiently powerful boost to the reform movement.'"[28]

Tell charged that Brennan researchers "deliberately faked" their results, systematically fudging, massaging, altering and jiggering the data to meet their needs. For instance, the raw data showed that between 38.5 to 40 percent of the ads barred by McCain-Feingold would be legitimate issue ads. Nevertheless, researchers managed to whittle this figure down to 7 percent in their final report.

Brennan's defenders argue that the inaccuracies in the Center's research were pointed out and corrected before they could affect any court decisions on McCain-Feingold. This may be true, but obviously the political agendas of the researchers could not help but impact the data all along the pipeline. Moreover, the mass media failed to give wide exposure to Brennan's scandalous conduct, and the glow of academic respectability which Brennan lent to the campaign finance reform movement plainly contributed to the passage of BCRA.

It seems unlikely that such an immense and multifaceted operation as Pewgate could have succeeded without a strong leader at the top. George Soros would doubtless agree with this statement. He has many times written forcefully on the importance of leadership. For instance, after Mikhail Gorbachev resigned from the presidency of the dying Soviet Union, Soros excoriated the fallen leader for his failure to take charge. In his 1991 book, *Underwriting Democracy*, Soros wrote:

> [Gorbachev] had a rather naïve belief in democracy: allow people to make their own decisions and they will make the right decisions. But business cannot be run on consensus. Within each organization, there must be a well-defined chain of command. In the absence of autonomous business organizations, there must also be a chain of command for the economy as a whole. If the economy is to be restructured, someone must be in charge of the restructuring. No attempt was made to establish an authority suited to the purpose.[29]

According to Soros, "someone must be in charge" and there must be a "well-defined chain of command." Only thus can a leader coordinate many organizations to work together toward a common goal. Given his strong opinions on the subject, it is safe to assume that Soros would not have agreed to join forces with the other Pewgate foundations, unless he was satisfied that the effort was well-led and well-organized. Soros would not have invested his time and money in an operation which he viewed as leaderless, rudderless and haphazard. Who, then, was the leader?

As we have already seen, Pew officer Sean Treglia claims the honor. He boasts that he led the campaign from his perch at the Pew Charitable Trusts. We are inclined to doubt his claim, however. Treglia was and remains a low man on the totem pole, a position underscored by his impolitic out-of-school boasts. If anyone at Pew had the clout to lead such a nationwide effort, involving at least eight major foundations and some $140 million in expenditures over a ten-year period, it seems more likely that it would have been Treglia's boss, Rebecca W. Rimel, who became president and CEO of the Pew Charitable Trusts in 1994.

Even Rimel seems a poor candidate to have led Pewgate, however. A former nurse who became an assistant professor of neurosurgery, Rimel specialized in healthcare issues at Pew. She is more bureaucrat than entrepreneur. Moreover, as a self-styled "executive feminist," she opposes strong, top-down management on philosophical grounds. "Most other businesses have a pyramid structure, whereas ours is very flat," she told the feminist magazine *IRIS* in 2000.[30]

The second largest contributor to the Pewgate operation after the Pew Charitable Trusts was the Schumann Center for Media and Democracy, of which PBS journalist Bill Moyers has been president since 1990. Is it possible that Moyers was the true mastermind behind Pewgate? Probably not. Moyers is a journalist by training and experience. As with Rimel, nothing in his professional experience suggests that he has the leadership skills or the entrepreneurial derring-do to oversee a project of the magnitude, complexity and stunning audacity of Pewgate. He does, however, enjoy a close and long-standing relationship with another foundation head whose skills precisely fit the above description: George Soros. A former trustee of Soros' Open Society Institute, Moyers is a close Soros ally. As the Pewgate plot unfolded, it became increasingly clear that Soros played a much more pivotal role in the operation than his relatively modest cash contribution of $12.6 million might suggest.

In November 2000, Soros announced that he had conceived a master plan for saving the world. The announcement came in a brief epilogue to his book *Open Society: Reforming Global Capitalism*. However, Soros said he could not divulge the plan. It must remain secret for awhile. To reveal it, he implied, would be like advertising his intentions on the eve of a major stock-market play, where showing his hand might queer the deal. All the same, Soros could not resist tantalizing readers by dropping a small hint. He wrote: "I have a clear sense of mission for my foundation network. I shall not spell it out here because it would interfere with my flexibility in carrying it out—there is a parallel here with the problem of making public pronouncements when I was actively engaged in making money—but I can state it in general terms: *to foster the civil society component of the Open Society Alliance.*" [emphasis added][31]

What sort of hint was that? How did Soros intend to save the world by fostering the "civil society component" of his global network? Soros was using NGO-speak. To ordinary people, his words were gibberish. However, to global activists immersed in the worldwide "community" of "United Nations-associated" "non-governmental organizations" (NGOs), the term "civil society" is a familiar and oft-used buzz phrase. On the most literal level, "civil society" simply refers to those necessary elements of a just and humane society that are independent of the government. On a deeper level, however, the term "civil society" refers to the peculiar conceit of the NGO community that it represents the conscience of the world, that its network of UN-affiliated non-profits are veritable outposts of civilization standing like radical Fort Apaches on a barbarous frontier where racism, sexism, homophobia, theocracy, corporate greed and cultural intolerance run rampant.

The analogy with Fort Apache is not trivial, for it is the plain intent of the NGO community to colonize and civilize the benighted nations of the world. Often this means confronting governments that fail to live up to its own UN-approved standards of behavior. Holding such governments "accountable" is a major part of what NGOs do, and many do not shrink from encouraging active resistance to governments they regard as violating the norms of "social justice"—the current code phrase for the leftist political agenda.

In the year 2000, George Soros was still an obscure figure in the United States. Most Americans had not heard of him, unless they read the financial pages. In that year, however, Soros dramatically raised his American profile.

During the 2000 election cycle, he first began to experiment with raising political contributions through "Section 527" committees. We shall say more about these committees in a later chapter. For now, we simply note that, for many years, a loophole in federal election law made such committees useful for raising political contributions above and beyond the legal limits, and the McCain-Feingold reform initially did nothing to change that fact.

During the 2000 election, Soros assembled a team of wealthy Democrat donors to help him push two of his favorite issues—gun control and marijuana legalization. He raised the money through 527 committees. One of Soros' 527s was an anti-gun group called The Campaign for a Progressive Future, which sought to neutralize the influence of the National Rifle Association by targeting political candidates whom the NRA endorsed. Soros' Campaign for a Progressive Future also funded political ads and direct mail campaigns in support of state initiatives favoring background checks at gun shows.

Democrats had backed off the gun control issue when candidate Al Gore learned that 40 percent of union households owned guns. However, Soros was no party Democrat. He personally seeded The Campaign for a Progressive Future with $500,000.[32] Also during the 2000 election, Soros and his associates funneled money into pro-marijuana initiatives, which appeared on the ballot that year in various states.[33]

It was also during the 2000 election that Soros made his most dramatic move yet to win support for the McCain-Feingold Act. He did this by sponsoring the so-called "Shadow Conventions." Organized by author, columnist and socialite Arianna Huffington, the Shadow Conventions were counter-cultural events that gave a spotlight to radical opponents of the electoral mainstream, most of them from the Left.

In an effort to lure news crews away from the national party conventions, Huffington held her "Shadow Conventions" at the same time and in the same cities as the Republican and Democratic events in Philadelphia and Los Angeles. Huffington was a newcomer to the Left. Until her husband was defeated in his Republican bid for a California Senate seat, she was a prominent conservative figure whose cult-like adoration of Newt Gingrich evoked non-partisan titters among the cognoscenti. At the Shadow Conventions, the new Arianna told reporters: "I have become radicalized."[34]

Some media commentators played the Shadow Conventions for laughs. Yet its fumings supported a serious radical agenda, which Soros evidently endorsed. The Shadow Conventions promoted the view that neither Democrats nor Republicans served the interests of the American people. US politics needed a third force to break the deadlock. Among the issues highlighted at the Shadow Conventions were special interest lobbies, marijuana legalization, corporate control of American society and the allegedly growing concentration of wealth. Most speakers and delegates at the Shadow Convention hewed to a hard-left line, their views resonating with the "Free Mumia" chants that erupted periodically from the crowd and with Jesse Jackson's incendiary charges that Republicans were racists. Comic activist Al Franken provided the entertainment.

Despite the multitude of issues raised, both Shadow Conventions had a clear, overriding theme, which was campaign finance reform. The keynote speaker at the Los Angeles Shadow Convention was Senator Feingold and the keynote speaker at the Philadelphia Shadow Convention was Senator McCain.

Both Senators spoke on the supposedly urgent need to pass the legislation that would become the McCain-Feingold Act. Feingold said, "I am in Los Angeles as a Democratic Party delegate for a reason and I'm enthusiastic about the efforts of my party to win the election in the fall. But my friends, I confess to you that as I came in to L.A. yesterday, I had a real feeling of disappointment with what has happened to our conventions, to our government, and to our democracy. It seems that this convention nearby here is all about money, and especially, corporate money. This is why I believe there are Shadow Conventions. This is why I believe there are strong protests at both national conventions."[35]

In fact, as Senator Feingold was well aware, the reason there

were Shadow Conventions had nothing to do with popular outrage over money in politics. Quite the contrary. Like the campaign finance reform movement itself, the Shadow Conventions
were a *manifestation* of money in politics. Without funding from
George Soros' Open Society Institute and other Pewgate foundations, the Shadow Conventions could not and would not have
occurred, any more than McCain-Feingold could eventually have
passed into law.

In fact, few signs of any populist zeal for campaign finance
reform could be observed at either event. When John McCain
spoke at the Philadelphia Shadow Convention, he was nearly
driven from the stage by hecklers angry over his sponsorship of
the Navajo-Hopi Relocation Act, which would force many Indian
families off their land. Cries of "Indian killer" peppered the auditorium during his speech.[36] Reporter Matt Labash who attended
the event wrote, "On the second day, the shadow people get down
to the serious business of campaign finance reform. Very serious,
in fact. So serious that nobody seems actually to want to show up,
so the shadow conveners cordon off the back two-thirds of the
auditorium's seating with duct tape, forcing people to sit up front
so as not to spoil the photo-op."[37]

Public apathy toward campaign finance reform, however
widespread, did not prevent McCain-Feingold from being
enacted as the law of the land. McCain-Feingold passed not
because the American people wanted it, but because George Soros
and his Pewgate allies wanted it.

According to Arianna Huffington, major funders of the
Shadow Conventions included the Open Society Institute, the
Pew Charitable Trusts, the Carnegie Foundation, and the Arc
Foundation.[38] According to *Time* magazine, the largest single con-
tributor to the Shadow Conventions was Soros' Open Society

Institute, which put up about a third of the total cost.[39] At this time, few journalists knew who George Soros was. But columnist Robert Novak did and castigated John McCain for appearing at what he presciently dubbed "The Soros Convention."[40]

In the final analysis, the Shadow Conventions were symbolic affairs. They represented no party and nominated no candidates for office. But they put America on notice that a third force had entered the political arena. That force was George Soros.

•

9

THE CONNECTION

H arold Ickes shuns publicity. He does not like or trust reporters. Even those interviewers who sympathize with Ickes's left-wing politics find him elusive, brusque, sarcastic and uncooperative. During the 2004 presidential campaign, Ickes granted an interview to *New York Magazine* writer Michael Crowley. The hapless scribe placed a digital audio recorder on the table between himself and Ickes. Ickes eyed the device "quizzically," according to Crowley. Then he said, "That's a pretty nifty little deal there. Boy." This manner Crowley described as "disarmingly folksy." But suddenly Ickes' voice grew hard and "penetrating dark eyes" met Crowley's. "I'm usually off the record," said Ickes. "So there's no sense in turning the f---ing thing on."[1]

Nowadays Ickes must acclimate himself to a great deal more publicity than he tolerated in the past. His role as unofficial CEO of George Soros' Shadow Party has put him at the forefront of an historic power struggle. Now, in or out of election season, any move by Ickes draws attention from the press. After John Kerry had won the Democratic party nomination to be its 2004 candidate, Democratic strategist Howard Wolfson suggested that, outside the official Kerry campaign, Ickes "is the most important person in the Democratic Party today."[2] With Kerry out of the picture, Wolfson can repeat that same claim today without condition or qualifier. Ickes is indisputably "the most important person in the Democratic Party," bar none. As always, throughout his career, Ickes' importance lies primarily in his willingness to do what others fear to do.

As the liaison between Soros' Shadow Party and "Hillaryland"—insider jargon for Hillary's official political machine—Ickes operates in a gray area of the law, where almost anything he does could plausibly be interpreted as a violation of the McCain-Feingold Act. He provides for Soros and Hillary—that is, for the Shadow Party and the Democrats—the coordination that these allied networks desperately require, but which they are forbidden by law from achieving. This is the type of job that Ickes does best. As a political operative, he has always moved along the fringes of the law. For him, it is familiar terrain.

Like most Shadow Party leaders, Ickes began his political career in the Sixties Left. He was recruited in 1964 by Stanford University professor Allard Lowenstein, a Democrat activist whose skill at luring young people into radical causes earned him the sobriquet "the Pied Piper." Under Lowenstein's guidance, Ickes turned up on every noteworthy political battlefront of the Sixties and early Seventies. He served as a Freedom Rider in the Deep South, registering black voters for the Student Non-Violent Coordinating Committee (SNCC). In 1965, Ickes traveled to the Dominican Republic, where he lent assistance to a *junta* of leftist colonels seeking to oust the sitting government. Some of the rebels displayed a worrisome degree of sympathy for Castro's revolution. The plot was foiled when President Johnson landed 20,000 Marines on the island.[3]

Ickes next followed Lowenstein to New York, where they went to work organizing resistance to the Vietnam War. Angry over Johnson's prosecution of the war, Lowenstein had started a "dump Johnson" campaign, which proved remarkably popular among left-wing Democrats. Lowenstein's project eventually crystallized around the candidacy of Senator Eugene McCarthy, a radical dove who demanded unconditional US withdrawal from Vietnam. With

Lowenstein pulling strings for him behind the scenes, Ickes became co-manager of McCarthy's New York presidential campaign.[4] Later, Ickes worked for another anti-war candidate, George McGovern, who ran on a campaign slogan of "Bring America Home" in 1972.

It was through his involvement in the Vietnam protest movement that Ickes met Bill Clinton. Both found themselves working together on Operation Purse Strings in 1972. This was a grassroots lobbying effort aimed at pressuring Congress to cut off aid to Cambodia and South Vietnam.[5] The campaign eventually succeeded and both governments fell, with catastrophic consequences for the Cambodians and Vietnamese.

It was Ickes' later stint as a labor lawyer that appears to have left the deepest stamp on his character. During the years when Ickes represented labor unions for a living, many unions were controlled or influenced by New York's "five families"—the Gambino, Colombo, Lucchese, Genovese and Bonanno crime syndicates. Union bosses were often hand-picked by the mob. These Mafia-anointed bosses embezzled union dues, robbed pension funds, planted friends and associates in lucrative "ghost jobs" on union payrolls, rigged bids on work contracts, and extorted payoffs from businesses by threatening strikes. The biggest losers in the labor racket were the rank-and-file union members. Mob-run union bosses grew rich on kickbacks and payoffs. But the cozy deals they cut with employers left workers out in the cold. Union members who protested mob corruption were threatened, beaten and, when necessary, killed.

Today's labor movement remains as corrupt as Ickes found it in the 1970s. It is true that organized crime and its union rackets took a drubbing from the Reagan Justice Department during the 1980s but—to paraphrase Mark Twain—reports of organized crime's demise have been greatly exaggerated. Federal prosecutors jailed many crime bosses, but others replaced them. During the Clinton years, a new generation of 21st-century racketeers spread its tentacles from Wall Street to Silicon Valley. This is a world with which Harold Ickes is familiar.

A 1971 graduate of Columbia University law school, Ickes joined the Mineola, Long Island law firm Meyer, Suozzi, English & Klein in 1977. Meyer Suozzi is an important cog in New York's Democratic machine. It was founded in 1960 by the late John Francis English, a lifelong Democrat operative, who was a close advisor to all three Kennedy brothers, John, Robert and Teddy. English counseled Robert Kennedy to run for the Senate in New York in 1964. He served both JFK and RFK as a strategist on their presidential campaigns. When English died of liver cancer in 1987, Senator Ted Kennedy praised him as "a hero" to the Kennedy family. "There were two Jacks in my life and now both of them are gone," Kennedy lamented.[6]

English met Harold Ickes in 1968. He admired Ickes' work on the McCarthy campaign. No doubt, English was equally impressed by Ickes' pedigree as a Washington insider. Ickes' father, also named Harold, served as Secretary of Interior for Franklin Delano Roosevelt and Harry Truman from 1933 until 1946.

Meyer Suozzi's labor practice has brought controversy to the firm through its long history of representing corrupt unions under mob control. Because of it, New York attorneys have bestowed upon Meyer Suozzi the irreverent nickname "The Firm"—a reference to the 1993 film by that name, starring Tom Cruise and Gene Hackman as attorneys trapped in a white-shoe law firm serving Mafia dons.[7]

Ickes started as an associate at Meyer Suozzi in 1977, became a partner in 1980 and headed the firm's labor practice from 1982 to December 1993, overseeing a staff of nine lawyers serving nearly 200 union clients.

Through his labor practice, Ickes represented numerous clients with ties to the New York crime families.[8] Ickes justifies his work during those years by arguing that unions need representation, and that dealing with unions often means dealing with the mob. He told the *Washington Post* in 1993, "It is very important that law firms such as mine, which are known for their integrity, provide honest and competent legal representation to unions and their memberships. If we abandoned our clients in the face of allegations of corruption, it would leave union members at the mercy of only corrupt lawyers."[9]

This is disingenuous, at best. If Ickes wanted to help unions, he would help them get rid of mob control, as did Bobby Kennedy when he was Attorney General. All too often, Ickes has done the opposite. He has represented, and thus protected, the very individuals who were corrupting unions and terrorizing honest workers. On at least one occasion, his actions on behalf of mob-connected union bosses have moved federal officials to accuse Meyer Suozzi's labor practice of obstructing federal law enforcement.

This occurred in connection with Ickes' work for the Teamsters. Ickes has represented a number of Teamsters locals long viewed by federal prosecutors as hotbeds of mob racketeering. Among these were Teamsters Locals 295 and 851, which represent air freight workers at New York City airports, and reputedly run the air freight rackets in New York. Both unions have been under mob control for decades, according to federal investigators.[10] The US Justice Department attempted to clean up these unions by placing them under federal supervision, in an arrangement known as a trusteeship.

After Local 295 boss Anthony Calagna—an associate of the

Lucchese crime family—was convicted of extortion in 1992, a federal judge placed Local 295 under the supervision of two trustees, Thomas P. Puccio (a former federal prosecutor) and Michael J. Moroney (a former Labor Department investigator). The trustees Puccio and Moroney quickly identified Harold Ickes and his law firm Meyer Suozzi as obstacles in their efforts to clean up Local 295. They told the court that Meyer Suozzi had shown "hostility to the trusteeship," and demanded that the firm cease representing Locals 295 and 851, citing Meyer Suozzi's "past practices" and the firm's "lack of independence" from the Mob.

Another Ickes client was Teamsters Local 560 in Union City, New Jersey, long reputed to be dominated by the Genovese crime family. Local 560 plays a dark role in the Teamsters saga. When former Teamsters president Jimmy Hoffa attempted to regain control of the union in 1975, the mob resisted him. Seeking allies, Hoffa arranged a meeting in Detroit to make peace with one of his chief rivals, Anthony "Tony Pro" Provenzano, who had headed Local 560 since the 1950s. In the words of a senior official of the Newark US Attorney's office, Provenzano was "one of the most notorious, high-ranking members of the Genovese [organized-crime] family."[11]

When Hoffa arrived at the Detroit meeting place, Provenzano was not there. He was home in New Jersey. Hoffa never returned from that meeting. Prosecutors did not succeed in pinning Hoffa's disappearance on Provenzano. However, they eventually managed to convict him of extortion, labor racketeering and of ordering Teamsters rival Anthony Castellito strangled to death with piano wire. Incarcerated for these crimes on 18 November 1980, Provenzano died in prison on 12 December 1988. The fall of Provenzano did not end mob domination of Teamsters Local 560, and the Genovese crime family remained in control throughout the period that Harold Ickes and Meyer Suozzi represented it.

Perhaps the most notorious of Ickes' clients was Arthur Armand Coia, who became president of the Laborers International Union of North America (LIUNA) in February 1993. Coia ruled LIUNA with an iron fist, under the watchful eye of the union's real masters, the Patriarcha crime family of Providence, Rhode Island. In a 1994 civil racketeering complaint, Justice Department investigators accused Coia of having "associated with, and been controlled and influenced by, organized crime figures." The complaint further charges that Coia "employed actual and threatened force, violence and fear of physical and economic injury . . ." to keep his troops in line. At Coia's command, LIUNA locals throughout upstate New York were ordered to pay tribute to mob bosses in Buffalo.[12]

Ickes also represented Local 100 of the Hotel Employees and Restaurant Employees Union (HERE), identified by federal investigators as a mob fiefdom under joint control of the Colombo and Gambino crime families. Before Gambino boss Paul Castellano was gunned down in 1985, investigators taped Castellano stating that Local 100 was "my union and I don't want anything happening to it."

Ickes' work has brought him perilously close to prosecution, but when the pressure was on, he always displayed a Houdini-like gift for evading authorities. "There are more than a couple of prosecutors in this city who believe that the only thing separating Harold Ickes and a jail cell is his ability to go strong and silent in the face of tough questions," noted *New York Post* columnist Mike McAlary in 1993.[13]

Ronald Reagan waged unrelenting war on union corruption. His Task Force on Organized Crime pummeled mob bosses and labor racketeers with an onslaught of federal RICO suits. In 1985, James Harmon of the President's Commission on Organized Crime was able to announce that, "Approximately 10 percent of the Mafia's overall strength is under indictment."[14] George Bush Sr. continued the assault.

Unfortunately, the forces of corruption would soon launch a counterattack. And when they did, no Ronald Reagan stood in the breach to stop them. Bill and Hillary Clinton took a dramatically different approach to labor racketeering than any of their White House predecessors, including Democrats like the Kennedy brothers. In exchange for record-breaking campaign contributions from union treasuries, Clinton effectively killed the federal effort to clean up unions. Michael Moroney, the former Labor Department investigator who accused Meyer, Suozzi, English & Klein of mob complicity, wrote in 1999, "Reagan's Organized Crime Commission wanted Justice to use civil racketeering laws to clean up the national Teamsters unions. George Bush's Justice Department launched the case. But the Clinton administration sees anti-labor rackets laws as a political profit center. . . ."[15]

Under Clinton, the mobsters returned in force. So did left-wing militants of a sort whose influence had not been seen in organized labor since the 1940s. A marriage of convenience arose between union radicals and Mafia bosses whose corrosive effects have reduced the labor movement to little more than a gigantic ATM, dispensing limitless quantities of cash to Democrat fund-raisers and left-wing causes.

Political radicals took control of the labor movement in 1995 when John Sweeney ousted AFL-CIO president Lane Kirkland, in what has been called a "palace coup." Kirkland understood that the greatest threat to organized labor came from forces—organized crime and political radicals—that undermined the movement from within. When Polish shipyard workers, led by Solidarity leader Lech Walesa, ignited a wave of strikes against communist oppression in 1980, Kirkland put the AFL-CIO's formidable resources squarely behind Walesa, pouring money into his movement and arguably doing more than any other private individual to bring down the Soviet empire.

The political Left hated Kirkland for his anti-communist stand, and the mob never forgave him for cooperating with Reagan's Organized Crime Task Force. Therein lay the seeds of the coalition that would one day end Kirkland's reign.

The anti-Kirkland forces made their move in January 1994. Planted stories in the press cited anonymous sources within the AFL-CIO blaming Kirkland for declining union membership. The proportion of union members in the US labor force had declined from 31 percent in 1960 to 15 percent in 1994. In fact, the long-term decline of union membership largely resulted from labor's success at winning US industrial workers the highest wages in the world—higher on average than most white-collar workers in America. Prosperity had taken the fight out of America's working class. In addition, many states had passed right-to-work laws that ended the practice common in many unionized businesses of forcing workers to join the union as a condition of employment.

Blaming Kirkland for these macro-economic circumstances was hardly fair. But the insurgents needed a scapegoat, and Kirkland—nearing retirement at age 73 and lacking the will for another fight—was an easy target. Militant union leaders pressured Kirkland to resign, airing their complaints in a public manner calculated to humiliate the grand old man of labor. In an effort to outwit his opponents, Kirkland agreed to step down in favor of his right-hand man Thomas R. Donahue, whom Kirkland trusted to carry on his policies. But Donahue lacked Kirkland's authority. When he stood for election on 31 October 1995, SEIU president John Sweeney beat Donahue handily, becoming president of the 13-million-member AFL-CIO. Sweeney and his "New Voice" insurgents have dominated organized labor ever since.

Sweeney's "New Voice" movement drew its name from a campaign manifesto published by United Mine Workers president Richard Trumka in June 1995. In it, Trumka called for "a new leadership" that would "make the AFL-CIO a strong, new voice for working Americans." What Trumka meant by a "new voice" was apparent from his own left-wing views and from the number of former SDS radicals he had placed on the union payroll. The "New Voice" movement itself, however, is a diverse coalition, uniting left-wing militants, old-style mob bosses, and those—like Sweeney himself—who seem a cross between the two.

Presidents of the three largest unions in the AFL-CIO led the Dump Kirkland insurgency. They were Ron Carey of the 2.3-million-member International Brotherhood of Teamsters; Gerald W. McEntee, president of the 1.2-million-member American Federation of State, County and Municipal Employees (AFSCME); and Sweeney, who, before ascending to the AFL-CIO presidency, had led another government union, the Service Employees International Union (SEIU) with 1.1 million members. Combined with a number of smaller unions, the insurgents controlled more than half of the AFL-CIO's 13.3 million members.

Much has been made of Sweeney's political radicalism. A card-carrying member of the Democratic Socialists of America (DSA), Sweeney opened the AFL-CIO's door to Communist Party organizers for the first time since the 1950s, allowing Communists to distribute literature at his conventions and recruit workers to their cause. As an organizer, Sweeney has all but abandoned the private sector, whose shrinking industrial base offers little room for union growth. The "New Voice" Movement targets government workers through public-sector unions such as AFSCME and SEIU, whose business model relies upon a perverse feedback loop which rewards government unions financially the farther left they drift.

Because they represent government workers, unions such as AFSCME and SEIU have a vested interest in supporting Democrat politicians who promise to raise taxes and put more people on the government payroll. The more people federal, state and local governments hire, the more members public-sector unions can acquire, and the more taxpayer money they can garnish from those union members' government paychecks in the form of mandatory dues. The formula is working, for the time being. Because the public sector is currently the only part of the US economy whose payrolls are growing, government unions such as AFSCME and SEIU are the only unions increasing their membership. Their success, in turn, exerts a leftward pressure on the labor movement as a whole.

It also fuels the broader radical movement in society at large. When anti-globalization rioters shut down Seattle during the 1999 meeting of the World Trade Organization, leftists were thrilled at the sight of Sweeney and McEntee and their union followers marching in solidarity with anarchists, eco-terrorists and Ruckus Society vandals amid the smoke of burning storefronts and the stench of tear gas. Enraptured by Sweeney's militancy and the promise of a "blue-green coalition" of unions and eco-activists, liberal journalists neglected to scrutinize the business side of Sweeney's "New Voice" operation. This was a serious oversight, for behind the façade of street marches and protest songs, organized crime has regained its choke hold over American labor.

Sweeney's tolerance for mob activity carries a strong element of self-interest. His old local, SEIU 32-BJ, was founded by Lucky

Luciano. FBI investigators have identified the local as a center of Genovese crime family activity. Years after leaving Local 32-BJ to become SEIU president, Sweeney continued drawing a salary from the local—a second salary, in addition to what he was paid as president. Gus Bevona, Sweeney's hand-picked successor to head Local 32-BJ, made sure that Sweeney got his cut. Such "double-dipping" is a time-honored tradition among unions—but not one that inspires confidence in Sweeney's "progressive" leadership.

Adding to this already sordid picture is the fact that known mob cronies such as Teamsters president Ron Carey and LIUNA president Arthur Armand Coia have played significant roles in Sweeney's "New Voice" movement from the beginning. As one insider explained to a reporter, "Picking Sweeney is a signal. The fact that he lived with Bevona and had his hand in the cookie jar makes it clear to people like Coia that, hey—we may be talking revolution in the streets, but we ain't talking about cleaning up unions."[16]

Following Bill Clinton's election in 1992, labor lawyer Ickes was widely expected to get the job of deputy White House chief of staff. He had managed Clinton's New York campaign, run the Democratic Convention, and overseen the Clinton transition team. However, shortly before Clinton announced his White House appointments, unknown sources began leaking reports of Ickes' mob connections to the press—sources widely believed to be connected with his enemies in the Democratic Party.[17] Ickes was too hot to handle. Clinton declined to name him to any White House post, pending the results of further investigation.

In a pattern that was to become all too familiar during the Clinton years, Ickes and his law firm were soon "cleared" of all allegations, based on an "investigation" whose thoroughness was open to some question. Court officer Mary Shannon Little was assigned to investigate. "Based on the evidence available to date, there is no evidence of criminal misconduct on the part of Harold Ickes or Meyer, Suozzi, English & Klein," she wrote in a November 1993 memorandum. However, the 57-page Little report was sealed. When the Long Island newspaper *Newsday* sued to unseal it, a federal appeals court ruled against *Newsday*. While acknowledging that the report contained "various accusations" against Ickes, the court pointed out that much of the text had been redacted or blacked out and that it "would circulate accusations that cannot be tested by the interested public because the sources and much of the subject matter are shrouded by the redactions . . ."[18]

Thus Meyer Suozzi managing partner William Cunningham III—who would later serve as treasurer for Hillary Clinton's Senate campaign—announced on 18 November 1993 that Ickes had been cleared of all charges. Of course, this was not exactly true. The only person with complete knowledge of the evidence for and against Ickes was court officer Mary Shannon Little.

On 4 January 1994, a very happy Ickes began his first day of work at the White House, as deputy chief of staff for political affairs and policy, where he served until January 1997. Bill and Hillary Clinton found many uses for Ickes' peculiar talents. Ickes himself wryly referred to his role as "director of the sanitation department," because so many of his duties involved suppressing Clinton scandals and defusing federal investigations.[19] "Whenever there was something that [Bill Clinton] thought required ruthlessness or vengeance or sharp elbows and sharp knees or, frankly, skulduggery, he would give it to Harold," former Clinton advisor Dick Morris told *Vanity Fair* in 1997.[20]

When he arrived in the White House, Ickes brought his mob connections with him. Even before Bill Clinton's election, mobsters and labor racketeers had begun courting the First Couple. With a Justice Department RICO suit hanging over his head, LIUNA boss Arthur Armand Coia was particularly eager to curry favor with Bill Clinton. Ickes served as the Clintons' go-between with crooked unions such as LIUNA and the Teamsters. Coia donated over $1 million in union funds to the Democrats in 1994. More importantly, he backed John Sweeney's takeover of the AFL-CIO—a move that would put tens of millions of dollars more within the Clintons' reach. Coia and Clinton became quite friendly, exchanging costly gifts such as customized golf clubs. In the end, Coia got what he wanted. In 1995—after investigating Coia and LIUNA for three years—Janet Reno's Justice Department abruptly decided not to press any charges against him.[21]

Teamsters' president Ron Carey also needed a helping hand. He was up for reelection in 1996 and James P. Hoffa—son of the legendary Teamster chief—was challenging him. Carey needed money and lots of it. The union treasury was full, but the law forbade using members' dues to campaign for union office. What to do? The answer was an elaborate scheme to launder union funds through Democrat-friendly organizations, then siphon them back into Carey's campaign.

In 1996, Carey laundered nearly $1 million through a daisy-chain of left-wing non-profit groups that included Ralph Nader's Citizen Action, the National Council of Senior Citizens, Teamsters for a Corruption Free Union, Project Vote (an ACORN front group)—and also the AFL-CIO and the Democratic Party itself. Kickbacks and barter arrangements made it worth everyone's while. Every participant in the daisy-chain got a piece of the action. Everyone was happy, and Carey won the election.[22]

The "Teamstergate" conspirators might have gotten away

with it, but for one rank-and-file union member who resented the misuse of his dues and decided to blow the whistle. In the end, seven conspirators were convicted in federal court, but almost all were low-level players. Trial testimony directly implicated Teamsters president Ron Carey, AFL-CIO president John Sweeney, AFSCME president Gerald McEntee, SEIU president Andrew Stern, UMW president Richard Trumka, and 1996 Clinton-Gore reelection manager Terry McAuliffe. Of these, only Ron Carey was eventually indicted. The rest got off scot-free.

"Not long ago, Teamster scandals were the work of wise guys with names like Jimmy the Weasel, Fat Tony, Tony Ducks or Tony Pro," mused Jim Larkin in the leftist journal *In These Times*. "The current one, surprisingly enough, is the work of people associated with the Democratic Party, Citizen Action, liberal unions and other progressive causes."[23] Larkin's article bore the plaintive headline, "What Went Wrong." What appears to have gone wrong is that the wise guys were now running the White House.

By the mid-1990s, Ickes was heading the Clintons' fundraising machine, collecting record-breaking quantities of soft money. Much of the soft money Ickes raised was used to buy "issue advocacy" ads—the same sorts of ads which the Soros-funded Brennan Center later condemned as "sham issue" ads, demanding their criminalization.[24]

Federal investigators began zeroing in on Ickes in 1996. He suddenly became a liability. Immediately after Bill Clinton's re-election in November 1996, the President fired him. But Ickes escaped prosecution. Despite pressure from within her own Justice Department, Janet Reno refused to appoint a special prosecutor to investigate him.[25] He went back to work for Meyer, Suozzi, English & Klein and today runs the firm's Washington office.

Ickes would not be out of politics long. Hillary Clinton had need of his services. From the beginning, Ickes' truest loyalty was to Hillary. The *Boston Globe* called him "a special favorite of the president's wife."[26] In the Clinton White House, Ickes quickly gravitated to Hillary's end of the operation. He served initially as "health care czar," charged with drumming up political support for Hillary's floundering Health Security Act. Hillary later placed Ickes in charge of a special unit within the White House Counsel's office, dedicated to suppressing Clinton scandals. In his work for this special unit, Ickes reported directly to Hillary Clinton.

Hillary recruited Ickes as chief campaign advisor for her 2000 Senate run. According to Ickes, he accepted the job after a four-hour meeting with Hillary on 12 February 1999—the same day that the US Senate voted on Bill Clinton's impeachment. "I'm really doing this out of my friendship for Hillary, pure and simple," Ickes told the Associated Press on 17 June 1999. "She called and there was no way I was going to say no to Hillary."[27]

As Hillary's unofficial campaign chief, Ickes brought to bear all the clout and connections he had accumulated through thirty-three years of bare-knuckled power struggles in the Empire State. Ickes enlisted the help of his old union allies. A statewide get-out-the-vote drive conducted by canvassers from the radical ACORN network and its front group the Working Families Party proved pivotal in Hillary's Senate victory. Former Meyer Suozzi managing partner William Cunningham III served as Hillary's campaign treasurer.

Getting Hillary elected to the US Senate was a major coup for Ickes. But bigger jobs lay ahead. George Soros was readying his Shadow Party for action, and Ickes possessed just the sorts of talents Soros needed.

10

THE
SHADOW PARTY

T his is not a normal election. These are not normal times," George Soros told the Associated Press on 10 June 2004.[1] Soros indicated with these words that he intended to take off the gloves. In his view, America had entered an extreme crisis, which called for extreme measures. He would not be bound, in this contest, by an inappropriate reverence for legal niceties.

"I do not accept the rules imposed by others," he wrote in *Soros on Soros*. "If I did, I would not be alive today. I am a law-abiding citizen, but I recognize that there are regimes that need to be opposed rather than accepted. And in periods of regime change, the normal rules don't apply. One needs to adjust one's behavior to the changing circumstances."[2]

The McCain-Feingold Act went into effect on 6 November 2002. After spending eight years and countless millions of dollars getting McCain-Feingold passed, Soros immediately began evading its restrictions on political contributions. Over the next year, the term "shadow party" began creeping into the press. In the 5 November 2002 *Washington Post*, writer Thomas B. Edsall wrote of "shadow organizations" springing up on both sides of the political fence to circumvent McCain-Feingold's soft money ban.[3] Lorraine Woellert of *Business Week* appears to have been the first journalist to apply the term "shadow party" specifically to the Democrat network of 527 groups that Soros was assembling. She did so in a 15 September 2003 article titled, "The Evolution of Campaign Finance?"[4] Other journalists followed her example.

Theoretically, the McCain-Feingold Act banned unlimited,

soft-money contributions to politicians and political parties. Only hard-money contributions were allowed, which were strictly limited in size (an individual donor could give $2,000 to a candidate, $5,000 to a political action committee and $25,000 to a political party in any single election cycle, all of which had to be reported to the Federal Election Commission). In practice, however, Soros demonstrated that one could get around this restriction simply by giving money to political front groups that were supposedly independent of any party.

Ironically, considering widespread Democrat support for McCain-Feingold, its stipulations put the Democrats at a fundraising disadvantage. Historically, Republicans have enjoyed a 2-1 advantage over Democrats in raising hard-money contributions from individual donors. Democrats have relied much more heavily on large, soft-money contributions, especially from unions.

Before McCain-Feingold, government unions used to lavish multi-million-dollar contributions on the Democratic Party—money that the unions drew from their members through mandatory dues. The unions still collected their membership dues, but, under McCain-Feingold, they could no longer pass that money along to the Democratic Party, at least not directly. The Soros solution? Give it to his Shadow Party conduits instead.

During the 2004 election cycle, the Shadow Party used various expedients to evade the McCain-Feingold limits. Primarily, it works through independent non-profit groups which supposedly have no connection to the Democratic Party, either structurally or through informal coordination. Most of its big fundraisers during the 2004 election were "527 committees"—named after Section 527 of the IRS code, and useful to the Shadow Party because they were not required to register with the Federal Election

Commission nor—except in special circumstances—to divulge their finances to the FEC. The FEC recently cracked down on 527s, but many other sorts of non-profit groups exist which can fill the same role.

Another expedient used by the Shadow Party is to claim that it is not engaged in electioneering at all. Most Shadow Party groups say they are soliciting funds not to defeat a particular candidate, but to promote "issues" and non-partisan get-out-the-vote drives. Of course their issue promotions, in most cases, turn out to be attacks on the opposing candidates, and their get-out-the-vote drives use sophisticated demographic marketing techniques to target exclusively Democratic constituencies. All this casts doubt on the Shadow Party's claim to be aloof from the electoral struggle and therefore exempt from FEC regulation. However, a pliant Federal Elections Commission conveniently declined to rule on the Shadow Party's legality until after the election, when it would no longer matter.

McCain-Feingold also bars the Republican Party from raising soft money. However, Republicans never had a problem raising individual contributions for their candidates and never made a habit of raiding union treasuries for "soft money." Thus Republicans felt less urgency than Democrats to seek alternative fundraising methods, and, during the 2004 race, they proved slower in pursuing the 527 circumvention route around the McCain-Feingold provisions. To this day, Republicans have never built a network of independent, non-profit fundraising groups comparable in numbers or scale to the Democrat Shadow Party.

To the extent that the Shadow Party can be said to have an official launch date, 17 July 2003 probably fits the bill.[5] On that day, a team of political strategists, wealthy donors, left-wing labor leaders and other Democrat activists gathered at George Soros'

Southampton estate called El Mirador, on Long Island. Aside from Soros, the most noteworthy attendee was Morton H. Halperin, whom Soros had hired the previous year to head the Washington office of his Open Society Institute.

It was at this meeting that Soros laid out his plan to defeat George Bush in the coming election.[6] No one has published a full list of the attendees at the meeting, but partial lists are available in accounts that appeared in the *Washington Post* and the *Wall Street Journal*. These include an impressive array of former Clinton administration officials, among them Halperin, who—despite his disloyalty as a Pentagon official during the Vietnam War (or more likely because of it) served eight years under Clinton: first as Under Secretary of Defense for Policy and finally as Director of Policy Planning for the Clinton State Department.

The guests at Soros' estate also included Clinton's former chief of staff John Podesta; Jeremy Rosner, former special advisor to Clinton's Secretary of State Madeline Albright; Robert Boorstin, a former advisor to Clinton's Treasury Secretary Robert Rubin; and Steven Rosenthal, a left-wing union leader who served the Clinton White House as an advisor on union affairs to Labor Secretary Robert Reich. Carl Pope, executive director of the Sierra Club, and Ellen Malcolm, founder and president of Emily's List, also attended the meeting, as did prominent Democrat donors including auto insurance mogul Peter B. Lewis, founder and CEO of RealNetworks Rob Glaser, Taco Bell heir Rob McKay, and Benson & Hedges tobacco heirs Lewis and Dorothy Cullman.

Months earlier, Soros had hired two political analysts to probe Bush's defenses. They were Tom Novick, a lobbyist for the Western States Center—a group of radical environmentalists in Oregon—and Democrat media strategist Mark Steitz, president of TSD Communications in Washington DC, whose clients have included the Democratic National Committee and the Clinton presidential campaigns of 1992 and 1996. Both Novick and Steitz were present at the Southampton meeting to brief the team in person.

Working independently, the two analysts had reached similar conclusions. Both agreed that Bush could be beaten. Voter turnout was the key. The analysts proposed massive get-out-the-vote drives among likely Democrat voters in seventeen "swing" or "battle-ground" states: Arizona, Arkansas, Florida, Iowa, Maine, Michigan, Minnesota, Missouri, Nevada, New Hampshire, New Mexico, Ohio, Oregon, Pennsylvania, Washington, West Virginia, and Wisconsin.

"By morning," reports Cummings, "the outlines of a new organization began to emerge, and Mr. Soros pledged $10 million to get it started." The name of that organization was America Coming Together (ACT)—a grassroots activist group designed to coordinate the Shadow Party's get-out-the-vote drive. ACT would dispatch thousands of activists—some paid, some volunteers—to knock on doors and work phone banks, combining the manpower of left-wing unions, environmentalists, abortion-rights activists and minority race warriors from civil rights organizations.

ACT was not exactly new. A group of Democrat activists had been trying for months to get it off the ground. But, until George Soros stepped in, ACT had languished for lack of donors. Laura Blumenfeld of the *Washington Post* describes the scene at the 17 July meeting at Soros' El Mirador estate:

> Standing on the back deck, the evening sun angling into their eyes, Soros took aside Steve Rosenthal, CEO of the liberal activist group America Coming Together (ACT), and Ellen Malcolm, its president. . . . Soros told them he would give

ACT $10 million. . . . Before coffee the next morning, his friend Peter Lewis, chairman of the Progressive Corp., had pledged $10 million to ACT. Rob Glaser, founder and CEO of RealNetworks, promised $2 million. Rob McKay, president of the McKay Family Foundation, gave $1 million and benefactors Lewis and Dorothy Cullman committed $500,000. Soros also promised up to $3 million to Podesta's new think tank, the Center for American Progress, which would function as the policy brains of the new network.[7]

The Shadow Party had been born. Three weeks later, on 8 August, the *New York Times* announced the official roll-out of America Coming Together (ACT), describing it as a political action committee led by Ellen Malcolm and Steven Rosenthal.

Soros next summoned California software developer Wes Boyd to meet him in New York on 17 September. Boyd was best known among computer users for his "Flying Toasters" screen saver. The political world knew him as founder of the radical website MoveOn.org, the Internet force behind Howard Dean's anti-war presidential campaign. Boyd had launched the website during the Clinton impeachment trial in 1998, offering a petition to censure the President and "move on" to more important matters. Hundreds of thousands of readers responded, and Boyd quickly began milking his growing readership for membership fees and political contributions. His website raised millions for Democrat candidates in three national elections—two midterms and one presidential race. When they met in New York, Soros offered Boyd a deal. He and his associate Peter Lewis would donate $1 to MoveOn.org for every $2 Boyd could raise from his members, up to $5 million total from Soros and Lewis combined. Boyd accepted.[8]

By November 2003, the Shadow Party was ready to go public. Soros calculated that the best way to launch his network would be to issue a public statement, calling attention to the record-breaking contributions he had pledged to the Shadow Party. Such an announcement would "stimulate other giving" from Democrat donors still sitting on the fence, Soros thought.[9]

He chose the *Washington Post* to carry his message. Soros sat down with reporter Laura Blumenfeld and issued his now-famous call for regime change in the United States. "America under Bush is a danger to the world," Soros declared. "Toppling Bush," he said, "is the central focus of my life . . . a matter of life and death. And I'm willing to put my money where my mouth is." Would Soros spend his entire $7-billion fortune to defeat Bush, Blumenfeld asked? "If someone guaranteed it," Soros replied.[10]

George Soros is an exacting taskmaster. In return for his money, he demands productivity. What he requires of employees and business associates in the investment world, Soros also demands from the political operatives he funds. "Mr. Soros isn't just writing checks and watching," noted *Wall Street Journal* reporter Jeanne Cummings. "He is also imposing a business model on the notoriously unruly world of politics. He demands objective evidence of progress, and assigned an aide to monitor the groups he supports. He studies private polls to track the impact of an anti-Bush advertising campaign, and he is delivering his money in installments, giving him leverage if performance falters."[11]

Under Soros' guidance, the Shadow Party infrastructure had assumed a coherent shape by early 2004. Making up its framework were seven ostensibly "independent" non-profit groups, which, at the time, constituted the network's administrative nexus. Let us call them the Seven Sisters. In chronological order, based upon their launch dates, they are:

1. MoveOn.org (launched 22 September 1998)

2. Center for American Progress (launched 7 July 2003)

3. America Votes (launched 15 July 2003)

4. America Coming Together (launched 17 July 2003)

5. The Media Fund (launched 5 November 2003)

6. Joint Victory Campaign 2004 (launched 5 November 2003)

7. The Thunder Road Group LLC (launched early 2004)

With the exception of MoveOn.org—based in Berkeley, California—all Seven Sisters maintained headquarters in Washington DC. Testifying to the close links between these groups were their interlocking finances, Boards of Directors and corporate officers. In some cases, they even shared office space.

For example, two of the Seven Sisters—The Media Fund and Joint Victory Campaign 2004—shared an office in Suite #1100 at 1120 Connecticut Avenue, NW. Three other groups—America Coming Together, America Votes and The Thunder Road Group— leased offices in the Motion Picture Association Building at 888 16th Street, NW. It is tempting to consider that the clustering of these three groups in a building owned by the Motion Picture Association of America (MPAA) may not be coincidental. The MPAA has long enjoyed a cozy relationship with the Democratic Party; many high-ranking Democrats have slipped comfortably from government jobs into glamorous posts in the MPAA's upper management.

In March 2004, for instance, Dan Glickman succeeded Jack Valenti as MPAA president. Valenti was a Democrat lobbyist and former aide to President Lyndon Johnson. Glickman was formerly a Democratic Congressman from Kansas, who later served as

Secretary of Agriculture in the Clinton White House. Now, as MPAA president, Glickman holds what is arguably the most powerful position in Hollywood.

The Shadow Party draws much of its funding from the entertainment world. Between August 2000 and August 2004—the period when Soros was assembling his shadow network—Jane Fonda was the fourth largest donor to Democrat 527 groups, having contributed $13 million, according to the Center for Public Integrity. Larger contributors soon overtook her.

According to Political Money Line, $78 million of the money raised through pro-Democrat 527s during the 2004 election cycle came from just five donors: George Soros—$27,080,105; Progressive Insurance chairman Peter Lewis—$23,997,220; Hollywood producer Stephen L. Bing—$13,952,682; Golden West Financial Corporation founders Herbert and Marion Sandler—$13,007,959.[12]

Below is a brief overview of the Seven Sisters and their function in the Shadow Party network. The profiles appear in chronological order, according to their launch dates.

MOVEON.ORG

"It feels so bourgeois!" exclaimed a man who had just made the first campaign contribution of his life. Recorded by *LA Weekly* writer Brendan Bernhard, this man's outburst bespeaks a mass phenomenon for which MoveOn.org can largely take credit.[13]

More than a website, MoveOn.org is a movement cleverly tailored to lure the young, the Net-savvy and the self-consciously fashionable into supporting mainstream Democrats such as John Kerry—the sort of candidate whom today's digital hipsters would normally dismiss as a square. MoveOn's peculiar contribution to the Shadow Party is its ability to draw into the political process America's ever-growing hordes of self-absorbed cyber-existentialists—"tech-savvy progressives," in the words of Salon.com writer Michelle Goldberg—and convince them that a vote for the Democrats is a blow against middle-class conformity. MoveOn is the Joe Camel of the Shadow Party, playing to the deep-seated antipathy that bohemians of every age group harbor toward all things normal, wholesome, traditional and adult.

Regarding MoveOn's success at harnessing popular entertainment to the Democrat cause, whether in the form of rock-concert fundraisers or Bush-bashing ads with an MTV edge, the *LA Weekly*'s Bernhard concludes, "[I]t's all part of a giant, perhaps unprecedented effort by the country's intellectual and artistic communities to unseat the conspicuously unintellectual, inartistic man in the Oval Office."

High-tech entrepreneur Wesley Boyd and his wife Joan Blades created MoveOn. Their software company Berkeley Systems Inc. of Berkeley, California made a fortune in the early '90s with its "After Dark" screensaver, featuring the famous animated "flying toasters." When the screensaver market peaked in 1994, Berkeley Systems rolled out a successful line of CD-ROM computer games.[14] Company sales had reached $30 million annually by the time Boyd sold Berkeley Systems in 1997 for $13.8 million.[15]

Idle, wealthy and still full of fight, Boyd and Blades sought new challenges. Angered by the Clinton impeachment, the couple wrote a one-sentence petition and e-mailed it to friends, who then e-mailed it to others in chain-letter fashion. It said, "Censure the president and move on to pressing issues facing the nation." At the same time, Boyd and Blades launched a website enabling people to sign their petition electronically. To their astonishment, 100,000 supporters registered in the first week.

Boyd and Blades realized they were onto something. They launched MoveOn.org on 22 September 1998. One month later, on 23 October they rolled out MoveOn PAC, a federal political action committee designed to draw political contributions from MoveOn's fast-growing membership. MoveOn PAC raised millions of dollars for Democrat candidates in the elections of 1998, 2000 and 2002. By the time Wes Boyd met with Soros in the fall of 2003, MoveOn boasted an e-mail list of more than 2.2 million members in the US and over 800,000 abroad.[16] The lean-and-mean operation rented no office space. Its ten full-time staffers worked from home, staying in touch via e-mail, instant messaging and weekly conference calls.[17]

MoveOn's fundraising feats impressed Beltway strategists. On 17 April 2004, MoveOn held a national "Bake Sale for Democracy," in which members conducted more than 1,000 bake sales around the country, raising $750,000 in a single day for MoveOn's anti-Bush campaign.[18] When a Republican redistricting plan threatened Democratic incumbents in the Texas state senate in May 2003, an appeal from MoveOn brought in $1 million in contributions in two days, to support the beleaguered Democrats.[19]

In 2002, Boyd and Blades hired 32-year-old Zack Exley as MoveOn's organizing director. A computer programmer and Web designer by trade, Exley had gained national attention during the 2000 campaign when he launched GWBush.com, a website featuring doctored photographs portraying candidate Bush as a dope fiend. Exley was a hardened activist of the Left. Trained by the AFL-CIO, he had worked as an undercover union organizer for five years, and had also done a stint training activists for the Ruckus Society, an anarchist group whose violent tactics first caught the public eye during the 1999 riots against the World

Trade Organization meeting in Seattle.[20] Exley brought a ruthless edge to MoveOn's fundraising and propaganda drives, which soon aroused the admiration of mainstream Democrats. In May 2003, the Howard Dean presidential campaign hired Exley away from MoveOn for two weeks in order to turbo-charge Dean's Web operations. Exley finally left MoveOn for good in April 2004 to become Director of Online Communications and Online Organizing for the Kerry-Edwards campaign.

In the meantime, George Soros had incorporated MoveOn into his Shadow Party. Following the 17 September 2003 meeting between Soros and Boyd mentioned above, Soros and his associates poured nearly $6.2 million into MoveOn over a period of six months, according to the Center for Public Integrity. The contributions included $2.5 million from George Soros personally, $2.5 million from Peter B. Lewis of Progressive Insurance, $971,427 from Stephen Bing of Shangri-La Entertainment, $100,000 from Benson & Hedges tobacco heir Lewis Cullman, and $101,000 from Soros' son Jonathan, an attorney and financier recently promoted to deputy manager of Soros Fund Management LLC.

Jonathan Soros became personally involved with MoveOn.org's activities. In December 2003, he collaborated with techno-rocker Moby to organize "Bush in 30 Seconds," an online contest for the best 30-second anti-Bush TV ad. MoveOn agreed to air the winning commercial on national television. Among the 1,500-odd submissions to the contest were two ads juxtaposing footage of George W. Bush and Adolf Hitler. MoveOn posted these ads on its site. Under pressure from Jewish groups and Republicans, MoveOn pulled the Hitler ads and apologized for them.[21]

Despite such gaffes, MoveOn need not worry about its media image. Major networks and newspapers pour forth an endless flood of free publicity for the group. Calculated in terms of equivalent advertising fees, the millions MoveOn raises in political contributions doubtless pales in value beside the worshipful profiles and saccharine coverage that major media never tire of bestowing upon Boyd and Blades' website and political campaigns.

CENTER FOR AMERICAN PROGRESS

The Center for American Progress is widely understood to be what one inside source called, "the official Hillary Clinton think tank"—a platform designed to highlight Hillary's policies and to enhance her prestige as a potential presidential candidate.[22]

Robert Dreyfuss reported in the 1 March 2004 edition of the *Nation*, "The idea for the Center began with discussions in 2002 between [Morton] Halperin and George Soros, the billionaire investor. . . . Halperin, who heads the office of Soros' Open Society Institute, brought Podesta into the discussion, and beginning in late 2002 Halperin and Podesta circulated a series of papers to funders."[23]

Soros and Halperin then recruited Harold Ickes—chief fundraiser and former deputy chief of staff for the Clinton White House—to help organize the Center. It was launched on 7 July 2003 as the American Majority Institute, but has operated under the name Center for American Progress since 1 September 2003.

The official purpose of the Center was to provide the Left with something it supposedly lacked—a think tank of its own. Where was the Left's Heritage Foundation? asked Soros and Halperin. Of course, the Left had plenty of think tanks, including the Brookings Institution, the Urban Institute, the Economic Policy Institute, the Center on Budget and Policy, the Institute for Policy Studies, and the Progressive Policy Institute—not to mention the Kennedy School for Government at Harvard and numerous similar academic institutions firmly under leftist control. But Shadow Party leaders seemed to be looking for something different—something that no existing institution on the Left offered—perhaps a think tank tied directly to their own political operations.

Regarding the alleged need for the Center, Hillary Clinton told Matt Bai of the *New York Times Magazine* on 12 October 2003, "We need some new intellectual capital. There has to be some thought given as to how we build the 21st-century policies that reflect the Democratic Party's values."[24] Expanding on this theme, Hillary subsequently told the *Nation's* Dreyfuss, "We've had the challenge of filling a void on our side of the ledger for a long time, while the other side created an infrastructure that has come to dominate political discourse. The Center is a welcome effort to fill that void."[25]

Soros and Hillary seemed to understand the need for the new Center, even if they did not always succeed in explaining it to others. They found fault with every existing left-wing think tank. Even Bill Clinton's personal favorite, the Progressive Policy Institute, was too moderate, too middle-of-the-road for their purpose. But what was their purpose?

Hillary Clinton tries to minimize the depth of her involvement with the Center for American Progress—as indeed she habitually does in all matters concerning the Shadow Party. Beltway insiders are not fooled, however. Persistent press leaks confirm that Hillary calls the shots at the Center—not its director, John Podesta. "It's the official Hillary Clinton think tank," an inside source confided.[26]

Many ideological purists on the Left dismiss the Center as a platform for Hillary's presidential ambitions. No doubt, they are right. Dreyfuss notes the abundance of Clintonites on the Center's staff, among them Clinton's national security speechwriter Robert Boorstin, Democratic Leadership Council staffer and former head of Clinton's National Economic Council Gene Sperling, former senior advisor to Clinton's Office of Management and Budget Matt Miller, and so on. Commented the *Nation*'s Dreyfuss, "The center's kickoff conference on national security in October, co-organized with *The American Prospect* and the Century Foundation, looked like a Clinton reunion featuring Robert Rubin, Clinton's Treasury Secretary; William Perry, his Defense Secretary; Sandy Berger, his National Security Adviser; Richard Holbrooke and Susan Rice, both Clinton-era Assistant Secretaries of State; Rodney Slater, his Transportation Secretary; and Carol Browner, his EPA administrator, who serves on the center's board of directors." Hillary Clinton also attended the event.

"In looking at Podesta's center," Dreyfuss muses, "there's no escaping the imprint of the Clintons. It's not completely wrong to see it as a shadow government, a kind of Clinton White-House-in-exile—or a White House staff in readiness for President Hillary Clinton."[27]

Another of the Center's missions is to carry out "rapid response" to what it calls conservative "attacks" in the media. The Center's website vows to build its capacity for "responding effectively and rapidly to conservative proposals and rhetoric with a thoughtful critique and clear alternatives." To this end, the Center offers a stable of talking heads—coiffed, credentialed and fully briefed—available for appearances on national talk shows. Notable among the Center's line-up of talking heads are the *Nation*'s Eric Alterman—who claims expertise on the subjects of media and democracy—and Morton H. Halperin, who offers to speak on national security.

The Center for American Progress immediately helped to launch a fraternal project, Media Matters for America, better known for its website MediaMatters.org. Inasmuch as Media Matters aspires to serve as a media watchdog, monitoring the inaccuracies of "rightwing" journalists for ethical infractions and errors, it is peculiar that writer David Brock is appointed its President and CEO. Brock is a former conservative journalist who defected to the left amidst an outpouring of dramatic public confessions that he had built his career on lies, writing political hit pieces filled with flimsy evidence. Whatever Brock lacks in credibility, he more than makes up for in currying influence. Brock told the *New York Times* that he conferred with Senator Hillary Clinton, Senator Tom Daschle and former Vice President Al Gore before launching the website.[28]

The *New York Times* generously provided a 1,041-word feature article to announce Brock's grand opening in May 2004: "Mr. Brock's project was developed with help from the newly formed Center for American Progress.... Podesta has loaned office space in the past to Mr. Brock and introduced him to potential donors." Brock received $2 million for the start-up. His donors include friend-of-Hillary Susie Tompkins Buell, co-founder of the fashion company Esprit; Leo Hindery Jr., former CEO of the scandal-ridden Global Crossing; and San Francisco philanthropist James C. Hormel, whom Clinton appointed ambassador to Luxembourg in the 1990s.[29]

Media Matters quickly acquired a reputation for lock-step partisanship and reckless disregard for the truth. Brock and his team seem to sleepwalk through their work, rubberstamping, with mind-numbing monotony, virtually every conservative utterance that finds its way into major media as a "lie," a "smear," a "slander," or a "falsehood."

One of Brock's first projects was to exert pressure on Congress and Defense Secretary Donald Rumsfeld to ban Rush Limbaugh from American Forces Radio and Television Service—thus depriving the troops in Iraq of one of the few radio programs they are allowed to hear which wholeheartedly supports them and the cause for which they fight. At the time Brock began his campaign, only one hour of Limbaugh's three-hour show was broadcast on only one of AFRTS's thirteen radio channels, five days per week— constituting less than one percent of the network's total weekly programming.[30] Nevertheless, that was one percent too many for the Shadow Party and its operatives.

Shortly after Media Matters began its campaign, Democrat Senator Tom Harkin of Iowa obligingly proposed an amendment to the 2005 Defense Authorization Act mandating "political balance" on AFRTS. The Senate approved Harkin's amendment unanimously on 16 June. It stopped short of banning Limbaugh outright, but the amendment effectively required AFRTS to balance Limbaugh with more left-wing commentary. Given the fact that one of the network's two news channels was airing National Public Radio 24 hours per day, seven days per week, it is hard to imagine how AFRTS could have been expected to broadcast more left-wing commentary than it already was.[31] Even so, Senator Harkin complained in a 17 June Senate speech, "[T]here is no commentary on the service that would even begin to balance the extreme right-wing views that Rush Limbaugh routinely expresses on his program."[32]

AMERICA VOTES

America Votes is an umbrella group encompassing a national coalition of grassroots get-out-the-vote organizations. It was formed on

15 July 2003, as the Democratic primaries got into high gear to help coordinate the activities of the growing number of non-profit groups that now constituted the Shadow Party. During the 2004 election cycle, its website claimed that America Votes commanded the political loyalty of "more than 20 million Americans in every state in the country" through its 33 member organizations.

The McCain-Feingold soft-money ban took effect on 6 November 2002. Shortly thereafter, Democrat operative Gina Glantz called a meeting at the Washington restaurant BeDuCi's. Glantz was then an official of the left-wing government union SEIU. She subsequently became a key strategist for the Howard Dean campaign. Attendees at Glantz's meeting included Clinton operative Harold Ickes, SEIU president Andrew Stern, Steven. Rosenthal, Ellen Malcolm and Carl Pope. Glantz argued that the proliferating Democrat 527 committees needed a central command structure—an "umbrella group"—to avoid duplicating efforts and wasting money. Everyone liked her idea, but no donors stepped forward. Glantz's idea for an umbrella group languished for the next eight months.[33]

In describing the genesis of America Votes, the *Texas Monthly* listed a cast of characters similar to those who attended Glantz's meeting—but with one noteworthy addition: Jim Jordan. When the Shadow Party launched America Votes, Jordan was still John Kerry's campaign manager. He was not fired from that job until 9 November—nearly four months later. If indeed Jordan helped launch America Votes while working as Kerry's campaign manager, he violated FEC regulations, which bar coordination between campaign officials and independent political committees.[34]

The *Texas Monthly* further reported that the group decided to appoint Cecile Richards—then deputy chief of staff for House minority leader Nancy Pelosi—to head America Votes. "We wanted to find a way to bring progressive groups together for the election. . . . It was a monster coalition, and we universally agreed that Cecile was the best person to coordinate it," said Ellen Malcolm. Richards' primary job would be to keep the organization's thousands of activists from duplicating efforts. "With America Votes, we really have a way now to settle who is in which neighborhoods, who is taking which precincts," Richards explained. "And the role of our state directors is to hold those folks accountable for what they said they'd do."[35] Member organizations of the America Votes coalition during the 2004 election cycle are listed below:

1. ACORN (Association of Community Organizations for Reform Now)

2. ACT (America Coming Together)

3. AFL-CIO (American Federation of Labor—Congress of Industrial Organizations)

4. AFSCME (American Federation of State, County and Municipal Employees)

5. AFT (American Federation of Teachers)

6. ATLA (Association of Trial Lawyers of America)

7. Brady Campaign to Prevent Gun Violence

8. Clean Water Action

9. Defenders of Wildlife Action Fund

10. Democracy for America

11. EMILY'S List

12. Environment 2004

13. The Human Rights Campaign

14. League of Conservation Voters

15. The Media Fund

16. The Million Mom March

17. MoveOn.org Voter Fund

18. Moving America Forward

19. Music for America

20. NAACP—National Voter Fund

21. NARAL Pro-Choice America

22. National Education Association

23. National Jewish Democratic Council

24. National Treasury Employees Union

25. Partnership for America's Families

26. People for the American Way (PFAW)

27. Planned Parenthood Action Fund

28. Service Employees International Union (SEIU)

29. Sierra Club

30. USAction

31. Voices for Working Families

32. Young Voter Alliance

33. 21st Century Democrats

Cecile Richards had a personal as well as an ideological ax to grind against President George W. Bush. She is the daughter of former Texas governor Ann Richards, whom Bush soundly defeated in 1994, ending her political career.

Like many of Bush's harshest critics, Cecile Richards harbors a deep antipathy toward the so-called "Christian Right." After her mother's 1994 defeat, Richards founded the Texas Freedom Network, a grassroots organization aimed at countering the political influence of conservative Christians, especially on school boards. Richards subsequently moved to Washington DC, where she served as organizing director of the AFL-CIO, then as a pro-abortion activist for the Turner Foundation and Planned Parenthood, and finally as deputy chief of staff for Democrat minority whip Nancy Pelosi, soon to become minority leader. Richards held that post for eighteen months, before joining America Votes.

George Soros' son, Jonathan, has donated $250,000 to America Votes. Several of the organization's top donors, such as Rob McKay and Robert Glaser, are also close Soros associates.

AMERICA COMING TOGETHER

Only two days after the team from BeDuCi's restaurant launched America Votes, George Soros held his 17 July meeting in Southampton, where he and his associates pledged $23.5 million to America Coming Together and $3 million to "the official Hillary Clinton think tank," the Center for American Progress. Internal Revenue filings give 17 July 2003 as ACT's official launch date. However, the public announcement did not come until 8 August 2003, when the *Washington Post* announced the roll-out of a new political action committee, naming as its co-founders Ellen Malcolm and Steven Rosenthal.[36]

On the surface, America Coming Together was simply one of 33 member organizations under the umbrella of Cecile Richards' America Votes. However, ACT played a special role among the affiliate groups during the 2004 election. As the *Wall Street Journal* explained, affiliates such as Planned Parenthood and the NAACP pay $50,000 apiece for the privilege of joining America Votes, for which they gain access to ACT's high-tech, get-out-the-vote system.

The *Journal* describes an encounter between Rebecca Barson, an official at Planned Parenthood of Northern New England, and cyber-activist Rob O'Brien from ACT, whom it describes as a "tattooed young man sporting a black t-shirt and earring," with a laptop computer. Ms. Barson wants to canvass single, local young women, ages 18-30, who are registered Democrats and likely to respond to a pro-abortion message. Mr. O'Brien hits a few keys on his laptop and, voila, up pop the names of 812 local women answering Ms. Barson's target profile to a "T," their addresses marked by dots on a street map. From that point, the *Journal* explains, "it was up to Planned Parenthood—and a host of affiliated liberal organizations working with ACT to divide up the terrain—to reach the voters, assess their political inclinations and cajole supporters to vote on Nov. 2."

"This is the first time we've really done field work on this level," Ms. Barson told the *Wall Street Journal*. "We would never be able to afford the voter file and mapping software on our own."[37] It all sounds so exciting and cutting-edge—applying state-of-the-art splinter-group marketing techniques to a political campaign. But columnist Craig McMillan of WorldNetDaily.com sees a more sinister dynamic at work. Voter registration drives are considered non-partisan, and therefore permissible to 501(c)(3) non-profit groups such as Planned Parenthood. Thanks to ACT's software, however, Democrat activists such as Ms. Barson can now go through the motions of pretending to carry out a non-partisan voter registration drive while in fact targeting only single Democrat women who, if they can be prodded to vote at all, will surely vote only for Democrat candidates.

In McMillan's view, the transaction between Ms. Barson and her be-earringed young friend from ACT constitutes but the tip of an iceberg of corruption. When they pay their $50,000 membership fees to America Votes, what those Democrat non-profit groups really appear to be purchasing is access to a cornucopia of "illegal coordination" via "private cell-phone conversations, within encrypted e-mails, and on password-protected websites."[38] In short, their fees buy access to the Shadow Party and its resources.

During the 2004 campaign, America Coming Together claimed on its website to be running, "the largest voter contact program in history." America Coming Together coordinated, facilitated and provided foot soldiers for the Shadow Party's "ground war"—its grassroots voter mobilization drives, using manpower both from its own ranks and from its "partner" organizations in America Votes. America Coming Together claimed to employ over 1,400 full-time canvassers during the 2004 election cycle, as well as thousands of volunteers working from 55 offices throughout the battleground states. Its website boasted that the voters it mobilizes "will derail the right-wing Republican agenda by defeating George W. Bush and electing Democrats up and down the ticket."

In order to ensure that the voters it mobilized would cast their ballots only for Democrats, ACT canvassers focused on "swing" voters (which it defined as "pre-retirement women" and "younger voters," whom its website described as less likely to be politically informed than other demographic groups). It also targeted "Democratic base voters"—such as African-Americans and Hispanics—"who vote Democratic but need extra contact to persuade them to vote."

America Coming Together and its affiliate groups used intrusive, high-pressure tactics to register and mobilize voters, both by phone and by door-to-door canvassing. Not only did its canvassers register voters, but they compiled extensive personal dossiers on them—including such private information as their driver license numbers, social security numbers, and favored candidates in the election—information that could be retrieved on demand through canvassers' hand-held Palm Pilots. Follow-up was key to its get-out-the-vote strategy. According to its website, its canvassers extracted firm "promises" from individual voters, then followed up to make sure that "promises are kept."

ACT's website does not explain precisely how its canvassers went about enforcing the "promises" they exacted. However, the menacing demeanor of at least some ACT canvassers no doubt proved motivating to many voters. On 23 June 2004, the Associated Press revealed that an undetermined number of ACT's fulltime canvassers were felons, convicted for crimes that included burglary, assault and sex offenses.[39]

JOINT VICTORY CAMPAIGN 2004

Harold Ickes formed the Joint Victory Campaign 2004 on 5 November 2003—the same day that he also formed The Media Fund, which focuses on campaign messages. Joint Victory was the chief fundraising entity for the Democrat Shadow Party. A 527 committee, it was run jointly by America Coming Together and The Media Fund. Joint Victory collected contributions for these two groups and divided the money between them, whence the funds were disbursed further down the line, as needed. In 2004 alone, Joint Victory channeled more than $53 million into the Shadow Party network—$38.4 million to The Media Fund and $19.4 million to American Coming Together.

Since it was little more than a money conduit, Joint Victory drew less press attention than its sister organizations but surfaced briefly in a 5 February 2004 *Washington Post* editorial questioning the shadowy nature of its financial transactions.[40] The editorial noted that a mysterious 527 committee calling itself the Sustainable World Corporation had suddenly sprung into existence in Houston, Texas on 10 December 2003. Seven days later, it donated $3.1 million to Joint Victory Campaign 2004, which then divided the money between ACT and the Media Fund. The *Post* failed in its attempt to discover the source of the $3.1 million donation.[41]

When the *Post* called Harold Ickes, it was lucky enough to catch him in a candid and forthcoming mood—which is not his usual posture toward the press. Though under no legal obligation to answer the *Post*'s question, Ickes generously explained that Houston investor Linda Pritzker of the Chicago Hyatt hotel family was the mystery benefactor behind Sustainable World Corporation. "It's nice that Mr. Ickes answered. But a system that permits these kinds of huge donations to be made under a cloak of anonymity is deeply troubling," commented the *Post*. Janice Ann Enright—Ickes' partner in the Washington lobbying firm The Ickes and Enright Group—also acted as Treasurer for the Joint Victory Campaign 2004.

THE MEDIA FUND

While Malcolm, Glantz and Rosenthal were cobbling together the coalition of labor unions, pro-abortion activists and environmentalists which would later emerge as the Shadow Party's ground war operation, America Votes, Ickes sought to organize a message arm to conduct the campaign air war. He first informally called it a "presidential media fund"—a 527 committee that would raise money for campaign advertising for the anti-Bush presidential campaign. Unable to think of a catchy name, Ickes finally just settled on The Media Fund, launching it on 5 November 2003.

The Media Fund functions as an in-house campaign advertising agency for the Shadow Party. The Fund conceptualizes, produces and places political ads on television, and in print media and on the Internet. "The Media Fund is the largest media buying organization supporting a progressive message," says its website. Ickes explained to *New York Magazine* in a 28 June 2004 interview, "The goal of the Media Fund is to create, test, and then air ads that raise issues that we think are important in this election. . . . [However,] we are not in the business of electing or defeating candidates."[42] Ickes had to add that last sentence for legal purposes. Such paper-thin disclaimers form the Shadow Party's only bulwark against federal prosecution under the McCain-Feingold Act. Ickes' denial notwithstanding, electing and defeating candidates is of course The Media Fund's sole purpose.

The Media Fund was extremely active in creating and airing attack ads against President Bush in battleground states. It largely defined the message of the Kerry campaign. Drawing on top talent from Madison Avenue advertising firms, The Media Fund sought to convince Americans that President Bush was pursuing what its website called a "radical agenda," which has "given us a country less secure, a foreign policy in disarray, record job losses, deficits that mortgage our children's future, environmental policies that abandon common sense and attacks on civil liberties that undermine the very premise of our democracy."

The Media Fund received over $51.6 million in donations during the 2004 election cycle. Much of the money is hard to trace, however, since it was first laundered through Joint Victory Campaign 2004. Soros' money has doubtless found its way into the mix. Soros poured millions into Joint Victory Campaign 2004, as did close Soros associates Peter B. Lewis and Stephen Bing.

THE THUNDER ROAD GROUP

Launched in early 2004, The Thunder Road Group was the last of the Seven Sisters to appear, but arguably the most vital of the lot. The *Boston Globe* called Thunder Road the "nerve center" of the Shadow Party—its unofficial headquarters: "[The Thunder Road Group] is an operation unlike any other in politics, devising strategy, message, and public relations services for the 527s."[43]

A soup-to-nuts political consultancy, Thunder Road combined the roles of strategic planning, polling, opposition research, covert operations and public relations. It coordinated strategy for The Media Fund, America Coming Together and America Votes. Its founder Jim Jordan was frequently quoted in the press as a spokesman for other Seven Sister groups.

Jordan is an attorney long active in Washington as a Democrat spin doctor. Among other high-profile assignments, Jordan handled press relations for the Senate committee investigating DNC fundraising in 1997 and for the House Judiciary Committee during the Clinton impeachment. Riding the whirlwind of

Clinton-era scandals gave Jordan a zest for what he calls "intense political, hand-to-hand combat."[44]

Jordan attained his highest public profile when he served for nearly a year as John Kerry's campaign manager. This lasted from December 2002 to November 2003, when Kerry's sinking poll numbers led him to fire Jordan and his top staff and replace them with a team provided by his political patron Ted Kennedy. Mary Beth Cahill, Stephanie Cutter, Bob Shrum and other well-known Kennedy operatives quickly took control of the Kerry campaign. Former New Hampshire Governor Jeanne Shaheen, national chairwoman of Kerry's campaign, was credited with masterminding the putsch. *New York Times* columnist William Safire commented on Kerry's new chief, "Cahill has impeccable far-left credentials, from Emily's List fund-raising to Representative Barney Frank's staff."[45]

Less than a month passed before Harold Ickes and Ellen Malcolm recruited Jordan to handle publicity and strategy for the Shadow Party (specifically for The Media Fund, ACT and America Votes). In order to handle the growing volume of work pouring in from his newfound friends, Jordan launched his own company in early 2004. He named it Thunder Road after a Bruce Springsteen lyric: "It's a town full of losers, and I'm pulling out of here to win."

By the end of July, Jordan had already collected $1.7 million in consulting fees in addition to his $85,000 salary at that time.[46] Jordan's group was involved in "opposition research"—the term of art for dirt-digging among political consultants. Some reports indicate that Jordan's covert operations went beyond the garden variety of Washington smear-mongering. For instance, the *American Spectator* reported that Jordan may have helped stage-manage the media circus that disrupted the work of the 9-11 Commission, nearly bringing the investigation to a standstill.[47]

Even before Condoleezza Rice made her opening statement to the Commission, Thunder Road operatives began bombarding reporters with e-mails attempting to discredit her. The e-mails continued for the entire three hours that Rice testified. The *American Spectator* reported that a staffer for America Coming Together said, "We'd heard that [former National Counterterrorism Coordinator Richard] Clarke had some help with writing his testimony and in prepping for the questioning. . . . The rumor is that he ended up getting some help from Kerry's people, but indirectly through Thunder Road."[48]

Richard Clarke's testimony to the Commission later turned out to be rife with contradictions and misinformation, as the Commission's final report makes clear. If indeed the Thunder Road Group helped prepare that testimony, then it helped obstruct an investigation of grave importance to America's national security.

Why did Soros spend seven years and millions of dollars pushing a soft-money ban through Congress, only to turn around in 2004 and mount an equally ambitious effort—through the Shadow Party—to circumvent that ban and bankroll the John Kerry campaign? Many critics have accused Soros of "hypocrisy" for playing both sides of the McCain-Feingold fence. These critics misunderstand the subtlety of Soros' strategy.

By pushing McCain-Feingold through Congress, Soros cut off the Democrats' soft-money supply. By forming the Shadow Party, Soros offered the Democrats an alternate source—one which he personally controlled. As a result, the Democrats are now heavily—perhaps irretrievably—dependent on Soros. It seems reasonable to suppose that from its inception, campaign finance reform was a Soros power play to gain control of the Democratic Party.

With Ted Kennedy nearing retirement and the Kennedy clan

in overall decline, no dynasty of comparable wealth or ambition has stepped forward to lead the Democratic Party. George Soros may have his eye on the empty space. Soros was 72 years old when he launched the Shadow Party at his Southampton estate. He has five children, three by his first wife Annaliese and two by his second wife Susan. In September 2004, Soros effectively placed his two oldest sons in charge of his financial empire. Robert Soros, then 41, and Jonathan Soros, then 34, officially took over the day-to-day investment decisions of Soros Fund Management, as its chief investment officer and deputy chairman respectively.[49]

Robert and Jonathan have also followed their father into politics. As we have already mentioned, Jonathan Soros is a MoveOn.org activist, a financial sponsor of MoveOn, and a contributor to other Shadow Party groups. His brother Robert is focusing, for the time being, on state-level politics. Robert and his wife Melissa gave $100,000 to the New York State Democratic Campaign Committee in 2004. "I live in New York and understand the importance of state government," Robert explained to the *New York Post*.[50]

A cover story for the *New York Times Magazine* of 25 July 2004—on the very eve of the Democratic Convention's opening ceremonies in Boston—provided a glimpse of the Soros-related tidal force now sweeping the destinies of Democrats and their Party in its wake. The story, written by Matt Bai, was titled, "Wiring the Vast Left-wing Conspiracy." It might just as well have been called, "The Democratic Party is Dead—Long Live the Shadow Party!" for that was what its contents conveyed.[51]

"As Democrats converge on Boston this week to hold their party convention and formally anoint Kerry as their nominee, all the talk will be of resurgence, unity and a new sense of purpose. Don't be fooled," wrote Bai. "The Democratic Party of the machine age, so long dominant in American politics, could be holding its own Irish wake near Boston's North End. The power is already shifting—not just within the party, but away from it altogether."

Bai described the collapse of traditional Democrat power: "Since the 1950s, when nearly half of all voters called themselves Democrats, nearly one in six Democrats has left the party, according to a University of Michigan study, while Republican membership has held close to steady.... The Democratic Party has seen an exodus of the white working-class men who were once their most reliable voters. In the suburbs . . . the percentage of white men supporting the party has plummeted 16 points just since Bill Clinton left office. . . . [Democrats] have spent most of the last decade in the minority, and during that time they have never enjoyed a majority of more than a single vote."[52] Bai summed up the damage: "Thirty years ago, Democrats could claim outright control of 37 state legislatures, compared with only 4 for Republicans; Democrats now control just 17." Democratic strategist Pat Caddell agreed: "The deterioration is steady, and it's spreading like a cancer. So much for thinking that if we could just go back to the glorious 90s, the party would be fine. The 90s were our worst decade since the 1920s."

According to Bai, the last best hope for "progressive" politics in America lay in what he called the "vast left-wing conspiracy," by which he means the network of independent, non-profit issue groups controlled by Soros, Ickes and their allies: the Shadow Party.

The Shadow Party's independence, however, is a double-edged sword for Democrats. On the one hand, it allows Democrats to circumvent the law, by delegating what amounts to a new form of "soft-money" fundraising to an outside entity. On the other hand, the same process makes the Democratic Party so dependent on the entity that some Shadow Party operatives on the left were asking the question whether they even needed the Democrats at all. Why not form a Third Party?

"This is like post-Yugoslavia. We used to have a strongman called the party. After McCain-Feingold, we dissolved the power of Tito," exulted Soros supporter and former Sixties radical Andrew Stern, president of the Service Employees International Union (SEIU), which spent $64 million to beat Bush in 2004. Shadow Party co-founder Harold Ickes extolled the activist spirit that MoveOn.org's online activists brought to political organizing. He told Bai, "When you go out and talk to them, people are much more interested in something like MoveOn.org than in the Democratic Party. It has cachet. There is no cachet in the Democratic Party. MoveOn raised a million dollars for a bunch of Texas state senators, man. Plus their bake sale. If they continue with their cachet and really interest people and focus their people on candidates—boy, that's a lot of leverage. No party can do that. And what the political ramifications of that are. . . ." Ickes' voice trailed off. He shrugged. "Who knows?"

Bai's article shined a spotlight on the rising Young Turks of the Shadow Party such as Silicon Valley entrepreneur Andrew Rappaport and Jonathan Soros. According to Bai, these young leftists "have come to view progressive politics as a market in need of entrepreneurship, served poorly by a giant monopoly—the Democratic Party." The solution? "People like Andy Rappaport and Jonathan Soros might succeed in revitalizing progressive politics—while at the same time destroying what we now call the Democratic Party."

SEIU leader Andrew Stern agreed with Bai. Despite the $64 million he poured into the Kerry campaign, Stern seemed oddly apathetic toward the party Kerry represents. "There is an incredible opportunity to have the infrastructure for a third party," he told Bai. "Anyone who could mobilize these groups would have the Democratic Party infrastructure, and they wouldn't need the Democratic Party." It would be a radical dream come true.

What exactly would a third party—guided by George Soros and his radicals—seek to accomplish that today's Democrats cannot or will not? The possibilities are both limitless and disturbing. In the past, Bai explains, contributions to the Democratic Party simply vanished down a black hole, to be spent as Party leaders saw fit. The independent issue groups allow "ideological donors" such as George and Jonathan Soros to apply their money to specific projects which enable them to shape Party goals and strategy—or to by-pass the Party altogether and form a new electoral force.

New Democrat Network president Simon Rosenberg told Bai that independent groups would be free to attack ideological foes with a forcefulness mainstream Democrats would never dare display. Insurgents such as Rosenberg are looking for a "more defiant kind of politics," that confronts head-on the "sharp ideological divide between them and the Rush Limbaugh right," notes Bai.

In the final analysis, the movers and shakers of the Shadow Party may or may not decide to go it alone, forming a Progressive Party to the left of the Democrats as the Communists did in 1948 behind the candidacy of Henry Wallace (Wallace lost and the Progressive Party disintegrated after a pitiful showing in the 1952 elections). The defiant statements to Matt Bai, on the other hand, might merely have been shots across the bow—warnings to Democrat moderates to take the Shadow Party and its left-wing agenda seriously, or risk a devastating party split. Either way, the Shadow Party emerged as a winner from the 2004 campaign as a force that is here to stay. It has created a new power base for the Left, independent of the mainstream party apparatus—a leverage point from which to drive the party—and the nation's politics—in an ever-more-radical direction.

It seems unlikely that further changes in the campaign finance laws will hamper the Shadow Party's operations any more than did the original McCain-Feingold Act. Senators McCain and Feingold have been instruments of Soros' campaign finance movement since at least 1994. From the beginning, they have faithfully echoed Soros' line and played by Soros' rules. He has nothing to fear from them. Every new law they promulgate leaves a multitude of loopholes, which the Shadow Party is well-equipped to exploit.

On 6 April 2006, for instance, the US House of Representatives approved new rules for 527s limiting individual donations to $25,000 per year for get-out-the-vote efforts and $5,000 per year for support of particular candidates. The bill would bar unions and corporations altogether from donating to 527s. Senators McCain and Feingold have proposed a similar measure in the Senate. In short, it is reasonably certain that the next time the Shadow Party goes into action, 527 committees will no longer serve as its primary fundraising vehicles.

It is unclear how these reforms will affect the Seven Sisters groups previously described, but they will certainly not harm the Shadow Party as a whole. Harold Ickes says he intends to keep the Media Fund running, and Soros contributed $500,000 to America Votes on 25 November 2005. Meanwhile, Soros' minions are already developing new instruments to fill the gap left by the 527s. For example, 501(c)(4)s.

In David Soares' election as Albany county district attorney as described in Chapter 3, a Soros-funded group called the Drug Policy Alliance Network gave $81,500 to his campaign. The

Network donated this money indirectly, giving it to an ACORN front called the Working Families Party, which thereupon passed the money to the candidate's organization.

When the scandal first surfaced, Soares' opponents accused the Drug Policy Alliance Network of exceeding the $5,000 cap on corporate donations in New York State. This seemed a logical objection, inasmuch as the Drug Policy Alliance Network is a corporation and its donation of $81,500 exceeds the maximum of $5,000 by approximately sixteen-fold. In his defense, the Network's executive director Ethan Nadelmann argued that his organization was not bound by New York State's corporate donation cap since his Drug Policy Alliance Network was registered as a 501(c)(4).[53] Under federal law, 501(c)(4)s have no contribution limits and no disclosure requirements regarding donors. The New York State Supreme Court accepted Nadelmann's argument, thus setting a precedent for future elections.[54] Armed with a favorable court ruling, the Shadow Party will almost certainly use 501(c)(4)s as its new vehicle for unlimited political fundraising, on the local, state and federal level.

Some Shadow Party operations are being transferred to private, for-profit companies. For instance, Harold Ickes announced on 8 March 2006 that he is launching a new company called Data Warehouse, with financial backing from Soros. According to the *Washington Post*, Ickes' company will "compile huge amounts of data on Americans to identify Democratic voters." Its database will "allow political field operatives" to "tailor messages to individual voters and households" and "home in on precisely the voters they wish to reach." By tapping into "the growing volume of data available from government files and consumer marketing firms," as well as conducting its own surveys, Ickes' firm will compile such information on voters as, "the kind of magazines they receive, whether they own guns, the churches they attend, their incomes, their charitable contributions and their voting histories." Ickes will sell this information initially to "politically active unions," and "liberal interest groups," he says.

The *Post* notes that "Washington operatives" are speculating that Ickes "is acting to build a campaign resource for a possible 2008 presidential run by Hillary Clinton." Ickes and Hillary have both expressed dissatisfaction with the Democratic Party's existing voter database. "It's unclear what the DNC is doing. Is it going to be kept up to date?" says Ickes, noting that an out-of-date database is "worse than having no database at all."[55] This is but one more step in the Shadow Party's displacement of the Democratic Party itself.

While some of its institutional components are changing, the Shadow Party's lines of authority remain as clear as they were when the network was first assembled at Soros' El Mirador estate in Southampton. All lines of authority lead to Soros. Concealing this fact has become a high priority of the new order. At some point during the 2004 campaign, its spin doctors appear to have realized that they had an image problem that would not go away. As one hostile columnist put it, "Soros' gaunt visage, thousand-yard stare, thick Central European accent, levitating gray hair and megalomaniacal pronouncements weirdly echo those of the 'Dr. Strangelove' character in Stanley Kubrick's 1964 Cold War classic."[56] However one might critique the Soros persona, there was no question that having a world-famous billionaire at its center was not the best way to present a movement for "reform."

Sensitive to the problem, Shadow Party operatives have gone out of their way to deny connections to the kingfish or his billions. When David Horowitz accused *Media Matters'* David Brock of being a Soros operative, Brock's website posted a disclaimer the very next day, stating, "To date, neither *Media Matters* nor its president and CEO David Brock has received any money from Soros or from any organization with which he is affiliated." This was untrue. The Center for American Progress helped launch *Media Matters*, contributing money, free office space and other material assistance. Not only was the Center launched with $3 million of Soros seed money, but its co-founder, Morton Halperin, also serves as director of US advocacy for Soros' Open Society Institute. Another Soros-funded outfit that contributed generously to Brock's startup is MoveOn.org.[57] When confronted with these facts by Cybercast News Service, *Media Matters* backpedaled and e-mailed a revised disclaimer, which read, "*Media Matters for America* has never received funding directly from George Soros."[58]

The revised disclaimer may or may not be true, but either way, it is irrelevant. Albany county district attorney David Soares can also say that he never received $81,500 "directly" from George Soros nor even from anyone funded by Soros, since Soros cohort Ethan Nadelmann laundered his contribution through the Working Families Party. All the same, no one in New York has any doubt about who is pulling David Soares' strings, nor should anyone doubt who provides David Brock with his marching orders.

The habit of implausible denial, of course, begins with Soros himself. He has repeatedly claimed a distaste for politics, and announced his imminent departure from political activism, only to turn up later pouring more money into Shadow Party organizations. After an interview with him in July 2004, *New York Times* reporter Matt Bai wrote, "Strangely, for someone who is supposedly staging a hostile takeover of an entire party, Soros said he is only nominally a Democrat, and he evidenced an obvious distaste for the business of politics. 'I hate this kind of political advertising,' he said at one point, complaining about the anti-Bush attack ads he had paid for. 'I always hated it, but now that I've sort of been involved in it, I hate it more.' Soros said his only goal is to get rid of Bush, whom he believes is endangering American democracy. After that, he said, he didn't expect to continue meddling in politics at all, and in fact, he seemed eager to be rid of it."[59]

Even more preposterously, Soros claimed in October 2005, "I am a political neophyte. . . . This is not my strength. I'm eager to get out of this partisan position that I'm pigeonholed into. I heartily dislike it. I've always been against dividing the world into 'us' versus 'them.' So this 'us'-versus-'them' campaign is very uncomfortable for me."[60] This from the man who had made it his life mission to defeat George Bush, called the President "a danger to the world," and characterized his struggle against Bush as "a matter of life and death." One month after expressing his eagerness to leave "partisan" politics behind him, Soros donated half a million dollars to America Votes, the umbrella group that coordinates all other groups in the Shadow Party in their political campaigns. Three months after that, Soros announced that, together with Peter Lewis, Rob Glaser and other Shadow Party donors, he would lead a multimillion-dollar bailout of the ailing and highly partisan Air America Radio Network, which was specifically designed by liberals ("us") to counter Rush Limbaugh and conservative talk radio ("them").[61] When George Soros has an idea to sell or an agenda to explain, the prudential rule is *caveat emptor*.

11

GOING GLOBAL

When Soros announced his crusade against George Bush in the *Washington Post* of 11 November 2003, he said that ousting Bush from the White House "is the central focus of my life . . . a matter of life and death."[1] So excited were media commentators at the prospect of Soros writing checks for the Democrats, that few stopped to consider, much less worry about, the wildly overheated language Soros had employed. Was defeating George Bush really a matter of "life and death?" Did Soros really believe that? And, if so, what did he mean by it?

Soros answered that question in an updated preface to the 2003 edition of his book *The Alchemy of Finance*. In it, Soros admitted that his greatest fear was that the Bush Doctrine would succeed—that Bush would crush the terrorists, tame the rogue states of the Axis of Evil, and usher in a golden age of what Soros calls "American supremacy." While insisting that "the concept" of "American supremacy" is "flawed" and bound to "fail in the long run," Soros nevertheless admits that it might succeed in the short run, and he dreads the possibility. "What I am afraid of is that the pursuit of American supremacy may be successful for a while because the United States in fact enjoys a dominant position in the world today."[2]

The reason Soros fears US victory in the War on Terror is that such a victory would end the current crisis—that is, the national security crisis that began with the terror attacks of 11 September 2001. Like Richard Cloward and Francis Fox Piven, Soros has a radical vision of how America—and the global community—

should change. Like them, he understands that the best time to implement radical change is during times of upheaval. The exploitation of crisis is central to Soros' strategic thinking. "Usually it takes a crisis to prompt a meaningful change in direction," Soros wrote in his 2000 book *Open Society*.[3]

When the Asian currency crisis erupted in 1997, Soros thought that his opportunity had come, and dashed off what he described as an "instant book," *The Crisis of Global Capitalism*, released in 1998, in which he predicted the imminent collapse of the global financial system. Soros pointed to the financial turmoil that had swept through Asia "like a wrecking ball," impoverishing the once-mighty Asian Tigers, forcing Russia into default, and pushing the giant US hedge fund Long-Term Capital Management to the brink of bankruptcy. All of this was bad enough, but worse lay ahead, Soros warned. As the "contagion" of collapsing credit spread around the globe, it would ultimately strike America, producing a "recession," followed by a long, lingering and intractable "depression." Soros fretted that financiers like himself were largely to blame, for they had allowed greed to overwhelm their humanity. "The (global capitalist) system is deeply flawed," he wrote. "As long as capitalism remains triumphant, the pursuit of money overrides all other social considerations."[4]

Needless to say, the book got a mixed reception from many economists and financial reviewers who had previously admired Soros. However, his book did find some admirers on the Left. Reporting in the *South China Morning Post*, Hong Kong's English-language newspaper, Greg Torode recounted a conversation with a certain "Vietnamese Communist Party cadre" who preferred to remain anonymous. Torode writes, "It is an odd experience to hear a solid Vietnamese Communist Party cadre quoting George Soros and Karl Marx in the same argument, but it is starting to happen.

'The concerns Mr. Soros is raising can be found in our long-standing ideology,' one old party friend said over bitter Vietnamese tea as he digested the commentary springing from the fund manager's latest work, *The Crisis of Global Capitalism.* 'Pure capitalism is not enough. A new way must be found if we are to survive,' he continued, surrounded by rows of mouldering party tracts in the shade of an old Hanoi villa. 'Here,' he said, blowing dust off one ancient volume. 'I believe it is known as the post-capitalist phase. Pure capitalism has proved ineffective. Marx knew this all along. This Soros is not so stupid.'"[5]

Suddenly Soros was everywhere, hawking his book on major talk shows and calling for new planet-wide regulatory bodies capable of restraining the destructive impulses of global investors such as himself. The *New York Times* reported on 14 November 1998 that, coincidentally or not, in response to the growing worldwide recession, President "Clinton has proposed a 'third way' between capitalism and socialism."[6] At this point, most Americans were too distracted by the Monica Lewinsky scandal to notice the revelation concerning Clinton's economic plans, but whatever his intentions, he never got a chance to implement them. Much to the surprise of Soros and other Wall Street Cassandras, the US economy proved resilient. Frightened investors from many nations poured their money into US assets, transforming America into a haven of prosperity in the economic storm.

The crisis passed with no further talk of jettisoning capitalism—at least for the time being. "So will it be business as usual in 1999?" Soros asked acidly in a *Financial Times* op-ed of 4 January 1999. "The recent dramatic volatility in financial markets is but a distant memory. The miseries of Russians and Indonesians seem far away. But the global financial system still has fundamental flaws. Unless these problems are addressed and we learn the lessons of the past year, the system is liable to collapse."[7] No one listened. The crisis had passed, and with it Soros' moment of opportunity. It had not lasted long enough, nor frightened people badly enough, to ensure their cooperation. Promoters of the "Third Way"—and of other radical schemes for reforming the world financial system—would have to wait for another opportunity.

"The richest 1 percent of the world's population receive as much as the poorest 57 percent," Soros laments in his 2002 book *George Soros on Globalization.*[8] Closing the gap between rich and poor nations will require putting curbs on what Soros calls "global capitalism." Particularly egregious, in Soros' view, is the effect of global capitalism on social security. The free flow of capital across borders reduces "the ability of the state to provide social security to its citizens," he argues.[9]

In one respect, Soros is correct. Tax-based, pay-as-you-go social security systems of the sort that Otto von Bismarck introduced in Germany in 1889 and Franklin Delano Roosevelt brought to America in 1935 require massive taxation of working people in order to support those who are not working. In a high-tech, global marketplace, people in the upper tax brackets quickly learn to shelter their earnings from the tax collector through such expediencies as investing in offshore derivatives markets. Self-serving actions of this sort threaten the entire concept of a pay-as-you-go social safety net. As long as taxpayers can hide their assets from the government, no country can possibly collect enough taxes to provide cradle-to-grave security for its underclass. As Soros puts it, "The globalization of financial markets has rendered the welfare state that came into existence after World War II obsolete because the people who require a social safety net cannot leave the country, but the capital the welfare state used to tax can."[10]

Soros' solution to this problem is to turn the entire planet into a giant welfare state. In order to squeeze the necessary taxes from today's globalized investor class, Soros calls for the creation of global institutions with the authority to track down and confiscate capital from anyone, anywhere in the world. To this end, Soros recommends the formation of what he calls an Open Society Alliance, a global network of likeminded nations, corporations and NGOs that would operate first within the framework of the United Nations, but would later replace the UN, taking on all its current functions and more. According to Soros, this Open Society Alliance would employ various sorts of "carrots and sticks" to keep its members in line.[11] "It would offer incentives where possible but would not shy away from enforcement where necessary," he writes.[12]

The engine of Soros' Open Society Alliance would be what he calls "a kind of international central bank," operating under the auspices of the International Monetary Fund. Soros has proposed calling this new bank the International Credit Insurance Corporation.[13] It would facilitate the global redistribution of wealth by making loans to poor countries that would be guaranteed by rich countries.[14] The bank would even have the ability to issue its own global currency, denominated in SDRs or "Special Drawing Rights," which Soros aptly describes as a kind of "artificial money" currently used by IMF member nations to make payments to each other.[15]

The obvious problem for Soros' vision of a global welfare state is that free-minded Americans will resist it. Americans remember the social and economic destruction wrought by 40 years of Great Society entitlements. Having finally closed the door on the 40-year catastrophe that was the American welfare state, why would Americans support a plan to make the welfare state global? What could possibly induce them to undertake yet another massive experiment in socialist redistribution, this time on a global scale? Soros has an answer: terrorism.

In the 1960s, with America's inner cities exploding into violence, the architects of Lyndon Johnson's Great Society argued that the best way to stop the rioting would be to pump money into the ghettos. Soros is advancing a globalized version of the same argument: that the best way to fight terrorism is to pump money into impoverished regions of the world where terrorism tends to flourish.

In his 2002 book *George Soros on Globalization*, Soros explains that, in a global capitalist system such as ours, which concentrates wealth and power in the hands of a few, we must expect that some "people may rebel against the system" by forming groups such as al-Qaeda. Rather than "repressing" such rebellions after the fact, Soros recommends "removing the root causes" of terrorism, such as "poverty, ignorance" and the like.[16] This will cost money, of course. Soros' new global bank will provide that money, and people like Soros will decide how to put that money to use, channeling much of it into lucrative "public/private partnerships" in troubled parts of the world.[17] In fact, it is precisely through the manipulation of such "public/private partnerships" that Soros became the 28th richest man in America. Small wonder that he would wish to expand and empower the global lending system that he spent his entire career learning how to exploit. Soros knows better than most the multitude of opportunities a global welfare state could provide for global social workers like himself to do well by doing "good."

In some of its parts, *George Soros on Globalization* reads like a resumé, in which Soros argues that his qualifications uniquely suit him to play a personal role in implementing the global programs he proposes. Regarding his call for a reorganization of international financial and trade institutions, Soros writes, "I believe I have some unusual qualifications for this project. I have been a successful practitioner in global financial markets, giving me an insider's view of how they operate. More to the point, I have been actively engaged in trying to make the world a better place. I have set up a network of foundations devoted to the concept of open society. I believe that the global capitalist system in its present form is a distortion of what ought to be a global open society. I am only one of many experts on financial markets, but my active concern with the future of humanity sets me apart from others."[18]

The 9/11 attacks occurred while Soros was still writing *George Soros on Globalization*. The book was published in March 2002, while bodies were still being unearthed from Ground Zero. Hence, in that book, Soros presents his thoughts on the 9/11 attacks with a freshness and candor missing from his later statements. Above all, the reader comes to understand that Soros views the 9/11 attacks as an opportunity. Throughout the book, he expresses repeatedly his hope that the attacks may serve to convince the American people of the need for a global welfare state. Soros writes, "September 11 has shocked the people of the United States into realizing that others may regard them very differently from the way they see themselves. They are more ready to reassess the world and the role that the United States plays in it than in normal times. This provides an unusual opportunity to rethink and reshape the world more profoundly than would have been possible prior to September 11."[19]

On the same page, Soros states that, thanks to the terror attacks, "The present moment is auspicious for gaining a hearing" for his concept of a world reserve bank capable of issuing "artificial money" in the form of SDRs (Special Drawing Rights).[20]

Indeed, Soros made a strong pitch for this proposal in his Hong Kong speech of 19 September 2001, only eight days after the 9/11 attacks—the same speech, quoted in Chapter 1, in which he argued against invading Afghanistan, and called on America to refrain, in general, from military retaliation against the terrorists. In that speech, Soros made essentially the same proposal for a new world reserve bank that he has been making at regular intervals since 1997, though he now couched his arguments in the language of a post-9/11 world. Soros said:

> [I]t is not enough to fight terrorism, we must also address the social conditions that provide a fertile ground from which volunteers who are willing to sacrifice their lives can be recruited. And, here, I think I do have something to contribute to the debate. . . . I propose issuing Special Drawing Rights or SDRs that the rich countries would pledge for the purpose of providing international assistance. This is an initiative that could make a substantial amount of money available almost immediately. . . . If the scheme is successfully tested, it should be followed by an annual issue of SDRs and the amounts could be scaled up so that they could have a meaningful impact on many of our most pressing social issues. This is the cornerstone of my plan. . . . Improving social conditions will not prevent people like Bin Laden from exercising their evil genius. But it will help to alleviate the grievances on which extremism of all kinds feeds.[21]

In his speech, Soros revealed that his plan was already in motion. In order to implement it, he needed three things: 1) Ratification by an 85 percent supermajority of the member states of the International Monetary Fund, 2) approval by the US Congress, and 3) approval by the president of the United States. In

Hong Kong, Soros announced that IMF "[m]embers having 71 percent of the total vote needed for implementation have already ratified the decision. All it needs is the approval of the United States Congress. I propose that President Bush introduce and Congress approve a special allocation of SDRs and all the richer members of the IMF pledge to donate their SDRs for the alleviation of poverty and other approved objectives."[22]

Soros surely realized that President Bush had more pressing matters on his mind eight days after the 9/11 attacks. However, Soros was determined to strike while the iron was hot. And the iron had never been hotter, in Soros' estimation. In his book *George Soros on Globalization*, he wrote, "After 11 September, the American public has become more aware than before that what happens in the rest of the world can affect them directly and there are important foreign policy decisions to be made. *This awareness may not last long, and I am determined not to let the moment pass.*" [emphasis added][23]

Soros was proposing nothing less than a global war on poverty. Not coincidentally, the machinery for such a project was already grinding into gear, under the auspices of the United Nations. Even as Soros wrote, his dream was becoming a reality. The question one must ask, as always, is: what's in it for Soros?

When Lyndon Johnson launched his War on Poverty in 1964, he appointed Sargent Shriver "poverty czar" to run it. Shriver decided who would get the billions of federal dollars allocated to the program. Large portions of the billions in poverty funds found their way into the hands of radical activists such as George Wiley, Saul Alinsky and Wade Rathke, who used the money to fund strikes, demonstrations, protests, riots, and actions against the Vietnam War, as well as the building of a permanent, radical infrastructure in America, all at taxpayer expense.

Now the Shadow Party looks forward to a new round of public funding, which it can use to bankroll radical activists all over the world—once again, under the guise of fighting poverty. In September 2000, the United Nations officially declared war on poverty. It aims to cut desperate poverty in half by the year 2015. The UN will take from the haves and give to the have-nots. It has asked the richest nations of the world to contribute 0.7 percent of their Gross National Product each year, for a ten-year period, from 2005 to 2015. That averages out to about $235 billion per year, of which the United States would contribute about 60 percent, or $140 billion annually.[24] Who will dole out this vast sum of money? Who is the poverty czar? He is Jeffrey Sachs, Columbia University economist, long-time Soros associate and Shadow Party operative.

This is the same Jeffrey Sachs, formerly of Harvard University, whom George Soros hired to implement "shock therapy" programs in Poland and Russia, as described in Chapter 5. Sachs left Harvard in July 2002 to direct the Earth Institute at Columbia University. As noted in Chapter 5, Sachs earlier resigned as president of the Harvard Institute for International Development in May 1999, just as US Justice Department investigators were closing the noose on his corrupt Russian assistance program. Sachs claimed that he knew nothing of the epic pilferage perpetrated by his "development" team in Russia. We have no reason to doubt his word. However, as president of the Harvard Institute, Dr. Sachs surely should have paid closer attention to what his people were doing. Whatever his merits as an economist, Sachs does not inspire confidence as an administrator. He is not the sort of person one should entrust with the disbursement of $235 billion in foreign aid funds per year. Yet that is exactly what UN Secretary-General Kofi Annan has hired him to do.

After the UN General Assembly declared war on poverty on 8 September 2000, Secretary-General Kofi Annan created the United Nations Millennium Project to implement the program. He appointed Jeffrey Sachs as its director, placing him at the helm of what the *Canada Free Press* has called, "the largest global wealth redistribution program ever conceived."[25]

Following the 9/11 attacks, promoters of the UN's war on poverty began touting the Millennium Project as the best antidote to terrorism. "It's time to step up the global war on poverty," urged former Clinton advisor Laura D'Andrea Tyson in a *Business Week* article of 3 December 2001.[26] Like Soros, Tyson presented the UN Millennium Project as an anti-terror initiative, which would attack the root cause of terrorism: poverty. "As the war on terrorism has unfolded," she wrote, "Americans have been reminded once more that we live in a world of unprecedented opulence and remarkable deprivation, a world so interconnected that poverty and despair in a remote region can harbor a network of terrorism dedicated to our destruction. In such a world, our prosperity and freedom at home increasingly depend on the successful development of countries like Afghanistan. . . ."[27] Tyson went on to plug George Soros by name, promoting his plan to issue "artificial money," denominated in Special Drawing Rights or SDRs, in order to fund anti-poverty programs.[28]

Jeffrey Sachs also weighed in after the 9/11 attacks, hewing closely to the Shadow Party line. "The most important step is to avoid war . . . ," he wrote in September 2001. "The biggest mistake would be to launch a war in response to a terrorist attack. . . ." Instead, Sachs counseled America to "wake up from two decades of insufficient attention to the urgent needs of the world's poorest nations."[29] Elaborating in his 2005 book *The End of Poverty*, Sachs wrote, "Whether terrorists are rich or poor or middle-class, their staging areas—their bases of operation—are unstable societies beset by poverty, unemployment, rapid population growth, hunger, and lack of hope. Without addressing the root causes of that instability, little will be accomplished in stanching terror."[30]

Just as President Johnson's poverty warriors sought to quell black riots by buying off urban militant groups with federal grants, Sachs proposed pouring money into the world's hotspots, including those ruled by corrupt, tyrannical, anti-American regimes. Speaking before the Counsel on Foreign Relations in March 2006, Sachs said, "Every day we're threatening someone else with an aid cut-off. . . . This is what we tried to do in Haiti for 20 years: put on the spigot, turn off the spigot. Put it on and turn it off. Put it on and turn it off until the place is so unbelievably desperate [there are] no jobs, no incomes, no nothing. . . . [I]f you're turning this on and off, you never get development . . . you just get instability."[31]

Sachs proposes instead that we turn on the spigot and leave it on, no matter how badly the recipient country behaves. The more money we pump into a corrupt country, Sachs implies, the less corrupt it will become. "Africa's governance is poor because Africa is poor," he wrote.[32]

Just how much bad behavior Sachs is willing to tolerate from foreign aid recipients became clear in January 2006, when Hamas, a terrorist group dedicated to the annihilation of Israel, won a majority in the Palestinian parliament. Sachs argued in a column that the West should continue bankrolling the Palestinian Authority, even under Hamas rule. "Almost daily the United States and Europe brandish threats to impose economic sanctions . . . ," he wrote. "The most recent threats are towards the new Hamas-led government in Palestine. . . . Such tactics are misguided. . . . [C]utting aid is likely to increase turmoil. . . . A newly elected

Palestinian government should be treated, at least initially, with legitimacy."³³

These remarks raise the possibility that the Millenium Project would fund terrorists. The problem does not stop with Hamas. Funding political radicals is, in fact, a stated goal of Sachs' Millennium Project. In *The End of Poverty* he announces his intention to help "raise the voice of the poor." Sachs writes, "Mahatma Gandhi and Martin Luther King Jr. did not wait for the rich and powerful to come to their rescue. They asserted their call to justice and made their stand in the face of official arrogance and neglect. The poor cannot wait for the rich to issue the call to justice."³⁴ Therefore, Sachs will help them "issue the call."

In *The End of Poverty*, Sachs states that, after 9/11, "we needed to address the deeper roots of terrorism in societies . . . that are misused and abused by the rich world, as have been the oil states of the Middle East."³⁵ Sachs castigates "neoconservatives" for instigating the invasion of Iraq and accuses the United States of entering Iraq not "as a liberator, but rather as an occupier."³⁶

Since ascending to the post of global poverty czar, Sachs has carried on a non-stop campaign of recrimination against the United States—and against George W. Bush personally—accusing America of "grossly irresponsible neglect of the world's poor"³⁷ and excoriating it as "the developed world's stingiest donor."³⁸ Sachs is angry that America has failed to cough up the annual payment of 0.7 percent of its GNP, which he claims this country owes to his Millennium Project.

Actually, America owes nothing to Sachs or his program. It has entered no binding agreement to participate in the UN's global war on poverty. Each time America was pressed to join the program, it declined, agreeing only to a general expression of support. US diplomats wisely refrained from making any sort of binding commitment to a program whose expense was stratospheric and whose administrative vehicle, the United Nations, was notoriously corrupt. The Bush administration promised only to raise development aid to 0.15 percent of America's GNP, which it did in 2003.[39] A Shadow Party president, on the other hand, might yield to Sachs' demands, with or without a binding agreement.

Thus has Soros operative Jeffrey Sachs emerged as the new poverty czar, not of America alone, but of the world. Americans did not want the McCain-Feingold Act, but got it anyway. We did not particularly want the Motor-Voter law, but now we live with its results. We did not ask for a Global War on Poverty, yet we are getting one all the same. These are the instruments and products of Shadow Party rule.

12

VELVET
REVOLUTIONS

I n the pursuit of his utopia, Soros makes his own rules. He is not deterred by laws or governments that frustrate his designs. He will not hesitate to seek the forcible overthrow of governments he has decided are oppressive or unjust. He is a manipulator of all available means. He will pursue revolution from above, but also revolution from below, by whatever means are necessary. "Working with the government may be more productive, but working in countries whose government is hostile may be even more rewarding," explained Soros in *The Bubble of American Supremacy*. In hostile countries, he explained, "it is important to support civil society to keep the flame of freedom alive. By resisting government interference, the foundation may be able to alert the population that the government is abusing its authority."[1]

Keeping the "flame of freedom alive" and "resisting government interference" can take many forms—from importing unauthorized Xerox copiers, as he famously did in Hungary in 1984, to paying armies of tens of thousands of activists to take to the streets. Soros refers to such subversive operations as "mobilizing civil society." Whether by accident or design, Soros-funded protests have, at some times and in some parts of the world, taken distinctly violent turns.

On the positive side, Soros helped bankroll the "velvet revolution" that hastened the fall of a dying Communist regime and catapulted dissident playwright Vaclav Havel to the presidency of the Czech Republic in 1989. To this day, people throughout the former Soviet bloc often use the term "velvet revolution" to denote Soros-sponsored coups.[2] The term "color revolution" has also been applied to Soros' subventions because in at least three recent cases the rebels identified themselves with a color or flower, a red rose in Georgia, the color orange in Ukraine, and a yellow tulip in Kyrgyzstan. These episodes, which took place in the years 2003, 2004 and 2005 respectively, were called the Rose Revolution, the Orange Revolution and the Tulip or Yellow Revolution.

From the Solidarity movement in Poland in the 1980s to the failed effort to oust Belarusian president Alexander Lukashenko in March 2006, Soros' hidden hand has been at work in many upheavals in the former Soviet bloc. But the fall of Communism did not bring an end to Soros' programs of subversion, nor seem to lessen their pace. "My foundations contributed to democratic regime change in Slovakia in 1998, Croatia in 1999, and Yugoslavia in 2000, mobilizing civil society to get rid of Vladimir Meciar, Franjo Tudjman, and Slobodan Milosevic, respectively," Soros boasts.[3]

In devising his strategy for these mobilizations, Soros drew on the teachings of former Harvard University political scientist Gene Sharp. Imprisoned for nine months as a conscientious objector during the Korean War, Sharp later served as secretary to A.J. Muste, a self-proclaimed Christian pacifist who had been a co-founder of the Trotskyist Workers Party of America. Sharp developed practical methods for toppling governments without resort to arms, and in several works, including *The Politics of Non-violent Action* and *Waging Nonviolent Struggle,* established himself as a leading thinker on the mechanics of regime change through direct action. He founded the Boston-based Albert Einstein Institution in 1983 to promote his direct action techniques and collaborated with Soros in orchestrating Ukraine's

Orange Revolution and ousting Milosevic in the aftermath of the NATO intervention.⁴

The key to defeating a hostile government, Sharp taught, was to undermine its ability to fight its opponents. This was a slow process, requiring patient infiltration of strategic departments of the target government, especially the police, military and intelligence communities. By this means, the target regime could ultimately "be coerced, in the sense that their peoples, armies, and resources will no longer perform well enough to keep them in power . . ." wrote Peter Ackerman and Christopher Kruegler, two Sharp disciples, in their book *Strategic Nonviolent Conflict: The Dynamics of People Power in the Twentieth Century.*⁵

Soros' velvet revolutions closely followed Sharp's model, proceeding through steady infiltration, using humanitarian aid missions as his vehicles of choice. In a 1996 speech, Croatian president Franjo Tudjman described how this process unfolded in his country: "[Soros and his allies] have spread their tentacles throughout the whole of our society. Soros . . . had approval to . . . gather and distribute humanitarian aid. . . . However, we . . . allowed them to do almost whatever they wanted. . . . They have involved in their network . . . people of all ages and classes—from secondary school pupils and students to journalists, university lecturers and academics—trying to win them over by financial aid. These are people from all walks of life, from the cultural, economic, scientific, medical, legal and journalistic sphere. . . . [Their aim is] control of all spheres of life . . . setting up a state within a state. . . ."⁶

Tudjman vowed to root out Soros' operatives, but died of stomach cancer before he could finish the purge. A Soros-approved "velvet government" under President Stipe Mesic took power in January 2000.

Soros' approach to "democratic regime change" is not always

particularly democratic. In Serbia, for instance, Soros' protesters filled the streets of Belgrade to halt an election that was still in progress. The vote was close enough that Yugoslav law required a runoff election. But the activists of "Otpor"—a 70,000-member militant youth group that Soros had bankrolled—did not wait for the second vote. Yugoslavia's velvet revolution began on Election Day, 26 September 2000. Candidate Vojislav Kostunovic won 48.9 percent of the vote to Milosevic's 38.6 percent. However, Yugoslav law requires a 50 percent plurality to win. A run-off election was duly scheduled for 8 October, but Kostunovic refused to participate, citing exit polls that contradicted the official results.[7] In fact, both sides had engaged in ballot-stuffing, according to the respected British intelligence bulletin *Jane's Sentinel.*[8] Nevertheless, Soros-sponsored media noticed only Milosevic's vote-rigging and called for his resignation. Kostunovic demanded that Milosevic step down.[9]

Otpor activists gave lip service to the code of non-violence. Yet, when they staged their *coup* on 5 October 2000, many relied not on Kumbaya sing-alongs, but on fists, boots, guns and Molotov cocktails.[10] On 5 October, revolutionaries rioted in Belgrade, setting fire to the Federal Parliament Building and the headquarters of the state television network RTS.[11] *Janes' Sentinel* reports that Otpor-led units armed with AK-47s, mortars and shoulder-launched anti-tank weapons set up road-blocks around Belgrade.[12] At the same time, Otpor activists went out of their way to calm Serb police and, wherever possible, win their sympathy and support. This was in keeping with the teachings of Gene Sharp, whose treatise, *The Politics of Nonviolent Action*, Otpor leaders adapted into a short, Serbian-language *Otpor User Manual* distributed to their activists. In an admiring account of the coup, the *New Republic* wrote, "Otpor, after all, had launched the bloodless revolution par excellence—a combination of clever marketing and deft courtship of the Serbian police. . . . They had intentionally scattered their followers across Yugoslavia's provinces, not confining them to metropolises like Belgrade and Novi Sad. That way, the regime couldn't easily stamp them out. And they had heeded Sharp's chief injunction: They had cultivated the police and military. Otpor sent flowers to soldiers. Every demonstration used humor to convince police it meant them no physical harm. As [Sharp disciples] Ackerman and DuVall wrote in a recent op-ed, 'Regimes fall when their defenders defect.'"[13]

Otpor's bold tactics convinced Milosevic that a long and bloody struggle lay ahead. Rather than risk civil war or NATO intervention, Milosevic stepped down. The deposed president was arrested and packed off to Holland for trial before the International Criminal Court in The Hague. According to British journalist Neil Clark, Soros spent nine years laying the groundwork for the coup, during which time he supplied over $100 million to the Serb resistance. Clark wrote in the *New Statesman*: "From 1991, his Open Society Institute channeled more than $100m to the coffers of the anti-Milosevic opposition, funding political parties, publishing houses and 'independent' media such as Radio B92, the plucky little student radio station of western mythology which was in reality bankrolled by one of the world's richest men. . . ."[14]

Soros and his operatives freely admit that they helped fund and organize the anti-Milosevic activists, including the radical Otpor organization whose role proved decisive in the *coup*. "We were here to support the civil sector—the people who were fighting against the regime of Slobodan Milosevic. . . . Most of our work was undercover," said Velimir Curgus to the *Los Angeles Times*.[15] Curgus is an operative of the Soros Foundation Networks. During the insurgency against Milosevic, he was attached to Soros' Fund for an Open Society-Yugoslavia.

Soros' next exercise in "democratic regime change" occurred in the former Soviet Republic of Georgia. When Georgian President Eduard Shevardnadze—himself a figure in Russia's democratic revolution—rebuked Soros in mid-2002 for meddling in local politics, Soros, speaking at a Moscow press conference, bluntly warned him that his presidency hung by a thread. At the conference, Soros floated the idea that Shevardnadze might try to rig Georgia's 2003 elections. Soros vowed that he would "mobilize civil society" to thwart any vote tampering. "It is necessary to mobilize civil society in order to assure free and fair elections," Soros said. "This is what we did in Slovakia at the time of Meciar, in Croatia at the time of Tudjman and in Yugoslavia at the time of Milosevic." [16]

Soros made good on his threat. A newspaper story in Britain's *Globe and Mail* summarized the facts: "It was back in February that billionaire financier George Soros began laying the brickwork for the toppling of Georgian President Eduard Shevardnadze. That month, funds from his Open Society Institute sent a 31-year-old Tbilisi activist named Giga Bokeria to Serbia to meet with members of the Otpor (Resistance) movement and learn how they used street demonstrations to topple dictator Slobodan Milosevic." [17] In the summer Soros brought Otpor activists to Georgia to train 1,000 student activists.

Meanwhile, the Soros-funded television station Rustavi-2 began weekly broadcasts of a US-made documentary called *Bringing Down a Dictator*. The film presented a step-by-step account of the overthrow of Slobodan Milosevic. Its producer was Peter Ackerman, a former Sixties radical who later made a fortune as a stock trader, working for Michael Milken at the legendary junk-bond brokerage Drexel Burnham Lambert. When

Milken was jailed for regulatory infractions, Ackerman left the firm to take up a new profession—fomenting velvet revolution. His International Center on Strategic Non-Violence based in Washington DC trains activists from many countries in direct-action principles similar to those found in Gene Sharp's revolutionary handbooks.

Ackerman's documentary *Bringing Down a Dictator* proved critical in training the Georgian insurgents. "Every Saturday for months, the independent TV network Rustavi-2 broadcast *Bringing Down a Dictator*, followed by a segment in which Georgians would discuss the film's implications for their own movement," observed the *New Republic*. "In the ten frenetic days leading up to Shevardnadze's collapse, the network increased the frequency of broadcasts. . . ." One revolutionary leader told the *Washington Post*: 'Most important was the film. All the demonstrators knew the tactics of the revolution in Belgrade by heart because they showed [the film]. . . . Everyone knew what to do.'"[18]

By the time the elections were held, the plotters were ready. No sooner did Shevardnadze announce his victory than the Soros-funded television station Rustavi-2 began broadcasting exit polls that contradicted the official vote tally. The exit pollsters were also on Soros' payroll. Protesters filled the streets, led by Serbian-trained activists. Buses brought reinforcements from the countryside, and demonstrators laid siege to the Parliament building, charging voter fraud. Shevardnadze had little choice. Rather than plunge his country into civil war, he stepped down on 23 November. "I'm delighted by what happened in Georgia, and I take great pride in having contributed to it," Soros told the *Los Angeles Times*.[19]

Proponents of "strategic non-violence" argue that, if one must dispose of a rogue regime, it is better to do it through bribery, blackmail, phony polls, voter fraud and paid street demonstrations than through bloodier methods, such as invasion and armed coups. From the standpoint of *realpolitick*, it is possible to concede the point. But the civic lesson taught is not one in democratic process. A more difficult question remains: What constitutes a rogue regime? Who determines it?

"I believe deeply in the values of an open society," Soros told the *Washington Post* in August 2003. "For the past 15 years I have focused my energies on fighting for these values abroad. Now I am doing it in the United States."[20]

Coming from Soros, this is a troubling statement, since it is clear from his own words that Soros views America under George Bush in much the same terms that he viewed Serbia under Slobodan Milosevic, Georgia under Eduard Shevardnadze or Ukraine under Viktor Yanukovych.

Of course, Soros recognizes that his Bush problem will soon go away. Bush will step down voluntarily when his term of office expires in January 2009. Unfortunately, Soros has made clear that his crusade is not against Bush personally, but against the worldview Bush represents, and "American supremacy" beyond that.

Any president who embraces what Soros has described as "the bubble of American supremacy," is an enemy of the "open society" as Soros and his political allies define it. Indeed, any president who, like Bush, is a believing Christian, qualifies as an enemy of Soros' utopia as well. Just before the 2004 election, Soros told the *New Yorker*, "The separation of church and state, the bedrock of our democracy, is clearly undermined by having a born-again President. Our concern about Islamic fundamentalism is that there's no separation between church and state, yet we are about to erode that here."[21]

Are we indeed? Soros' inability to distinguish between the

Ayatollah Ali Khamenei and President Bush underscores the danger inherent in self-appointed—and invariably self-righteous—guardians of civic virtue and prophets of utopia. With every regime they topple, the impatience of these revolutionaries with the democratic process will inevitably intensify. They have already grown used to getting their way. Such power is intoxicating—and eventually blinding—especially when those who wield it believe they are fighting in a noble cause.

Soros and his brotherhood of virtue have already shown their impatience with the vagaries and frustrations of the democratic process in their country. When their will is thwarted at the polls, they declare that the opposition has not won a vote but engineered a *coup d'etat*. When a democratically elected leader pursues a war policy that Congress has ratified and that a vote of the American electorate has endorsed, that leader reminds Soros of "the Germans" and strikes him as such "a danger to the world" that removing him becomes "the central focus of my life."

Considering the methods Soros has employed in other lands, there is reasonable cause for concern. Already some of these methods are making their appearances in American politics. Bellicose charges of vote-rigging and calls for UN intervention as have been issued by high-ranking Democrats ring strangely on American ears. Yet, for George Soros, such overheated claims and appeals to extra-national authorities are political business as usual and have already had far-reaching consequences in places like Kyrgyzstan, Albania and Ukraine.

Defenders of Soros paint his velvet putsches as benevolent, arguing that Soros has freed millions from despots such as Slobodan Milosevic. Maybe so. But bad cases make bad law. America is no Yugoslavia and George Bush—however much his critics may despise him—is no tyrant. The distinction seems lost on Soros and his allies, who have never reconciled themselves to the results of two consecutive national elections in America. "President Bush came to office without a clear mandate—he was elected president by a single vote on the Supreme Court," Soros charged in 2004.[22]

On the night of the 2004 election, as Americans awaited the final vote count, PBS talk show host Bill Moyers joined a panel discussion on the *Charlie Rose Show*.

"I think if Kerry were to win this in a tight race, I think there'd be an effort to mount a *coup*, quite frankly," Moyers volunteered.

"What do you mean by a *coup*?" asked Rose.

"I mean that the right wing is not going to accept it," replied Moyers.[23]

Moyers' words sounded weirdly out of place in a discourse about the results of an American election. But in the Shadow Party universe, whose inhabitants regard the Bush Administration as an incipient police state and America as an imperial menace, they are not.

Bill Moyers is one of Soros' closest confidants and political collaborators, a former trustee of the Open Society Institute. It was Moyers who helped Soros orchestrate the campaign for the McCain-Feingold legislation that opened the door for the Shadow Party's power grab in 2004. During the 2004 campaign, only three men had frequent access to Soros, and Bill Moyers was one of them, along with Shadow Party operatives Harold Ickes and Peter Lewis.[24]

It is hard to know what drives Moyers' paranoid response, since the Republican record is one of actually conceding elections they may have won (e.g. Kennedy's 1960 squeak past Richard Nixon, or Ashcroft's 2000 Senatorial defeat by an illegal opponent). Indeed, the only attempt to reverse a national election in the last hundred years was undertaken by Al Gore in 2000, with his efforts to recount the vote in three hand-picked Florida counties. Moyers' worry could more reasonably be regarded as a projection—and a pre-emptive one at that, since charges of thefts and political *coups* have been the focus of left-wing responses to both recent presidential elections, including the one Moyers was anticipating that night.

Like Moyers, the entire Democratic Party pursued the strategy of the victim long before the first vote was counted. Democratic Party leaders deployed a "SWAT team" of 6,000 lawyers ready to challenge the election on any available pretext.[25] An official Democrat manual urged activists to charge voter intimidation even if none had occurred.[26]

This campaign to treat the elections as though they were taking place in a Banana Republic instead of the United States reached its apogee when Congresswoman Eddie Bernice Johnson of Texas sent a letter to United Nations Secretary-General Kofi Annan requesting UN monitors for the upcoming election: "We are deeply concerned that the right of US citizens to vote in free and fair elections is again in jeopardy," she appealed to a body whose Human Rights Commission was headed by the Libyan dictatorship.[27]

Indiana Republican Steve Buyer barely managed to short-circuit Johnson's proposal by cutting off her cash flow. Buyer added an amendment to a pending foreign aid bill, blocking any US official from using the designated funds for UN election monitors. Buyer's move infuriated Rep. Corinne Brown (D-Fla.), who charged that Republicans "stole the election" in 2000. In another echo of Moyers, she wrote: "I come from Florida, where you and others participated in what I call the United States *coup d'etat*. We need to make sure it doesn't happen again."[28]

When the Buyer Amendment came up for a vote, House Democrats voted overwhelmingly—by a ratio of 5 to 1—to keep the door open for UN election monitors. An astonishing 161 representatives—all Democrats—voted *against* Buyer's proposal. The measure blocking UN monitors passed by a slim 243-161. Only 33 Democrats broke with their party to support Buyer's amendment and oppose UN monitors.[29] Never before had US lawmakers sought so openly, and in such great numbers, to allow foreign meddling in a US election—let alone by a body as morally corrupt as the United Nations, run by tyrannical regimes.

The disruptions did not end there. After the election, insurgent Democrats challenged the electoral vote count on the Senate floor. Once again, they were voted down, but not before Hillary Clinton took the occasion to deliver a speech denouncing the US voting system.[30]

In a memoir of the left, an activist recalled, "In the Sixties, we had scorned liberals because they believed in the 'process'—the rule of law that created obstacles to our radical agendas."[31] A similar scorn can be observed in the Shadow Party ranks. For movement believers, an American election decides nothing—not the legitimacy of a president nor the policies he has pursued. The war in Iraq is "illegal" even if both parties in Congress authorized it before the fact, and even if American voters re-elected its commander-in-chief after the war had begun. In the minds of the Shadow warriors, the transcendent nobility of their goal—to end the oppression and menace of "American Supremacy"—will justify almost any political means.

And therein lies the danger of what Soros has wrought. He has assembled an army of radical allies who have long been at war with the American system, and he has done so because, notwithstanding his financial eminence, he is an outsider and a radical himself. Using the power of his great purse and his brilliantly manipulative institutional vision, Soros has constructed a party, a Shadow Party, unlike any in American history. It is not an American-style party that is accountable to the people and subject to their will, but is more like a Leninist vanguard party, fully as conspiratorial and just as unaccountable. Moreover, it is a party improbably constructed by a financial tycoon, skilled at the manipulation of money and markets. As only such an individual could, Soros has woven his conspiracy out of institutional elements plucked from every level of the existing social hierarchy. The Shadow Party thus has a dimension of which Leninists could never dream. It is the party of rebels but also the party of rulers— a corporate unity of capital and labor. And it has been insinuated into the heart of the American system.

.

We'd love to hear from you about your experience with this book. Please go to www.thomasnelson.com/letusknow for a quick and easy way to give us your feedback.

Love to read? Get excerpts from new books sent to you by email. Join ShelfLife, Thomas Nelson's FREE online book club. Go to www.thomasnelson.com/shelflife.

ACKNOWLEDGMENTS

We thank our literary agent Georges Borchardt, our editor Joel Miller, our publisher David Dunham, our project manager Alice Sullivan, and all the good folks at Thomas Nelson, Inc., especially executive vice president Michael Hyatt, whose vision and leadership has given us the Thomas Nelson, Inc. imprint.

Thanks also to *NewsMax* editor Christopher Ruddy for his kind permission to use portions of Richard Poe's article, "George Soros' Coup" (*NewsMax Magazine*, May 2004), parts of which have been reproduced in this book, especially in Chapter 5.

David Horowitz gives his personal thanks to his executive assistant Elizabeth Ruiz who kept at bay the forces of chaos while he labored on this book.

Richard Poe offers a special prayer of thanks to St. Jude, help of the hopeless, and offers this book in grateful devotion to Our Lady of Fatima.

NOTES

Introduction

1. Sam Hananel, "MoveOn to Democratic Party: 'We Bought It, We Own It,'" Associated Press, 10 December 2004.

Chapter 1: The Shadow Party's Lenin

1. George Soros, *George Soros on Globalization* (PublicAffairs, 2002), 21.
2. Allen R. Myerson, "Currency Markets; When Soros Speaks, World Markets Listen," *New York Times*, 10 June 1993, D1.
3. Ibid.
4. George Trefgarne and Marcus Warren, "Soros Sparks Turmoil in World Shares," *Telegraph* (London), 14 August 1998.
5. George Soros with Byron Wien and Krisztina Koenen, *Soros on Soros: Staying Ahead of the Curve* (John Wiley & Sons, 1995), 221.
6. Speech by Rep. Henry Gonzalez, *Congressional Record*, 18 June 1993.
7. Interview with George Soros, *Power Lunch*, CNBC, 20 May 2003.
8. Laurie Mylroie, *The War Against America: Saddam Hussein and the World Trade Center Attacks* (ReganBooks, 2001), 78–87.
9. Laurie Mylroie, "The World Trade Center Bomb: Who Is Ramzi Yousef? And Why Does It Matter?" *National Interest*, Winter 1995/1996.
10. Mylroie, *The War Against America*, 88–105.

11. Ibid., 4.

12. Micah Morrison, "The Iraq Connection," *Wall Street Journal*, 5 September 2002.

13. Susan Page, "Clinton: Don't 'Overreact;' Urges Calm After Bombing," *Newsday* (New York City edition), 2 March 1993, 5; John W. Mashek, "White House Feeling Tremors from Bombing," *Boston Globe*, 2 March 1993, 17; "Clinton Says He Thinks About Personal Safety," Associated Press, 2 March 1993; "Clinton Appeals to Americans: 'Don't Overreact' to Bombing," Associated Press, 1 March 1993.

14. Walter R. Mears, "Everyday Violence Greater Threat Than Terrorism," Associated Press, 2 March 1993.

15. Steven Emerson, *American Jihad: The Terrorists Living Among Us* (The Free Press, 2002), 29.

16. George Soros, *The Bubble of American Supremacy: Correcting the Misuse of American Power* (PublicAffairs, 2004), 18, 26.

17. E.S. Browning, "The World Will Be Watching As U.S. Stock Trading Resumes," *Wall Street Journal*, 17 September 2001.

18. Susan Pulliam, "Some Managers of Hedge Funds are Betting Against U.S. Stocks," *Wall Street Journal*, 20 September 2001.

19. Wes Vernon, "Soros: Patriotism Ends at the Stock Market," NewsMax.com, 25 September 2001.

20. Dirk Beveridge, "Soros: Attacks Will Speed Downturn," Associated Press, 19 September 2001.

21. Interview with George Soros by Andrew Stevens, The N.E.W. Show, CNNfn, Hong Kong, 19 September 2001.

22. Keynote Address by George Soros at The Asia Society Hong Kong Center 11th Annual Dinner, Hong Kong, 19 September 2001.

23. Jonathan R. Laing, "Securities Fund Shuns Wall Street's Fashions, Prospers in Hard Years," *Wall Street Journal*, 28 May 1975, 1, 23.

24. Brian Wesbury, "The Best Economic Stimulus: Victory," *Wall Street Journal*, 14 September 2001.

25. "Soros Calls for 'Regime Change' in US," BBC News, 30

September 2003.

26. Laura Blumenfeld, "Soros' Deep Pockets vs. Bush," *Washington Post*, 11 November 2003, A03.

27. Ibid.

28. George Soros, *The Bubble of American Supremacy: Correcting the Misuse of American Power* (PublicAffairs, 2004), 18.

29. Ibid., 22.

30. Ibid., 4.

31. Ibid.. 10.

32. Ibid., 12–13.

33. Ibid., xi.

34. Mark Tran, "Soros Prepared to Dig Deep to Oust Bush," *Guardian*, 29 January 2004.

CHAPTER 2: How Soros Works

1. Connie Bruck, "The World According to Soros," *New Yorker*, 23 January 1995, 64.

2. "Soros Gets Splattered in Ukraine," BBC News (online), 31 March 2004.

3. David Holley, "Soros Invests in His Democratic Passion: The Billionaire's Open Society Institute Network is Focusing on Central Asia Now," *Los Angeles Times*, 5 July 2004, A6.

4. Daniel Ellsberg, *Secrets: A Memoir of Vietnam and the Pentagon Papers* (Viking, 2002).

5. Ellsberg, *Secrets*, 2002; Seymour M. Hersh, "Kissinger and Nixon in the White House," *Atlantic*, May 1982.

6. Seymour M. Hersh, "Kissinger and Nixon in the White House," *Atlantic Monthly*, May 1982.

7. Aryeh Neier, *Taking Liberties: Four Decades in the Struggle for Rights* (PublicAffairs, 2003), xix–xxi.

8. US Supreme Court, *New York Times* Co. v. United States, 403 US 713 (1971).

9. Neier, *Taking Liberties*, 103–12.

10. United States District Court, Western District of Wisconsin, United States of America v. Progressive, Inc., Erwin Knoll,

Samuel Day Jr., and Howard Morland, No. 79–C–98 (1979).

11. Morton H. Halperin and Jeanne M. Woods, "Ending the Cold War at Home," *Foreign Policy*, Winter 1990–1991, 136.

12. Morton H. Halperin, Jerry Berman, Robert Borosage and Christine Marwick, *The Lawless State: The Crimes of the U.S. Intelligence Agencies* (Washington DC: Center for National Security Studies, 1976), 5.

13. Morton Halperin, "The Case Against Covert Action," *Nation*, 21 March 1987, 345.

14. Andrea Pringle, "George Soros Opens Washington Office: Wants Open Society Institute to Have Added Impact on Policy" (press release), Open Society Institute, Washington DC, 10 June 2002.

15. Statement of Dr. William F. Schulz, Executive Director, Amnesty International USA, Annual Report, 25 May 2005.

16. Press Release: "In New National Ad, ACLU Calls for Investigation Into President's Illegal Surveillance of U.S. Citizens," American Civil Liberties Union, 29 December 2005.

17. Byron York, "Soros Funded Stewart Defense," *National Review Online*, 17 February 2005.

18. Neier, *Taking Liberties*, 295–97.

19. David Hogberg, "Funding Terror Foundationally," *American Spectator*, 25 February 2005.

20. Speech by Gara LaMarche, "Another Way in Which 9/11 'Changed Everything': The Impact of Counterterrorism and Security Legislation on the Work of Human Rights Defenders," Human Rights House Foundation conference: "Activists Under Attack: Defending the Right to be a Human Rights Defender," Oslo, Norway, 13 October 2004.

21. Susie Day, "Inside the Mind of a (Confused) Terrorist Lawyer," *Monthly Review*, 25 November 2002.

22. Joseph P. Fried, "In Muslim Cleric's Trial, a Radical Defender; Left-Leaning Lawyer and Revolutionary Sympathizer Comes Back in the Limelight," *New York Times*, 28 June 1995.

23. George Packer, "Left Behind," *New York Times Magazine*, 22

September 2002.

24. "Moslem Militants Threaten Revenge Attacks on U.S.," Agence France Presse, 20 January 1996.

25. Julia Preston, "Tapes Focus Terror Case Against Sheik's Lawyer," *New York Times*, 4 October 2004.

26. Packer, "Left Behind."

27. United States v. Ahmed Abdel Sattar, et. al., pp. 7967–8.

28. Byron York, "Soros Funded Stewart Defense," *National Review Online*, 17 February 2005.

29. Erick Stakelbeck, "Cheerleaders for Terror," FrontPage Magazine.com, 17 July 2003.

30. Statement of the ACLU of Massachusetts Regarding the Prosecution of Lynne Stewart, 17 February 2005.

31. Byron York, "Soros Funded Stewart Defense," *National Review Online*, 17 February 2005.

32. BORDC website available at http://www.bordc.org/, [accessed 27 May 2006].

Chapter 3: Boring From Within

1. Louis Jacobson, "New Organization to Push Liberal Measures," *Roll Call*, 23 June 2005.

2. Jim Holt, "A States' Rights Left?" *New York Times Magazine*, 21 November 2004.

3. William F. Hammond Jr., "Soros Ranks Second in N.Y. in Last-Minute Donations," *New York Sun*, 2 November 2004, 5.

4. William F. Hammond Jr., "Soros Group Invests in D.A. Race," *New York Sun*, 9 September 2004, 2.

5. Marc Humbert, "Giuliani: Endorsement for Clinton Proves She's a Lefty," Associated Press, 28 March 2000.

6. John Bachtell, "A Turning Point in New York Politics," *People's Weekly World*, March 2000.

7. Marc Humbert, "Poll Shows Clinton-Giuliani Races Tightening As She Picks Up Support," Associated Press, 26 March 2000.

8. James Bradley, "Nader, Schmader!: A Third-Party Alternative? Try the Working Families Party," *Village Voice*, 1–7 November

2000.

9. Ben Smith, "Is the Party Over for Working Families Party Before It Starts?" *New York Observer*, 3 November 2003, 1.

10. Tracey Tully, "Labor Unions Pushing Third Party for Workers," *Times Union* (Albany), 26 June 1998, A1.

11. Steven Malanga, "The Council's Confederacy of Dunces," *City Journal*, Spring 2003.

12. R. Emmett Tyrrell, "The 'Millions for Reparations March' You Might Have Missed in the Papers," *New York Sun*, 19 August 2002, 6.

13. Sol Stern, "ACORN's Nutty Regime for Cities," *City Journal*, Spring 2003.

14. "The New York City Council and War," *Gotham Gazette*, 3 March 2003.

15. "New York City Council Passes Anti-War Resolution," Xinhua News Agency, 13 March 2003.

16. "New York City Council Passes Resolution Opposing Iraq War," Deutsche Presse-Agentur, 12 March 2003.

17. "New York Says No," *Liverpool Daily Echo*, 13 March 2003, 2.

18. Andrea Peyser, "Homegrown Weasels Stick It To Brave GIs," *New York Post*, 13 March 2003, 10.

19. "The New York City Council and War," *Gotham Gazette*, 3 March 2003.

20. Press Release: "New York City Joins 250 Communities Upholding Civil Rights and Liberties, Denouncing Parts of Patriot Act," Bill of Rights Defense Committee (BORDC), Northampton, Massachusetts, 4 February 2004.

21. Errol Louis, "Primary's Real Winners and Losers," *Daily News*, 17 September 2004, 53.

22. Jennifer Gonnerman, "The People's Prosecutor," *Village Voice*, 28 September 2004, 40.

23. Joel Stashenko, "Court Says Party Intruded on Democratic Primary," Associated Press, 14 October 2004.

24. William F. Hammond Jr., "Next Sheriff of Albany," *New York Sun*, 4 October 2004, 9.

25. "... And Those Who Evade the Law," *New York Post*, 18 October 2004, 34.

26. William F. Hammond Jr., "Next Sheriff of Albany," *New York Sun*, 4 October 2004, 9.

27. Ellis Hennican, "Upsetting the Applecart," *Newsday*, 15 October 2004, A08.

28. Carl Limbacher, "Threat by Hillary Pitbull Spitzer Could be a Crime, Says Top Lawyer," NewsMax.com, 28 July 2000.

29. Ibid.

30. Marc Humbert, "Spitzer Warns GOP To Not Use 9-11 For Politics," Associated Press, 29 July 2004.

CHAPTER 4: Soros and Hillary

1. Comments by George Soros, "Take Back America" Conference, Federal News Service, Washington DC, 3 June 2004.

2. Comments by George Soros, "Take Back America" Conference, 3 June 2004.

3. Byron York, *The Vast Left Wing Conspiracy* (Crown Forum/ Random House, 2005), 52.

4. Comments by George Soros, "Take Back America" Conference, 3 June 2004.

5. Author interview with Rachel Ehrenfeld, 7 February 2006.

6. Howard Fineman and Karen Breslau with Matthew Cooper, "Hillary's Tailored Universe," *Newsweek*, 11 May 1998, 32.

7. Barbara Olson, *Hell to Pay: The Unfolding Story of Hillary Rodham Clinton* (Regnery Publishing, 1999), 31-33, 46; Joyce Milton, *The First Partner: Hillary Rodham Clinton* (William, Morrow and Company, 1999), 22.

8. Barbara Olson, "Hill's College Thesis Reveals Her Mind," *New York Daily News*, 17 January 2000.

9. David Brock, *The Seduction of Hillary Rodham* (The Free Press, 1996), 19.

10. Saul Alinsky, *Rules for Radicals: A Practical Primer for Realistic Radicals* (Vintage Books, 1989: first edition 1971), xix.

11. Ibid., 163.

12. Ibid., 184–45.
13. Sanford D. Horwitt, *Let Them Call Me Rebel: Saul Alinsky—His Life and Legacy* (Vintage Books, 1989), 19, 27.
14. Ibid., 20.
15. Ibid., 15, 17, 27.
16. Ibid., 22.
17. Saul D. Alinsky, *Rules for Radicals* (Vintage Books/Random House, 1989: first edition 1971), 148, 150-51.
18. Ibid., 150.
19. Horwitt, *Let Them Call Me Rebel*, 85-7, 103, 186.
20. Ibid., 178, 194.
21. Ibid., 178, 193.
22. Ibid., 176–80.
23. Ibid., 451–505.
24. Peter Collier and David Horowitz, *The Kennedys: An American Drama* (Encounter Books, 2002: first edition 1984), 295-98.
25. Jacques Levy, *Cesar Chavez: Autobiography of La Causa* (W.W. Norton & Company, 1975), 99-148.
26. Saul D. Alinsky, *Rules for Radicals* (Vintage Books/Random House, 1989: first edition 1971), 173-74.
27. R. Emmett Tyrrell Jr. with Mark W. Davis, *Madame Hillary: The Dark Road to the White House* (Regnery Publishing, 2004), 59.
28. Richard L. Berke, "Little Left to Chance by Would-Be Party Leader," *New York Times*, 1 February 2001; Richard L. Berke, "Democrats Choose Close Friend of Clinton to Lead Party," *New York Times*, 4 February 2001.
29. Tyrrell, *Madame Hillary*, 21.
30. Ibid., 33.
31. Ryan Lizza, "Welcome to Hillaryland: A Guide to the Clinton Juggernaut," *New Republic*, 20 February 2006, 17.
32. Ibid.
33. Ibid.

CHAPTER 5: Inside Soros

1. George Soros, *Underwriting Democracy: Encouraging Free*

Enterprise and Democratic Reform Among the Soviets and in Eastern Europe (PublicAffairs, 1991), 170.

2. George Soros, *The Bubble of American Supremacy: Correcting the Misuse of American Power* (Public Affairs, 2004), 159.

3. Charles Johnson, "Yale's Brave New Constitution," LittleGreen Footballs.com, 9 April 2005.

4. Richard Poe, "Soros Rewrites U.S. Constitution," Moonbat Central.com, 9 April 2005.

5. R. Emmett Tyrrell Jr. with Mark W. Davis, *Madame Hillary: The Dark Road to the White House* (Regnery Publishing, 2004), 27–29.

6. Tresa Baldas, "Law School Turf War Ignites: The Federalist Society Vies with Emerging ACS," *National Law Journal*, Vol. 26, No. 34, 26 April 2004, 1.

7. Christian Bourge, "Liberal Think Tank Debuts," United Press International, 7 July 2003.

8. Sam Graham-Felsen, "The New Face of the Campus Left," *Nation*, 13 February 2006; Howard Kurtz, "A Column with Support at Both Ends," *Washington Post*, 14 February 2005, C01.

9. Lowell Ponte, "The ABC's of Media Bias," FrontPageMagazine. com, 14 October 2004; Richard Poe, "ABC News: The Soros Connection," RichardPoe.com, 14 October 2004; Greg Pierce, "Inside Politics: The Soros Connection," *Washington Times*, 15 October 2004, A08.

10. Scott Johnson, "The $80,000 Misunderstanding," powerline blog.com, 9 April 2005.

11. John Hinderaker, "What Liberals Want: A Progressive Conference on the Constitution Sheds Light on the Real Stakes Involved with the Judiciary," *Weekly Standard*, 19 April 2005.

12. Karl R. Popper, *All Life is Problem Solving* (Routledge, 1999), 110.

13. Michael T. Kaufman, *Soros: The Life and Times of a Messianic Billionaire* (Random House, 2002), 83.

14. Soros, *The Bubble of American Supremacy: Correcting the Misuse of American Power*, 13.

15. Douglas T. Miller and Marion Nowak, *The Fifties: The Way We*

Really Were (Doubleday, 1975), 15.

16. Soros, *The Bubble of American Supremacy: Correcting the Misuse of American Power*, ix.

17. George Soros, *Open Society: Reforming Global Capitalism* (PublicAffairs, 2000), 120.

18. Ibid., 122.

19. Ibid., 134.

20. Chris Hedges, "Honoring Investment that Paid," *New York Times*, 15 October 1990.

21. Soros, *The Bubble of American Supremacy*, 11–12.

22. Neil Clark, "Profile—George Soros: The Billionaire Trader Has Become Eastern Europe's Uncrowned King and the Prophet of 'The Open Society.' But Open to What?" *New Statesman*, 2 June 2003.

23. Kaufman, *Soros*, 293.

24. George Soros, *Open Society: Reforming Global Capitalism* (PublicAffairs, 2000), 122.

25. George Soros with Byron Wien and Krisztina Koenen, *Soros on Soros: Staying Ahead of the Curve* (John Wiley & Sons, 1995), 44.

26. Uriel Heilman, "In Rare Jewish Appearance, George Soros Says Jews and Israel Cause Anti-Semitism," Jewish Telegraphic Agency, 10 November 2003.

27. Ibid.

28. Speech by Dr. Mahathir bin Mohamad, Organization of the Islamic Conference (OIC) Summit 2003, Putrajaya, Malaysia, 16 October 2003.

29. Heilman, "In Rare Jewish Appearance, George Soros Says Jews and Israel Cause Anti-Semitism."

30. Ibid.

31. Michael T. Kaufman, *Soros: The Life and Times of a Messianic Billionaire* (Vintage Books/Random House, 2002), 167.

32. Ibid., 32.

33. Bruck, "The World According to Soros," 58.

34. Interview with George Soros, *Adam Smith's Money World*, Public Broadcasting Service, 15 April 1993.

35. George Soros interviewed by Steve Kroft, *60 Minutes*, CBS, 20

December 1998.

36. Kaufman, *Soros: The Life and Times of a Messianic Billionaire*, 52.

37. Soros, *Underwriting Democracy: Encouraging Free Enterprise and Democratic Reform Among the Soviets and in Eastern Europe*, 3–4.

38. Bruck, "The World According to Soros," 59.

39. Soros with Byron Wien and Krisztina Koenen, *Soros on Soros: Staying Ahead of the Curve* (John Wiley & Sons, 1995), 241.

40. Soros, *The Bubble of American Supremacy: Correcting the Misuse of American Power*, 19–21.

41. George Soros with Byron Wien and Krisztina Koenen, *Soros on Soros: Staying Ahead of the Curve*, 240.

42. Robert Slater, *Soros: The Unauthorized Biography* (McGraw-Hill, 1996), 20.

43. Kaufman, *Soros: The Life and Times of a Messianic Billionaire*, 102–28; George Soros with Byron Wien and Krisztina Koenen, *Soros on Soros: Staying Ahead of the Curve*, 213.

44. Michael Harrington, *The Other America* (Touchstone/Simon & Schuster, 1997: first edition 1962), 1–18.

45. Harrington, *The Other America*, 172.

46. Herbert Mitgang, *Dangerous Dossiers: Exposing the Secret War Against America's Most Dangerous Authors* (D.I. Fine, 1988).

47. Kaufman, *Soros*, 180.

48. Kaufman, *Soros*, 206–07; Mayer, *The Money Man*, 176.

49. Kaufman, *Soros*, 183.

50. Connie Bruck, "The World According to Soros," *New Yorker*, 23 January 1995, 61.

51. Kaufman, *Soros*, 180.

52. Barry Miles, *Ginsberg: A Biography* (Harper Perennial/Harper Collins, 1990), 528–29.

53. Jonathan R. Laing, "Securities Fund Shuns Wall Street's Fashions, Prospers in Hard Years," *Wall Street Journal*, 28 May 1975, 1, 23.

54. Robert Slater, *Soros: The Unauthorized Biography* (McGraw-

Hill, 1996), 163–189.

55. Slater, *Soros: The Unauthorized Biography*, 243.

56. Taki Theodoracopoulos, "Soros is Charitable up to the Tax Break," *Sunday Times* (London), 22 January 1995.

57. Soros, *The Bubble of American Supremacy: Correcting the Misuse of American Power*, 136.

58. Bruck, "The World According to Soros," 56.

59. *Russia's Road to Corruption: How the Clinton Administration Exported Government Instead of Free Enterprise and Failed the Russian People*, Speaker's Advisory Group on Russia, United States House of Representatives 106th Congress, Washington DC, September 2000.

60. Amy Borrus, "Clinton Can't Put Foreign Policy Off Any Longer," *Business Week*, 5 April 1993, 37.

61. Bruck, "The World According to Soros," 57.

62. Richard Poe, "George Soros' Coup," *NewsMax*, May 2004, 15; Author interview with Anne Williamson, 16 March 2004.

63. Interview with George Soros, *The Charlie Rose Show*, Public Broadcasting Service, 30 November 1995.

64. David Ignatius, "Who Robbed Russia? Did Al Gore Know About the Massive Lootings?" *Washington Post*, 25 August 1999, A17.

65. Jeffrey D. Sachs, *The End of Poverty* (Penguin Press, 2005), 109–130.

66. Soros, *Underwriting Democracy*, 31–33.

67. George Soros, "The Centre Cannot Hold," *Independent* (London), 15 July 1991, 19.

68. "Gorbachev Fails to Gain Financial Aid," *Globe and Mail*, 18 July 1991, A1.

69. Peter Reddaway, "Questions About Russia's 'Dream Team,'" Post-Soviet Prospects, vol. 5, no. 5, Washington DC: Center for Strategic and International Studies, September 1997.

70. Chrystia Freeland, *Sale of the Century: The Inside Story of the Second Russian Revolution* (Abacus/Time Warner, 2005: first edition 2000), 187; Harry Kreisler, "The Myths of Globalization,

Markets, Democracy and Ethnic Hatred: Conversation with Amy Chua," Institute of International Studies, UC Berkeley, 22 January 2004.

71. Williamson, *Contagion—The Betrayal of Liberty: Russia and the United States in the 1990s* (unpublished), Chapter 13; Janine R. Wedel, "The Harvard Boys Do Russia," *Nation*, 1 June 1998.

72. Janine R. Wedel, "The Harvard Boys Do Russia," *Nation*, 1 June 1998.

73. James Y. Stern, "Sachs Leaves HIID Amidst Justice Probe," *Harvard Crimson*, 7 June 1999.

74. Janine R. Wedel, "The Harvard Boys Do Russia," *Nation*, 1 June 1998; Mark Whitehouse, "Harvard Partners Accused of Theft," *Moscow Times*, 12 August 1997; Martin Finucane, "Feds Sue Harvard Over Russia Plan," Associated Press, 26 September 2000; "A Difference of Nomenclature: Harvard Should Have Dissolved Scandal-Plagued HIID Utterly and Completely," *Harvard Crimson*, 4 October 2000; Press Release: "Harvard Defendants Pay Over $31 Million to Settle False Claims Act Allegations," US Attorney for the District of Massachusetts, US Department of Justice, 3 August 2005; "Harvard Pays $26 Million to Settle False Claims Case," White Collar Crime Prof Blog, 8 August 2005; United States District Court, District of Massachusetts, Civil Action no. 00CV11977 DPW, United States of America, Plaintiff v. The President and Fellows of Harvard College, Andrei Shleifer, Jonathan Hay, Nancy Zimmerman, and Elizabeth Hebert, Defendants; "Yale Connection to Harvard Russian Fraud Case," YaleInsider.org, 21 September 2002.

75. Michael Lewis, "The Speculator: What on Earth is Multibillionaire George Soros Doing Throwing Wads of Money Around in Eastern Europe?" *New Republic*, 10 January 1994, 19.

76. David Lister and James Bone, "'Dirty Money' Scandal Could Top $100 Billion," *Times* (London), 1 September 1999; David Ignatius, "Who Robbed Russia? Did Al Gore Know About the

Massive Lootings?" *Washington Post*, 25 August 1999, A17.

77. "Hearing of the House Banking and Financial Services Committee," Federal News Service, 22 September 1999.

78. Anne Williamson, *Contagion—The Betrayal of Liberty: Russia and the United States in the 1990s* (unpublished), Chapter 13; Janine R. Wedel, "The Harvard Boys Do Russia," *Nation*, 1 June 1998.

79. Anne Williamson, *Contagion—The Betrayal of Liberty: Russia and the United States in the 1990s* (unpublished), Chapter 13; Janine R. Wedel, *Collision and Collusion: The Strange Case of Western Aid to Eastern Europe* (Palgrave/St. Martin's Press, 2001), 161–63; Janine R. Wedel, "The Harvard Boys Do Russia," *Nation*, 1 June 1998.

80. "Hearing of the House Banking and Financial Services Committee," Federal News Service, 15 September 1998.

81. John Tagliabue, "Soros Is Found Guilty in France On Charges of Insider Trading," *New York Times*, 21 December 2002, C1; Floyd Norris, "Insider-Trading Conviction of Soros is Upheld in France," *New York Times*, 25 March 2005, 4; Ambrose Evans-Pritchard, "French Court Orders Soros to Pay Pounds 1.6m Insider Trading Fine," *Daily Telegraph*, 25 March 2005, 033; Angela Doland, "French Court Upholds Soros' Conviction," Associated Press, 14 June 2006.

82. George Soros, *The Crisis of Global Capitalism: Open Society Endangered* (PublicAffairs, 1998), 196.

83. Faisal Islam, "Rich Man, Wise Man ...," *Observer*, 10 March 2002.

CHAPTER 6: Strategy for Regime Change

1. Teresa Watanabe and Hector Becerra, "500,000 Pack Streets to Protest Immigration Bills," *Los Angeles Times*, 26 March 2006.

2. Teresa Watanabe and Hector Becerra, "The Immigration Debate: How DJs Put 500,000 Marchers in Motion," *Los Angeles Times*, 28 March 2006.

3. Ben Johnson, "Who's Behind the Immigration Rallies?"

FrontPageMagazine.com, 29 March 2006.

4. Johnson, "Who's Behind the Immigration Rallies?"

5. Barbara Olson, *Hell to Pay: The Unfolding Story of Hillary Rodham Clinton* (Regnery Publishing, 1999), 101.

6. Edward Klein, *The Truth About Hillary* (Sentinel/Penguin Group, 2005), 78–82.

7. Klein, *The Truth About Hillary*, 243–44.

8. Juan Williams, "If Liberals Need Riots, Let Whites Do It; Want to Protest Reaganomics? Some Advice From Those Who Lit the Fire Last Time," *Washington Post*, 13 June 1982, C1.

9. Richard A. Cloward and Frances Fox Piven, "The Weight of the Poor: A Strategy to End Poverty," *Nation*, 2 May 1966, 510–517.

10. Richard Rogin, "Now It's Welfare Lib," *New York Times*, 27 September 1970, 31, 73–76, 80–83.

11. Nick Kotz and Mary Lynn Kotz, *A Passion for Equality: George Wiley and the Movement* (W.W. Norton & Company, 1977), 76, 79, 91.

12. Richard A. Cloward and Richard M. Elman, "The First Congress of the Poor," *Nation*, 7 February 1966, 148–151.

13. Premilla Nadasen, *Welfare Warriors: The Welfare Rights Movement in the United States* (Routledge, 2005), 39.

14. William Borders, "Welfare Militant On the Way Up: George Alvin Wiley," *New York Times*, 27 May 1969, 32.

15. Frances Fox Piven and Richard A. Cloward, *Poor People's Movements: Why They Succeed, How They Fail* (Vintage Books/Random House, 1979: first edition 1977), 277–78.

16. Rogin, "Now It's Welfare Lib," 31, 73–76, 80–83.

17. Mark Toney, "Revisiting the National Welfare Rights Organization," *ColorLines*, Volume 3, Number 3, Fall 2000; William Borders, "Welfare Militant On the Way Up: George Alvin Wiley," *New York Times*, 27 May 1969, 32.

18. Rogin, "Now It's Welfare Lib," 76.

19. Stern, "ACORN's Nutty Regime for Cities."

20. Cloward and Piven, "The Weight of the Poor: A Strategy to End

Poverty," 511–12.

21. Vincent Cannato, *The Ungovernable City: John Lindsay and the Struggle to Save New York* (Basic Books, 2002: first edition 2001), 541.

22. Steven Malanga, "The Myth of the Working Poor," *City Journal*, Volume 14, Number 4, Autumn 2004, 26–37.

23. Cannato, *The Ungovernable City*, 541.

24. Heather MacDonald, "Compassion Gone Mad," *City Journal*, Volume 6, Number 1, Winter 1996.

25. Cannato, *The Ungovernable City*, 539.

26. Stern, "ACORN's Nutty Regime for Cities."

27. Nadasen, *Welfare Warriors*, 34.

28. Marvin Olasky, *The Tragedy of American Compassion* (Good News Publishers, 1992), 180–183.

29. Speech by Rudolph W. Giuliani, "Reaching Out to All New Yorkers by Restoring Work to the Center of City Life," Republic National Bank, Manhattan, 20 July 1998.

30. Jason DeParle, "What Welfare-to-Work Really Means."

CHAPTER 7: Marching Orders

1. Jack Beatty, "The Language of the Unheard," *Nation*, 8 October 1977, 341–43.

2. Frances Fox Piven and Richard A. Cloward, *Poor People's Movements: Why They Succeed, How They Fail* (Vintage Books/Random House, 1979: first edition 1977), 20.

3. Piven and Cloward, *Poor People's Movements*, 4–5, 15, 23–24.

4. Guida West, *The National Welfare Rights Movement* (Praeger Press, 1981), vii-ix.

5. Richard Rogin, "Now It's Welfare Lib," *New York Times*, 27 September 1970, 80.

6. Saul D. Alinsky, *Rules for Radicals: A Pragmatic Primer for Realistic Radicals* (Vintage Books/Random House, 1989: first edition 1971), 128.

7. Alinsky, *Rules for Radicals*, 151–52.

8. "Welfare Politics," *Nation*, 18 December 1982, 643–45.

9. Richard A. Cloward and Frances Fox Piven, "A Movement Strategy to Transform the Democratic Party," *Social Policy*, Winter 1983, 3-14.

10. Ibid.

11. Premilla Nadasen, *Welfare Warriors: The Welfare Rights Movement in the United States* (Routledge, 2005), 202.

12. Gary Delgado, *Organizing the Movement: The Roots and Growth of ACORN* (Temple University Press, 1986), 45.

13. Nadasen, *Welfare Warriors*, 202.

14. Delgado, *Organizing the Movement: The Roots and Growth of ACORN*, 43–45.

15. William T. Poole, "The New Left in Government: From Protest to Policymaking," Heritage Foundation Report, Institution Analysis No. 9, November 1978; William T. Poole, "The New Left in Government, Part II: The VISTA Program as 'Institution-Building,'" Heritage Foundation Report, Institution Analysis No. 17, February 1982.

16. acorn.org [accessed 29 May 2006].

17. Sol Stern, "ACORN's Nutty Regime for Cities," *City Journal*, Spring 2003.

18. Wade Rathke, "Different Days on Park Avenue with Citibank," ChiefOrganizer.org, 1 April 2004.

19. Press Release from William Jefferson Clinton Foundation: "Announcement of Earned Income Tax Credit Awareness Program to Assist Hurricane Katrina Survivors," 3 February 2006; Wade Rathke, "Bill's 1st Grant," ChiefOrganizer.org, 13 February 2006.

20. John Fund, *Stealing Elections: How Voter Fraud Threatens Our Democracy* (Encounter Books, 2004), 23.

21. Fund, *Stealing Elections*, 23.

22. "Vote Fraud, Intimidation and Suppression in the 2004 Presidential Election," American Center for Voting Rights (ACVR), 2 August 2005; Jonathan Bechtle, "Voter Turnout or Voter Fraud?"

Organization Trends, Capital Research Center, April 2006.

23. Jeff Jacoby, "The Dumbing Down of Democracy," *Boston Globe,* 12 November 1996, A17.

24. Bill Theobald, "False Counts: Special Report; Bogus Names Jam Indiana's Voter List," *Indianapolis Star,* 5 November 2000, 01A.

25. Soros, *The Bubble of American Supremacy,* 9.

CHAPTER 8: Opening the Door

1. Ellen Goodman, "The Turn-Off Factor; Election '94: Sorting It Out," *Boston Globe,* 10 November 1994, 23.

2. Sidney Blumenthal, *The Clinton Wars* (Farrar, Straus and Giroux, 2003), 118–23.

3. Craig Crawford, "Special Interests' Money is on Health; In the Past 18 Months Special Interests Have Spent $100 Million to Influence the Debate on Health-Care Reform," *Orlando Sentinel,* 22 July 1994, A1.

4. Craig Crawford, "Campaign Coffers Get Healthy Dose of Special-Interest Money; Sen. Connie Mack Tops Florida Lawmakers in Campaign Donations from Opponents to Health Reform, a Consumer Group Says," *Orlando Sentinel,* 17 July 1994, A1.

5. Bennett Roth, "Study Faults Alternative Health Bill; Liberal Groups Say Texas Would be Loser Under GOP Plan," *Houston Chronicle,* 19 July 1994, A9.

6. Crawford, "Special Interests' Money is on Health."

7. Jill Zuckman, "Health Reform Ads Draw Criticism," *Boston Globe,* 26 July 1994, 5.

8. Speech by George Soros, Alexander Ming Fisher Lecture Series at Columbia Presbyterian Medical Center, 30 November 1994.

9. Ibid.

10. Elizabeth McCaughey, "No Exit: What the Clinton Plan Will Do For You," *New Republic,* 7 February 1994, 21.

11. Speech by George Soros, Alexander Ming Fisher Lecture Series

at Columbia Presbyterian Medical Center, 30 November 1994.

12. Sense of the Senate Resolution, Feingold (and others) Amendment No. 1803 (Senate—20 July 1995).

13. George Soros, *Open Society: Reforming Global Capitalism* (PublicAffairs, 2000), 147–48.

14. Supreme Court of the United States: McConnell, United States Senator, et. al. v. Federal Election Commission, et. al., (02-1674) 540 U.S. 93 (2003). Argued 8 September 2003—Decided 10 December 2003.

15. Supreme Court of the United States: McConnell et. al. v. Federal Election Commission, et. al., (02-1674) 540 U.S. 93 (2003). Opinion of Judge Scalia.

16. Declan McCullagh, "The Coming Crackdown on Blogging," CNet News.com, 3 March 2005.

17. David Pace, "FEC Won't Regulate Internet Politics," Associated Press, 27 March 2006.

18. Richard Poe, "Pewgate: The Battle of the Blogosphere," FrontPageMagazine.com, 25 March 2005.

19. Ryan Sager, "Buying 'Reform': Media Missed Millionaires' Scam," *New York Post*, 17 March 2005, 33.

20. Sean P. Treglia, "Covering Philanthropy and Nonprofits Beyond 9/11," (videotaped speech), "Philanthropy and Public Policy: Foundation Strategies for Social Change," Annenberg Center for Communication at the University of Southern California, 12 March 2004.

21. Sager, "Buying 'Reform.'"

22. "The Soros Agenda: Free Speech for Billionaires Only," *Wall Street Journal*, 3 January 2004; Byron York, *The Vast Left Wing Conspiracy* (Crown Forum/Random House, 2005), 62.

23. Sager, "Buying 'Reform.'"

24. Frank Greve, "Moyers' Objectivity as Journalist and Financier Questioned by Observers," Knight Ridder/Tribune News Service, 10 October 1999.

25. Ed Morrissey, "Inside McCain's Reform Institute," CaptainsQuartersBlog.com, 9 March 2005.

26. Treglia, "Covering Philanthropy and Nonprofits Beyond 9/11."
27. David Tell, "An Appearance of Corruption: The Bogus Research Undergirding Campaign Finance Reform," *The Weekly Standard*, Volume 8, Number 36, 26 May 2003.
28. Tell, "An Appearance of Corruption."
29. George Soros, *Underwriting Democracy: Encouraging Free Enterprise and Democratic Reform Among the Soviets and in Eastern Europe* (PublicAffairs, 1991), 53.
30. Erin Healy, "Interview with Rebecca Rimel: President and CEO, The Pew Charitable Trusts," *IRIS: A Journal About Women*, 30 April 2000, 8.
31. Soros, *Open Society: Reforming Global Capitalism*, 360.
32. Aimee Welch, "When Voters Are the Legislators," *Insight on the News*, 11 December 2000, 22.
33. Welch, "When Voters Are the Legislators."
34. Andrew Ferguson, "The Arianna Sideshow," *Time*, 31 July 2000, 22.
35. Speech by Senator Russ Feingold, Shadow Convention, Los Angeles, 13 August 2000.
36. Matt Labash, "The Other, Stupider Convention: Spend Enough Time with Arianna, Granny D., and Al Franken, and You, Too, Will Favor Legalizing Drugs," *Weekly Standard*, 14 August 2000, 23.
37. Labash, "The Other, Stupider Convention."
38. Jennifer Brown, "Alternative Conventions Plan Humor, Satire to Contrast with GOP, Dems," Associated Press, 10 July 2000; Charlie Mitchell, "'The Radical Center' Shadows GOP," *National Journal*, 31 July 2000; Anne-Marie O'Connor, "Concocting Satiric Counterpoint to Conventions," *Los Angeles Times*, 22 June 2000, B1.
39. Andrew Ferguson, "The Arianna Sideshow," *Time Magazine*, 31 July 2000, 22.
40. Robert Novak, "The Soros Convention," *Creators Syndicate, Inc.*, 17 July 2000.

CHAPTER 9: The Connection

1. Michael Crowley, "Shadow Warriors," *New York Magazine*, 12

August 2004.

2. Crowley, "Shadow Warriors."

3. John Aloysius Farrell, "The President's Get-It-Done Guy," *Boston Globe*, 15 October 1995, 14; William H. Chafe, *Never Stop Running: Allard Lowenstein and the Struggle to Save American Liberalism* (BasicBooks/HarperCollins, 1993), 257–61; Richard Cummings, *The Pied Piper: Allard K. Lowenstein and the Liberal Dream* (Grove Press, 1985), 272–74.

4. Daniel Wise, "Veteran 'Point Man' Ickes Gets New Battle Assignment," *New York Law Journal*, 28 December 1993, 1; William Bunch, "Convention '92: Harold Ickes; Clinton's Gardener; Ickes Will Manage Madison Square," *Newsday*, 29 June 1992, 19.

5. Dave Saltonstall, "Harold Ickes Knows All the Secrets, But Won't Tell Any," *Daily News* (New York), 10 October 2000, 30.

6. Mary Voboril, "Law Firm Celebrates 35 Years," *Newsday*, 16 September 1995, A27.

7. Micah Morrison, "Who is Harold Ickes?" *Wall Street Journal*, 26 October 2000.

8. Morrison, "Who is Harold Ickes?" William G. McGowan, "The Mob and the Deputy Chief of Staff; Harold Ickes Jr.," *Washington Monthly*, Volume 26, Number 7–8, July 1994, 9; Jerry Seper, "U.S. to Probe White House Aide's Former Law Firm for Mob Ties," *Washington Times*, 5 July 1994, A1.

9. Thomas B. Edsall and George Lardner Jr., "Clinton's Likely Assistant Defends Work for Union," *Washington Post*, 9 January 1993, A5.

10. Morrison, "Who is Harold Ickes?"

11. Al Gordon, "Anthony Provenzano, Suspect in Hoffa Disappearance," 13 December 1988, *Newsday*, 35.

12. Morrison, "Who is Harold Ickes?"

13. Mike McAlary, *New York Post*, 12 January 1993.

14. David M. Alpern, "A Godfather's Fall: Mob Under Fire," *Newsweek*, 30 December 1985, 20.

15. Michael Moroney, "Laboring Against America," *Rising Tide*,

Summer 1999.

16. Matt Labash, "John Sweeney and the State of His Union," *Weekly Standard*, 21 October 1996, 20.

17. Todd S. Purdum, "A Political Whodunit; Suspects Abound in the Downfall of Harold M. Ickes," *New York Times*, 14 February 1993, 41.

18. Deborah Pines, "Circuit Panel Bars Release of Report Involving Ickes," *New York Law Journal*, 12 December 1995, 1.

19. Michael Lewis, "Bill Clinton's Garbage Man," *New York Times*, 21 September 1997, 58.

20. Judy Bachrach, "Seduced and Abandoned," *Vanity Fair*, September 1997.

21. Jerry Seper, "Ickes' Links to Union Under New Scrutiny," *Washington Times*, 16 June 1996, A1.

22. Michael Ledeen and Mike Moroney, "The White House Joins the Teamsters," *American Spectator*, November 1998.

23. Jim Larkin, "What Went Wrong," *In These Times*, 3 November 1997, 18.

24. Dave Saltonstall, "Harold Ickes Knows All the Secrets, But Won't Tell Any," *Daily News* (New York), 10 October 2000, 30.

25. Brian Duffy, "Campaign Investigation of Ickes Reveals Evidence of Wrongdoing," *Wall Street Journal*, 3 August 1998.

26. John Aloysius Farrell, "The President's Get-It-Done Guy," *Boston Globe*, 15 October 1995, 14.

27. Marc Humbert, "Ickes, a Tenacious Operative, Mrs. Clinton's 'Oak Tree' in New York," *Associated Press State & Local Wire*, 17 June 1999.

CHAPTER 10: The Shadow Party

1. Amy Westfeldt, "Billionaire Puts His Money Where His Mouth Is—Toward Ousting Bush," *Associated Press*, New York, 10 June 2004.

2. George Soros with Byron Wien and Krisztina Koenen, *Soros on Soros: Staying Ahead of the Curve* (John Wiley & Sons, 1995), 145.

3. Thomas B. Edsall, "Campaign Money Finds New Conduits As Law Takes Effect: Shadow Organizations to Raise 'Soft Money,'" *Washington Post*, 5 November 2002, A02.
4. Lorraine Woellert, "The Evolution of Campaign Finance?" *Business Week*, 15 September 2003, 62.
5. Jeanne Cummings, "Soros Has a Hunch Bush Can Be Beat," *Wall Street Journal*, 5 February 2004.
6. Cummings, "Soros Has a Hunch Bush Can Be Beat."
7. Blumenfeld, "Soros's Deep Pockets vs. Bush."
8. Blumenfeld, "Soros's Deep Pockets vs. Bush;" Michelle Goldberg, "MoveOn Moves Up," Salon.com, 1 December 2003.
9. Cummings, "Soros Has a Hunch Bush Can Be Beat."
10. Blumenfeld, "Soros's Deep Pockets vs. Bush."
11. Cummings, "Soros Has a Hunch Bush Can Be Beat."
12. Byron York, *The Vast Left Wing Conspiracy* (Crown Forum/Random House, 2005), 8.
13. Brendan Bernhard, "Tempest in a Teapot," *LA Weekly*, 6 August 2004, 22.
14. Steve Ginsberg, "Expanding the House that 'Jack' Built," *San Francisco Business Times*, 26 January 1996, 7.
15. Bernhard, "Tempest in a Teapot;" Chris Taylor and Karen Tumulty, "MoveOn's Big Moment," *Time Magazine*, 24 November 2003, 32.
16. Bernhard, "Tempest in a Teapot."
17. Bernhard, "Tempest in a Teapot;" Taylor and Tumulty, "MoveOn's Big Moment."
18. Bernhard, "Tempest in a Teapot."
19. Taylor and Tumulty, "MoveOn's Big Moment."
20. Lowell Ponte, "Zack Exley: Kerry's Toxic Web Spider," FrontPage Magazine.com, 31 August 2004.
21. Renuka Rayasam, "Piqued? Make an Anti-Bush TV Spot," *Austin American Statesman*, 30 October 2003, A11; "RNC Attacks Bush-Hitler Ad," WorldNetDaily.com, 4 January 2004; "2nd Bush-Hitler Ad Posted," WorldNetDaily.com, 5 January 2004.
22. Christian Bourge, "Liberal Think Tank Debuts," United Press

International, 7 July 2003.

23. Robert Dreyfuss, "An Idea Factory for the Democrats," *Nation*, 1 March 2004, 18.

24. Matt Bai, "Notion Building," *New York Times Magazine*, 12 October 2003, 82.

25. Dreyfuss, "An Idea Factory for the Democrats."

26. Bourge, "Liberal Think Tank Debuts."

27. Dreyfuss, "An Idea Factory for the Democrats."

28. Jim Rutenberg, "New Internet Site Turns Critical Eyes and Ears to the Right," *New York Times*, 3 May 2004, 21.

29. Rutenberg, "New Internet Site Turns Critical Eyes and Ears to the Right."

30. Hans Nichols, "Limbaugh Stirs Democrats' Angst Over Forces Radio," *Hill*, 14 September 2004, 6; Suzanne Gamboa, "Liberals Want More Antidote for Limbaugh on American Forces Radio," Associated Press, 28 June 2004; Jake Thompson, "Limbaugh Protests Harkin Move," *Omaha World-Herald*, 19 June 2004, 04A.

31. Nichols, "Limbaugh Stirs Democrats' Angst Over Forces Radio" *Hill*; "Harkin Leads Senate in Unanimous Vote Demanding Political Balance on American Forces Radio and Television Service," *US Newswire*, 16 June 2004.

32. "Statement of Senator Tom Harkin on American Forces Radio," harkin.senate.gov, 17 June 2004. In the interests of full disclosure, it should be mentioned that both co-authors of this book have, on several occasions, been targets of stunningly mendacious hatchet jobs on Mr. Brock's website.

33. Jeanne Cummings, "A Hard Sell on 'Soft Money,'" *Wall Street Journal*, 2 December 2003; Michael Crowley, "Shadow Warriors," *New York Magazine*, 12 August 2004.

34. S.C. Gwynne (with reporting by Michael Hardy), "The Daughter Also Rises," *Texas Monthly*, August 2004, 112.

35. S.C. Gwynne, "The Daughter Also Rises."

36. Thomas B. Edsall, "Liberals Form Fund to Defeat President," *Washington Post*, 8 August 2004, A03.

37. John Harwood, "In Fallout from Campaign Law, Liberal

Groups Work Together," *Wall Street Journal*, 27 July 2004, A1.

38. Craige McMillan, "Making a List, Checking it Twice," WorldNet Daily.com, 29 July 2004.

39. David A. Leib, "Political Group Paid Felons for Door-to-Door Voter Registration Drive," Associated Press, 23 June 2004.

40. "Unsustainable Secrecy," *Washington Post*, 5 February 2004, A20.

41. Ibid., "Sustainable World Corp. lists only a post office box in Houston as its address. Directory assistance has no number for it. Searches of ordinary business databases come up empty. We tracked down Lewis Linn, the Houston accountant who is listed as its registered agent, and asked him about Sustainable World; he said he was bound by professional constraints to keep information about it confidential. Asked if he would check to see whether those behind Sustainable World would let him reveal their identity, Mr. Linn called back to say, 'I've talked to my clients, and they wish to remain private.'"

42. Crowley, "Shadow Warriors."

43. Brian C. Mooney, "Kerry's Ex-Manager Spurs Anti-Bush Effort," *Boston Globe*, 26 July 2004, A1.

44. John Mercurio and John Bresnahan, "Who's Who at the Party Campaign Committees?" *Roll Call*, 13 September 1999.

45. William Safire, "Never Love a Stranger," *New York Times*, 12 November 2003.

46. Alexander Bolton, "Parties' Loss is 527s Gain," *Hill*, 27 July 2004.

47. The Prowler, "The Collusion is Complete," *American Spectator*, 9 April 2004.

48. "The Collusion is Complete," *American Spectator*, 9 April 2004.

49. Riva D. Atlas, "2 Soros Sons Get More Control of the Business," *New York Times*, 6 October 2004, C1.

50. Fredric U. Dicker, "Soros Jr.'s Splurge—Tycoon's Son Spends Liberally on N.Y. Dems," *New York Post*, 10 August 2004, 6.

51. Matt Bai, "Wiring the Vast Left-Wing Conspiracy," *New York Times Magazine*, 25 July 2004, 30.

52. Ibid.

53. William F. Hammond Jr., "Soros Invests in D.A. Race," *New*

York Sun, 9 September 2004, 2.

54. Joel Stashenko, "Court Says Party Intruded on Democratic Primary for DA," Associated Press, 14 October 2004.

55. Thomas B. Edsall, "Democrats' Data Mining Stirs an Intraparty Battle," *Washington Post*, 8 March 2006, A01.

56. David Yeagley, "George Soros and the Sundance Kid," Front PageMagazine.com, 7 February 2005.

57. Byron York, "David Brock is Buzzing Again," *National Review*, 14 June 2004.

58. Marc Morano, "David Brock Group Backpedals on Soros Funding," Cybercast News Service, 3 March 2005.

59. Bai, "Wiring the Vast Left-Wing Conspiracy."

60. Jane Mayer, "The Money Man," *New Yorker*, 18 October 2004.

61. Brian Maloney, "Bailout: Soros, Lewis in Air America Election-Year Rescue," *Radio Equalizer*, 22 February 2006.

CHAPTER 11: Going Global

1. Laura Blumenfeld, "Soros's Deep Pockets vs. Bush," *Washington Post*, 11 November 2003, A03.

2. George Soros, *The Alchemy of Finance* (John Wiley & Sons, Inc., 2003: first edition 1987), 15.

3. George Soros, *Open Society: Reforming Global Capitalism* (PublicAffairs, 2000), 337.

4. George Soros, *The Crisis of Global Capitalism* (PublicAffairs, 1998), 102.

5. Greg Torode, "Hanoi Makes Its Marx in Soros Warning," *South China Morning Post*, 7 January 1999, 8.

6. Roger Cohen, "Redrawing the Free Market; Amid a Global Financial Crisis, Calls for Regulation Spread," *New York Times*, 14 November 1998, B9.

7. George Soros, "To Avert the Next Crisis: The IMF Should Be Transformed into An International Central Bank, so that it Can Act to Prevent Financial Crises as well as be the Lender of Last Resort to Distressed Countries," *Financial Times* (London), 4 January 1999, 20.

8. Soros, *George Soros on Globalization*, 7, 10, 20, 166.
9. Soros, *The Crisis of Global Capitalism*, 203.
10. Soros, *George Soros on Globalization* (PublicAffairs, 2002), 3.
11. Soros, *Open Society: Reforming Global Capitalism*, 346–47.
12. Soros, *George Soros on Globalization*, 177.
13. George Soros, "Avoiding a Breakdown: Asia's Crisis Demands a Rethink of International Regulation," *Financial Times* (London), 31 December 1997, 12.
14. Soros, *Open Society*, 276.
15. Soros, *The Crisis of Global Capitalism*, 177.
16. Ibid., 168, 179.
17. Ibid., 182.
18. Ibid., viii.
19. Ibid., xi.
20. Ibid., 28, 155.
21. Keynote Address by George Soros at The Asia Society Hong Kong Center 11th Annual Dinner, Hong Kong, 19 September 2001.
22. Ibid.
23. Soros, *The Crisis of Global Capitalism*, 155.
24. Jeffrey D. Sachs, *The End of Poverty: Economic Possibilities for our Times* (Penguin Press, 2005), 299–301.
25. Joseph Klein, "Global Wealth Redistribution Program, Millennium Development Project: Jeffrey Sachs' Hollywood Style Dud at the United Nations," *Canada Free Press*, 24 April 2006.
26. Laura D'Andrea Tyson, "It's Time to Step Up the Global War on Poverty," *Business Week*, 3 December 2001, 26.
27. Tyson, "It's Time to Step Up the Global War on Poverty."
28. Tyson, "It's Time to Step Up the Global War on Poverty."
29. Jeffrey D. Sachs, "International Economic Strategy After September 11," Project Syndicate, September 2001.
30. Sachs, *The End of Poverty*, 330–31.
31. Elizabeth H. Becker, "A Conversation with Jeffrey Sachs," Counsel on Foreign Relations, Washington DC, Federal News Service, 14 March 2006.

32. Sachs, *The End of Poverty*, 312.
33. Jeffrey D. Sachs, "Development Aid for Development's Sake," Project Syndicate, February 2006.
34. Sachs, *The End of Poverty*, 365.
35. Sachs, *The End of Poverty*, 216.
36. Sachs, *The End of Poverty*, 359.
37. Elizabeth Becker, "Banker Presses Aid for Poor to Fight Terror," *New York Times*, 22 April 2004.
38. Jeffrey D. Sachs, "Defeating Terrorism Through Global Prosperity," Project Syndicate, October 2001.
39. Klein, "Global Wealth Redistribution Program."

CHAPTER 12: Velvet Revolutions

1. George Soros, *The Bubble of American Supremacy* (PublicAffairs, 2004), 143.
2. Matt Welch, "Velvet President: Why Vaclav Havel is Our Era's George Orwell and More," *Reason Online*, May 2003; George Soros, *Underwriting Democracy: Encouraging Enterprise and Democratic Reform Among the Soviets and in Eastern Europe* (PublicAffairs 1991), 26–27.
3. Soros, *The Bubble of American Supremacy*, 132.
4. F. William Engdahl, "Revolution, Geopolitics and Pipelines," *Asia Times*, 30 June 2005; Michael Dobbs, "U.S. Advice Guided Milosevic Opposition: Political Consultants Helped Yugoslav Opposition Topple Authoritarian Leader," *Washington Post*, 11 December 2000, A01.
5. Peter Ackerman and Christopher Kruegler, *Strategic Nonviolent Conflict: The Dynamics of People Power in the Twentieth Century* (Praeger Publishers, 1993), 46.
6. "President Tudjman Criticizes Foreign Interference in Croatia's Media," BBC Summary of World Broadcasts, 11 December 1996.
7. "The Balkans," *Jane's Sentinel Security Assessments*, 30 November 2000.
8. *Jane's Sentinel*, 30 November 2000.

9. "Yugoslav Election Commission Sets Second Round, Says Opposition," CNN.com, 6:53 PM EDT (2253 GMT), 27 September 2000.

10. Bob Graham, Sue Masterman, "The Storming of Belgrade; Parliament and HQ Burn as Mobs Tell Milosevic to Go," *Evening Standard* (London), 5 October 2000.

11. Steven Erlanger and Roger Cohen, "From a Summons to a Slap: How the Fight in Yugoslavia Was Won," *New York Times*, 15 October 2000, 16.

12. *Jane's Sentinel*, 30 November 2000.

13. Franklin Foer, "Regime Change, Inc. : Peter Ackerman's Quest to Topple Tyranny," *New Republic*, 25 April 2005.

14. Neil Clark, "NS Profile—George Soros," *New Statesman*, 2 June 2003.

15. David Holley, "The Seed Money for Democracy," *Los Angeles Times*, 26 January 2001, A1.

16. Mark MacKinnon, "Georgia Revolt Carried Mark of Soros," *Globe and Mail*, 26 November 2003.

17. Ibid.

18. Foer, "Regime Change, Inc."

19. David Holley, "Soros Invests in His Democratic Passion: The Billionaire's Open Society Institute Network is Focusing on Central Asia Now," *Los Angeles Times*, 5 July 2004, A6.

20. Thomas B. Edsall, "Liberals Form Fund to Defeat President: Aim is to Spend $75 Million for 2004," *Washington Post*, 8 August 2003, A03.

21. Jane Mayer, "The Money Man: Can George Soros's Millions Ensure the Defeat of President Bush?" *New Yorker*, 18 October 2004.

22. George Soros, *The Bubble of American Supremacy*, 9.

23. *The Charlie Rose Show*, "President Bush and Senator Kerry Engaged in a Very Tight Race," Public Broadcasting Service (PBS), 2 November 2004.

24. Jane Mayer, "The Money Man," *New Yorker*, 18 October 2004.

25. David M. Halbfinger, "Kerry Building Legal Network for Vote Fights," *New York Times*, 19 July 2004.

26. Matt Drudge, "Kerry/Edwards Election Directive: Charge Voter Intimidation, Even if None Exists!" DrudgeReport.com, 14 October 2004.

27. "House Members Will Discuss Request to United Nations to Monitor Election: Rep. Johnson Spearheads Effort to Invite International Body," Office of Congresswoman Bernice Johnson, Press Release, 6 July 2004.

28. Alan Fram, "Fla. Lawmaker Says 2000 Election 'Stolen,'" Associated Press, 1:14 AM, 16 July 2004.

29. Fram, "Fla. Lawmaker Says 2000 Election 'Stolen.'"

30. John Nichols, "The Boxer Rebellion," *Nation*, 28 February 2005; Kenneth R. Bazinet with Richard Sisk, "Dems Lose W Elex Challenge," *Daily News* (New York), 7 January 2005.

31. David Horowitz, *Radical Son: A Generational Odyssey* (Free Press, 1997), 396.

INDEX